LINCOLN'S
POLITICAL THOUGHT

George Kateb

HARVARD UNIVERSITY PRESS

Cambridge, Massachusetts
London, England
2015

First printing

Library of Congress Cataloging-in-Publication Data
Kateb, George.
   Lincoln's political thought / George Kateb.
      pages cm
   Includes bibliographical references and index.
      ISBN 978-0-674-36816-3 (alkaline paper)
   1. Lincoln, Abraham, 1809–1865—Political and social views.
2. Lincoln, Abraham, 1809–1865—Philosophy.   3. Lincoln, Abraham,
1809–1865—Oratory.   4. United States—Politics and government—
1861–1865.   5. United States—History—Civil War, 1861–1865.   6. Slavery—
Political aspects—United States—History—19th century.   7. Political
science—United States—History—19th century.   I. Title.
      E457.2.K37 2015
      973.7092—dc23   2014005879

To the memory of my sister, Jeanette Farage

Contents

Preface

My aim in this work is to try to understand Lincoln's words. The premise is that his thought can be difficult to take in. My approach is that of a student of political theory. At the risk of disproportion and unexpected emphases, I have therefore concentrated on those many occasions when Lincoln spoke or wrote words of lasting theoretical interest; in whatever form, they often have the weight of writings in the canon. His thought was dominated by a commitment to human equality and the fate imposed on it by the existence of institutionalized slavery, the worst antithesis to human equality. I largely exclude Lincoln's views on a wide range of matters of public policy and party politics as not essential to my effort, no matter how important they were to Lincoln, his party, and the country.

I must admit that the cumulative effect of his words leads me to a less unmixed Lincoln than I began with. My intense admiration remains, but is now joined to some dismay. Despite the dismay, I believe with many others that he was a great man, a good man, and a great writer. There is no need to apologize for thinking that as president he made all the difference, if ever one person of politics could. In the words of William Herndon, his law partner and close associate, "his history after he had been sworn into office by Chief Justice Taney is so much a history of the entire country" (Herndon, 323). No all-incorporating or all-projecting egomania led Lincoln to say in the middle of his presidency that a heavy sense of his responsibility came over him whenever he considered "the great territory of the country—the large population, with the institutions which have grown up—liberty and religion to be maintained" (Remarks to New School Presbyterians, October 22, 1863, CW, 6:531). He was by far the best person that could have held the power he did, the best that could have been hoped for. He saved the Union and abolished slavery and was perhaps the only president who could have done both, and he did so in the only way he thought possible: by cautiously and in good time plausibly tying them together inextricably, while taking advantage of the South's adamant adherence to secession. Lincoln inextricably tied together what the majority in the North wanted (the preservation of the Union) with something this majority did not want, or want enough (the end of slavery), even if on average they were less intensely opposed to ending slavery than the great majority of whites in the South. He eventually felt that he was able to say, despite skepticism and opposition, that the Union could be preserved only by the military policy of emancipation, which prepared the way for complete constitutional abolition.

Let us see clearly that the South made it possible for Lincoln to tie the knot that he perhaps wanted from the start and certainly came to want eventually. For the sake of slavery, the people of the South seceded and created a new government; in refusing to give up secession until they were forced to surrender, they lost not only their government but also their slaves. The situation grew to be all or nothing for both sides: an upshot surprising to most people, if not to Lincoln. The refusal to compromise by the South from the beginning, and by Lincoln from the beginning, though not by the will of the majority in the North at almost any time, resulted in the triumph of equality of human status for all races and hence for their freedom. Lincoln's role was decisive. He did not seek or initiate armed confrontation but was ready, perhaps relieved, when it came. It was the only way out and forward.

Lincoln worried with a rare intensity about saving the Union and worried with an intensity shared only by a minority of whites about ending slavery. As president, he was held by an unusual double passion that verged on fanaticism, but it was not fanaticism because it grew from an intellectually established morality, not from an ideology of race. It was not mysticism, as some have said, that defined his passion for the Union; and his passion for ending slavery had nothing to do with mysticism. Both passions came from his moral commitment to human equality.

Against the belief that Lincoln's passion for the Union was not solely or even mostly moral, but was rather owed in largest part to the mysticism or mystique of the state, I suggest that perhaps the generosity he extended to defeated Confederate soldiers and officials after the war was over and the Union safe demonstrated a spirit free of vengeance. But the spirit of vengeance is a characteristic usually inseparable from such a mystique; the absence of this characteristic in Lincoln might indicate the absence of state-mystique as well. It would be even worse if for Lincoln the struggle had been a game that had to be won for the sake of winning—a mere test of wills—at any cost and apart from any principle or even any mystique, but not from mystification. I think it would be a mistake to work with such an assumption.

What I call the group ferocities that defined the period before the war were mostly (but not exclusively) extreme passions rooted in largely unexamined but nonetheless rationalized habits and conventions and therefore had to be immoral or amoral. The group ferocities of the South called forth Lincoln's reactive double passion in his conduct of the war and stamped the war years until the North achieved victory, but for a while he had to restrain the abolitionist passion of some of his allies in order to end slavery. Their passion, though also rooted in moral principle, not in, say, an ideology of progress, was so intense that it had the potentiality to become self-defeating fanaticism. Frederick Douglass said eleven years after Lincoln's murder that if Lincoln had "put the abolition of slavery before the salvation of the Union . . . he would have rendered resistance to rebellion impossible" (Douglass, 3). But Douglass also said that Lincoln's highest aim was always to preserve the Union, not to destroy slavery. This statement is technically correct and reflects what Lincoln kept on saying, but might underestimate Lincoln's tactical dexterity in yoking the cause of black freedom to the cause of the Union.

The irony is that Lincoln could abolish slavery only because he was not an abolitionist until near the end of his career. This statement means that he became president only because he was not an abolitionist or at least did not declare himself an abolitionist; he could begin to emancipate slaves only because he became president and could launch the work of total abolition only after reelection and victory in the Civil War. Until his reelection he presented himself therefore as the unintentional emancipator who had to claim that he acted out of necessity, that freedom for slaves was forced on him. However he presented himself, I do not think we can deduct from his merits; his achievement was too great. The further inference is that in the mid-nineteenth century and for the foreseeable future, perhaps even beyond the nineteenth century, there could have been no initial emancipator but Lincoln, accidental or not, and then no other road to total abolition in all the states, North and South, than his. If we cannot always read his intentions before and after he became president, we can have no doubt about the strength of his will. Who else electable in the North would have had his will? I say this, while aware that it is foolhardy to be confident about counterfactuals.

In a rare admission of personal limitation in the history of the American presidency, and during a war no less, he said to a US senator that he was not a man "great enough to comprehend this stupendous enterprise" and that he was not endowed with "sufficient wisdom to manage and direct it. I confess I do not fully understand and foresee it all" (undated, F, 336). His confession was testimony to his incorruptible sanity, his refusal to convert even with one part of his mind countless human particulars into one imperious blinding abstraction.

Lincoln's presidency illustrates the generalization that the cost of eliminating a terrible condition is frequently staggering: evil done to prevent or remove evil remains evil and is not washed clean by a good result. His whole political life illustrates the generalization that in democratic politics, perhaps in all politics, it is nearly impossible to do the right thing for the right reasons, actually held and honestly stated.

Acknowledgments

I want to thank Charles Beitz, David Bromwich, Sharon Cameron, John Seery, Mort Schoolman, and Jack Turner for reading the whole manuscript and raising questions that proved most fruitful. I also learned a good deal from two anonymous reviewers. John Kulka's help was as always of great benefit. Along the way, the following colleagues either read parts of the manuscript or otherwise assisted me in trying to formulate my arguments: Bryan Garsten, Stephen Macedo, Luke Mayville, Steven B. Smith, George Shulman, and David Tubbs.

LINCOLN'S POLITICAL THOUGHT

1

The Period of Lincoln

THE PERIOD OF LINCOLN, who lived from 1809 to 1865, was 1854 to 1865, from passage of the Kansas-Nebraska Act to his murder. The situation in which he found himself and tried to act politically was the most terrible in American history. He did not try to stay quietly out of it. He emerged as the dominant person in it. When he became president, Lincoln said of himself that he was doomed to deal with problems that had no precedent since the founding, and that far exceeded even those faced by George Washington (Farewell Address at Springfield, February 11, 1861, LA, 2:199; second version, LA, 2:734; also Address to the Ohio Legislature, Columbus, February 13, 1861, LA, 2:205). No other American president had ever begun his term with the threatened destruction of the Union by secession. It turned out that eleven states seceded, either after and because of his election or in the wake of the events at Fort Sumter, which began in earnest with the South's firing on the fort on April 12, 1861. The last state seceded in early June. By that time there were twenty-three states (including the new free state of Kansas) rather than thirty-four remaining peacefully in the Union.

When Lincoln decided to try to undo the secession—it is not clear that every Republican, or indeed anyone else who happened to be elected president, would have made the same decision—the culmination was a civil war on an extraordinary scale. War might have been foreseen, but not its scale, which would have been unimaginable. In thinking about the war, one is impelled to ask, how did the people on both sides endure the strangeness inherent in the very outbreak of the war within the boundaries and between the members of one polity, and then endure the mystery, the shock, of the piled-up horrors of the war? One splendid academic work is in fact permeated by an inward comprehension of those horrors. I refer to Drew Gilpin Faust's *This Republic of Suffering* (2008). The book is humanly adequate to the worst part of the period of Lincoln, the war itself; there is no cheering or cheerfulness in it; no satire or cynicism; it is a rare accomplishment.

It is possible that no Democratic president would have faced secession in 1860–1861, but the South refused to support Stephen Douglas in his presidential bid, as if some slave states (not all) wanted to lose the election because they needed an excuse to secede; they were, in Lincoln's words, possessed of "the naked desire to go out of the Union," even though they were threatened by no new law (November 15, 1860, F, 459). Lincoln won a majority in the Electoral College (180–123) with a plurality of close to 40 percent of the total popular vote. Douglas was the runner-up in popular votes but the last of four candidates in electoral votes. (The only state in which Douglas won a popular majority was New Jersey.) Then in time of war, Lincoln not only referred to the struggle as "the greatest difficulty that this country had ever experienced" but also added "or was likely to experience" (Remarks to Baltimore Presbyterian Synod, version 2, October 24, 1863, CW, 6:536).

To understand Lincoln's greatness, we must understand some of the main sources of the troubles that confronted the country and him. That means above all that we must understand that the problems were not merely problems in the everyday political sense. We must face ferocities, the group ferocities, and the countless individual traumas caused and prolonged by these ferocities, in the period leading up to and during the war. The ferocities were so raw and the traumas so severe they cannot possibly be shaped into just another academic subject. We scarcely know, with the requisite imaginative intimacy, what we are handling when we study this period. Yet we know enough to be able to believe that everything and everyone, conditions and people, were worse than we like to think. Still, the period must be addressed; the gorgon must not paralyze us; nor, contrastingly, should the passage of time soothe us too much. We must have a sense of retrospective urgency that does not really suit standard academic discourse.

The national situation created by the passage of the Kansas-Nebraska Act (1854) and the *Dred Scott* decision (1857) was politically intractable; a consensual democratic system could not deal with it, in large part because the South seemed to grow less appeasable with every success it gained. The Southern ferocities created secession and then carried over into the war with intensified force through action and reaction. In that war Northern group ferocities emerged with counterforce, guided and employed by Lincoln's double passion to save the Union and send slavery on the way to abolition, and most of the traumas suffered by countless individuals grew, North and South, while the traumas of slavery for the slaves went on and on, inadequately represented in the public mind. Political problems, though unprecedented in American history, raised with a new force numerous questions that were as old as reflection on political life: slavery, tyranny, causes of revolution, the rule of law, constitutional limits on the scope and methods of political power, social cohesion, political loyalty, the force of necessity, and the moral costs of violent means used to achieve disputed ends, even moral ends. Political theory came to life too vividly.

———

It might be tempting to reach for the category of tragedy to encompass the national situation, to face and perhaps grasp such terrible compressed eventfulness. After all, the strife took place in the house of the Union; North and South made up a kind of family; there had been awful overreaching by those who were finally defeated. But the overreaching that seemed fated was not fated, as in Greek tragedy. Still, the country seemed under a curse that compelled unwitting or fallible participants to bear the burden of an ordained pattern of action apart from or against their will. Was there not an unconscious and implacable force transmitted from one generation to the next? But just as there was no fate in the period of Lincoln, so there was no curse; there was only unbending human intention that persisted through the accumulation of appalling consequences. To be sure, Lincoln during the war employed the notion of God's providence, which ordained both slavery and the war that ended it, and Lincoln therefore appeared to remove responsibility for the whole situation from human beings and assign it to divinity and its unexplainable purposes. He entertained the idea that human beings were playthings in the hands of something much greater than they were.

Lincoln's idea of providential determinism, however, was distinct from tragic determinism; it was not tragic because the reason for the historical plot was perfectly knowable; it made no human sense except by reference to a freely chosen policy from the start, a policy that a few or some knew to be a policy of wrongdoing, while most did not care. He did not see the whites as living under a curse and helplessly working out its inevitable effects. They had no inkling that they were pursuing one thing while all along they were actually achieving another. The attribution of a curse would make it seem that if the whites really had free choice, they would not ever have enslaved blacks and kept them enslaved generation after generation. Lincoln almost said such a thing, but more often he said other things along the way that blamed human beings for slavery. Providential determinism enters the picture only during the war and is not allowed to blot out human responsibility, even at the risk of inconsistency. But if the notion of curse were right, I do not know what account would be made of the centuries-long suffering of blacks. The whites were cursed and had to enslave, and the blacks were cursed and had to be slaves? Victimizers and victims were equally innocent? But no curse should have long-standing benefits to any participants. Slavery had great benefits over the centuries until the war ended them, and they all went to the same race. In a tragedy the principals lose, or at least they lose far more than they gain. Also, unlike a tragic pattern, the plot in the period of Lincoln had a happy ending for the whites who were on the winning side of the war. As we will see, Lincoln was not of one mind on the transfer of human responsibility to providential design; he also held that people deserved punishment for holding slaves or aiding and benefiting from the institution of slavery. If providential determinism entered Lincoln's mind only during the war, his sense of human responsibility became all the more implacable during the war. The people cursed themselves; they brought their sufferings on themselves. Despite the undeniable suggestiveness of the metaphor of a curse on a whole society—as a way of referring to a misfortune too great to grasp or deal with and affecting everyone indiscriminately in the range of the curse—I think it is untenable; it is too flattering; consequently, so is the wish to use the concept of tragedy to cover the whole situation.

Furthermore, only if we insist on seeing the period as a struggle between whites and whites and leave out the slaves can we call the situation tragic. It was not only and not primarily the story of the sons of Oedipus in blue and gray. The sufferings that befell the free originated in the desire of some of them to deny freedom to a people not of their race. The desire was no mere flaw of character; it was the definition of the character. If brothers fought each other, their contest was over an unorganized and hence largely powerless third group, the black slaves, who were allowed to become fully active as fighters in their own cause only from the middle of the war but did not become a self-activating region-wide insurrectionary force. Of course many slaves made the courageous decision to try to escape; the Emancipation Proclamation was an incitement to run away, as was the war itself. But as James Oakes says, "most slaves never left their farms and plantations," and adds that "Slaves were more likely to be freed during the war by the arrival of the Union army than by escaping to it" (Oakes, 395, 410). The point is that at the beginning of the action, the participants were white, North and South, and they fought over the South's attempt to secede in order to strengthen the system in which millions of blacks were held in slavery.

The underlying causes of the action were two: the question of the integrity of the Union and the slaves' human status. Neither cause was pursuit of some high worldly value of the sort that tragic individual heroes contend for, like position or influence or honor or successful revenge. The integrity of the Union was countered by the South's wish to start an independent country. The dispute was not from its qualities tragic, though the consequences were immense. The question of status was, could blacks rightly be enslaved and treated like mere moveable property, like living instruments, or were they human beings who were profoundly wronged by being enslaved, as human beings of any color would be? To us, that looks like a rhetorical question, a question with a self-evident answer, but it was forced into being a genuine question at the time, and was answered in diametrically opposed ways.

Other elements that are usually important to tragedy were also missing. For example, only the slaves were used by forces they could not control; they were not tragic heroes at the mercy of the gods or the impersonal nature of things, but beings at the mercy of tenacious human will. In the earliest days in the history of the Republic, when it might have been comparatively easy to abolish slavery, slaveholders and their following sought every device, constitutional and political, by which to strengthen the institution of slavery. They did not try to avoid holding slaves; they did not discover, tragically, that every move they made away from the institution only fastened them more tightly to it. The slaves were cursed in the most secular sense, while the masters were not cursed in any sense. The suffering of whites on both sides in the Civil War was traumatic; they endured, if you will, tragic suffering, but suffering on such a scale is not well described as tragic. Furthermore, to kill when you think you have to kill may count to you as an individual as a tragic choice, but to the person killed, the fate exceeds tragedy because in secular understanding death is absolute loss, and absolute loss is not merely tragic.

Let us not be misled by the dignity of the idea of tragedy to misperceive the situation in which white human beings made free choices all along the way; above all, the choice to persist in the gratification of their desires at the expense of the humanity of another race. The helplessness of Southern whites in the face of slavery was a fiction—alas, a fiction that Lincoln was not always immune from and even did a fair amount to promote. I do not wish to deny, however, that Greek and Shakespearean tragedy could throw some light on the mentality of Lincoln as president (the inwardness of Hamlet would perhaps be the most apt; but as I will suggest at the end, there are other literary characters that come closer to putting us in mind of Lincoln because they explode the category of tragic hero); or could throw light on Lincoln's own characterization of the period; or even on such aspects of the Civil War as, for example, when brothers and relatives fought on opposite sides. But the idea of tragedy should not be used, I think, to encompass the totality of the situation or grasp its essence.

One plausible attempt to invoke Greek tragedy and epic as an appropriate comparison to Lincoln, and "his time, his death" was made by Walt Whitman, but his aim was to show that the stuff of American experience in this period was in truth heroic enough to be worthy of the greatest literature. I do not wish to disagree, except to say that great literature tends to leave out the nameless multitude, and even more, the nameless slaves. But it was Lincoln's sudden violent death that was uppermost in Whitman's mind. Whitman concentrates on the tragic element in Lincoln's murder, although Whitman extends his literary embrace to the whole period by saying that it was "more fateful than any thing in Eschylus—more heroic than the fighters around Troy." Whitman thought that Lincoln's death at the hands of a murderer unified the story of the period of Lincoln in a way that made it forever memorable and fit to be memorialized in great literary art. Although Whitman insisted that Lincoln could not possibly have been the whole story, Lincoln's sudden emergence and abrupt disappearance "stamps this Republic with a stamp more mark'd and enduring than any yet given by any one man," including Washington. "A long and varied series of contradictory events arrives at last at its highest poetic, single, central, pictorial denouement." The period is a "baffling, multiform whirl," but Lincoln's violent death gathered it into "one brief flash of lightning-illumination—one simple, fierce deed." The manner and timing of his death must appeal to the "imaginative and artistic senses," which give us access to the "immeasurable value and meaning of that whole tragedy." His death was the "suddenly ringing down the curtain," which closed "an immense act in the long drama of creative thought, and gave it radiation, tableau, stranger than fiction." Not even the death of Socrates or the murder of Julius Caesar "outvies that terminus of the secession war" ("Death of

Abraham Lincoln" [1879] in Whitman, 1045–1046). An involuntary martyrdom of an un-innocent man who died on the altar of revenge exacted for the humiliation of total defeat appears to serve Whitman's aesthetic purpose. If Lincoln had died much later and nonviolently, of what benefit to art would his life have been? Whitman almost makes us feel gratitude to John Wilkes Booth for creating the possibility of aesthetic magnificence.

More simply, much less aesthetically, Emerson in his eulogy of Lincoln said that the tale of the war and emancipation needed a moral. Was it found in the thought that "heaven, wishing to show the world a completed benefactor, shall make him serve his country even more by his death than by his life?" ("Abraham Lincoln" [1865] in Emerson, 921). It was time for Lincoln to die: "what remained to be done required new and uncommitted hands" (921). These are sorrowful words, yet cold, despite their sorrow, because of the salience of the country's urgent practical aim. Whitman's words also show coldness, but the source is a passion for aesthetic fulfillment. It is good but not surprising that Lincoln anticipated what Emerson and Whitman said. Some weeks after the Emancipation Proclamation, Lincoln told an abolitionist delegation, referring to General Frémont's earlier attempted local emancipation proclamation (which he had revoked), and perhaps subtly but more significantly referring to himself, that "the pioneer in any movement is not generally the best man to carry that movement to a successful issue . . . the first reformer . . . gets so bespattered that afterward, when people find they have to accept his reform, they will accept it more easily from another man" (January 25, 1863, F, 120).

One of the many questions Whitman raises for us is how far we should go to countenance the aestheticism that demands a heroic or martyred death to make a situation serious and an outcome definitive. I believe that we should not measure historical or experiential seriousness by the degree to which it inspires a literary response, no matter

how profitable that response might be to the cultivation of future generations. A more important question, however, is lurking in Whitman's
piece: would our estimation of Lincoln's greatness as a man and president be less, or at least more complex, if he had not died when and how
he did? Do we extend him forgiveness for his indulgence of racism, his
insistence that gradual emancipation would have been greatly preferable
to sudden emancipation, and that compensation to slaveholders who
voluntarily emancipated their slaves would be morally untroubling if it
were expedient? In any case, thinking about the period of Lincoln as a
tragedy should take into account Whitman's magnificent essay. Whitman's motive was not to raise the South to the level of the North and
thus make the adversaries into tragic equals but to emphasize the world-
historical greatness of Lincoln's achievement in commanding the defeat
of the South.

Of course there were numerous occasions of drama in the period of
Lincoln. He himself likened his debates with Douglas to "the successive
acts of a drama . . . to be enacted not merely in the face of audiences like
this, but in the face of the world" (sixth debate, October 13, 1858, LA,
1:738). The tendency of political participants to aestheticize politics is
irrepressible. But the whole situation with its ferocities and traumas
should nevertheless not be placed within the grasp of literary categories, which would be yet another kind of reductionism and which
would, like all other kinds, help us avoid reality by abandoning analysis
too soon.

We must now give attention to the specific group ferocities and their
consequent traumas that define the period of Lincoln.

Let us always think first of the trauma to the slaves before the war.
There were four million alive in 1860; then add the number of those
who were already dead by then and those who died on the way to their

enslavement. But the trauma of the slaves was not at the forefront of attention of anyone who was white and free, except the abolitionists, and they were a minority that did not include Lincoln in name, but only sometimes in effect. The Free Soil party was devoted not to abolition but to the exclusion of slavery from the territories. Furthermore, despite the condition of the slaves, slave psychology was not the story of this period before or during the war. The rebellious spirit of the downtrodden and their thirst for vengeance or compensation, their righteous anger or *ressentiment*, their envy, or their will to turn the world upside down by enslaving their former masters—all these possible effects of enslavement did not figure as political elements. There could not be a worse guide to slave mentality in the United States than Melville's story "Benito Cereno" (1855), where all the readers' sympathies are coaxed and build up for the white captains, not the black slaves, even or especially after you realize that what is going on is flawless playacting. You root for the rebel slaves to be subdued. The story was perverse in its timing and would always be mischievous in its effects, if taken at any time as an account of American slave psychology. Not the war, not even the Emancipation Proclamation or the victory of the North, unleashed widespread insurrections or rampages, which Lincoln took care not to incite. Slaves fled, but they did not show the remorseless bitterness of retaliation. They fought as soldiers, when given a chance, not as an enraged mob. They did not collectively initiate their own emancipation; they did not liberate themselves without external assistance, as did the group of slaves (temporarily) aboard the Spanish ship *San Dominick* in Melville's story (based on a real event that dated from 1805). There was no imitation of the Haitian revolution. There also was little direct expression of the excess that is supposed to burst out and has sometimes occurred because of the intoxication felt by newly freed slaves or other exploited people in the days, months, or even years after victory.

No, the story of the Lincoln period is to begin with made up of the group ferocities of whites in the slave states: their absolute determination to maintain and extend slavery from self-interest or selfishness as Lincoln said more than once, but also, as he said, from the desire to tyrannize over others whom they refused to see as fully human; and to retain a way of life that was interwoven with slavery, even though only a minority of Southern whites owned slaves. It was a way of life Southerners loved and became ever more attached to, just because they could not imagine living in a society where numerous blacks mingled with them as free people. It was not only that slavery provided the cheapest labor and the greatest profits; slavery was good as a matter of right because blackness was odious and deserved subjugation in every detail of life. Why not enslave them and only them? Then add slavery-centered insurgent regional patriotism that was far more ferocious than the national patriotism of the North. In a word Southern racism defined Southern ferocity and permeated all its other sources. To be sure, a concern for the trauma of the slaves figured only a little among Northern politicians in this period; elected abolitionists were not many; everyday political discourse remained largely unburdened by the slaves' trauma, or was forced by gag rules and informal censorship to remain so. Outside voices carried much of the moral burden of antislavery. The passage of the Kansas-Nebraska Act in 1854 changed the situation somewhat; it certainly aroused Lincoln's attention and elicited from him some moments of eloquence on the plight of the slaves; but at least a few politicians in the North had been attentive for a longer time.

Let me acknowledge that the word *racism* is anachronistic. It is first used in the early twentieth century, well after abolition, to name discriminatory and abusive treatment by one race of another. I use the word throughout, even though it is anachronistic, and to refer to treatment that went well beyond discrimination and abuse. *Racialism* would now be misleading, and *color consciousness* not adequate.

Of course, there was antiblack racism in every part of the Union, but almost no legal slavery outside the South and the border states. We do not have to go to the South for punitive and virulent racism and for an imperialism that was racially defined. We can go to Stephen Douglas, who spoke the sentiments of many whites in the North. He said on July 9, 1858, shortly after Lincoln's House Divided speech and before his debates with Lincoln, that he was "in favor of preserving not only the purity of the blood, but the purity of the government from any mixture or amalgamation with inferior races." He then pointed to bad effects of racial mixture in Mexico and Central and South America. The general result had been "degeneration, demoralization, and degradation below the capacity for self-government" (A, 23). In the same speech Douglas extended his vision to California and supported the denial of rights to "coolies." He despised the local people south of the United States but coveted their land; his contempt made the acquisitiveness unsinful in his eyes. In his opening speech in the third debate, he endorsed the seizure of Cuba, parts of Canada, and "islands elsewhere" (LA, 1:601). His imperialism was not only grandiose but also both sprawling and somewhat vague, so in love was he with white American vitality. Although deep racism was pervasive among whites in the country, it was not always so harsh or expressed with such candor by prominent people, as in Douglas's case. Only in the North did racism have to be insisted on, because the North tended to allow public opposition to racism and hence could favor the possibility of bad conscience that had then to be discredited or rebutted. Racism could not be taken for granted everywhere in the North as nature's unquestionable way. Still, the wonder is not that there were slave states, but that there were free ones.

The South kept entrenching ever more deeply the so-called necessity to maintain and extend slavery. Growing numbers of blacks made the prospect of living with them on any terms other than slavery impossible to imagine. The slave states would never voluntarily work

their way out of their necessity; it was their salvation on the way to becoming their ruin.

The mentality of secession was driven by a fierce spirit not unlike
the spirit that drove the American Revolution; a wish to break off, start
fresh, assert a distinctive group identity that felt the impositions of the
larger union as unacceptably foreign. It is much easier to understand
the South's urge to secede than the North's resistance to secession. (The
four-year persistence by both sides in the struggle is another question
and not quickly answerable.) Secession was a war for regional independence from the nation. But of course secession was an inverted
American Revolution; it was meant to strengthen the institution of
slavery at home and establish not human liberty wherever possible,
but eventually slavery in Mexico, the Caribbean, and northern South
America. From these ferocities, to which we must add, as Lincoln knew,
a much more earnest church-Protestant proslavery religiousness than
the North's, the traumas came. These are the traumas of the costs of
the war.

It is probable that more American men died, North and South combined, in the Civil War than in World War II. Until blacks were allowed
by the North to fight, the deaths on American soil were inflicted by
white men on other white men; the enemies resembled each other,
spoke the same language, often had British surnames in common,
"worshipped the same God" (in Lincoln's words from the Second Inaugural Address), and, most tellingly, had once been fellow citizens. In
most respects they were not mutually "other." They were not separated
by color, until from 1863 onward the North enlisted more than 175,000
blacks. The nation's whites were not prescriptively divided into hereditary or largely fixed classes, as were, say, the participants in the English
Civil War more than two centuries earlier. But a chasm existed between
slave society and free society that always showed itself politically and
eventually took on a fatal national political importance, when coexis-

tence gave way, under mounting Southern pressure to change the rules, and thus to irreconcilable antagonism. The South thought that there had to be two nations in place of one, so that its culture of racial superiority could be hegemonic within sovereign boundaries, and slavery could therefore remain entirely untroubled by antislavery legal restrictions, even the mildest, or by moral opprobrium.

Then add one other trauma before the war, the horror to conscience and fellow feeling that antislavery white men and women endured. To them, the wrong of slavery was not only a violation of an abstract principle of liberty, but unacceptable cruelty and degradation. Moral outrage was not confined to abolitionists, but they endured it with undiminishing shock because they could begin to imagine what it was like to be a black slave, or at least how black slaves felt, while many whites—indifferent or mildly hostile to slavery—could never put themselves in the place of blacks, slave or free. Most whites thought they were forever protected by white skin from bondage; the only slavery they could imagine experiencing was like the mild selective despotism the colonies suffered under the British in the eighteenth century, and which Southern whites now claimed the North was threatening to impose on them in the 1850s. Southern whites would not accept the condition that Lincoln, in reference to British rule, called being "political slaves" (letter to George Robertson, August 15, 1855, LA, 1:359); staying in the Union meant political slavery to them. They found such political slavery as intolerable as some in the North found Southern human slavery, but what had been felt about British rule was not *moral* horror. On the other hand, abolitionist moral horror and outrage, true objective emotional correlatives to slavery in the South, were in themselves a trauma that was inflicted by the assault on the humanity in others. From this trauma of empathy (or sympathy) came some of the Northern ferocity and will to inflict in turn the trauma of death and destruction on the South.

Was the white abolitionist desire for vengeance on slaveholders more fierce than that of the black slaves themselves? It is not impossible, as if empathically imagined suffering were sometimes worse—sharper and more devastating—than experienced suffering. I grant that what was at issue was perhaps some feeling a little different from empathy and closer to sympathy, but to such intense sympathy that one would find it intolerable to know that anyone was a slave. It might be impossible for a lucky person to think one's way into abject suffering or dehumanization and feel it as if it were happening to oneself, as empathy would require, even though not wanting it to happen to oneself is obviously not sufficient for not wanting it to happen to someone else. There must be sympathy for the work of empathy to succeed; the process is never automatic. When Northerners of decent or even privileged circumstances, however, did try to imagine themselves as slaves, they would do so as persons who had known a personal status and condition of life vastly better than that of the slave, and, unlike most slaveholders and their numerous supporters, could not bear the knowledge that anyone of any race endured such thorough deprivation. They hoped or imagined that they would have the will, if suddenly they had to experience it, to resent it and resist it, and hoped that slaves would do the same. The shock of entering imaginatively into the effort of comparing the new state of existence with the earlier, better one would prove too much to permit oneself to think that one could endure it with resignation. Perhaps it was in the name of such anticipated shock that the trauma, whether we call it empathy or sympathy, arose and took the white person closer to the slave. The reverse side of the coin is that we should not expect that people who experienced the worst condition of life, permeated by systematic dehumanization, to offer vigorous challenge to it. Rather we should expect resentment and resistance to their own condition from people in lower classes, but not the lowest like slaves. People in lower classes are in a position to experience vicariously something better than what they now have. They retain the ability to imagine a better life, and then perhaps to receive support from the empathic or sympathetic who are already more fortunate. When racism is at its strongest, it is one of the great standing barriers to both empathy and sympathy. Only when racism is mild does it permit the sympathetic feeling that though chattel slavery, the worst social condition, is not likely to befall oneself, no one should be subjected to it, because all races and groups are equally human. Perhaps this last description fits Lincoln.

Next, we must not forget the collective passion of patriotism, which is always a potential cause of ferocity. If the South's patriotism was regional, and the regional identity took precedence over national identity (if there had to be a choice), and existed before the Civil War, the North's patriotism was national, for the Union, and more abstract and required war or a direct threat to American soil to be aroused from its latency. But once aroused it was remarkable and instantaneous; most Northern soldiers were volunteers throughout the war, even though for short periods of enlistment and with high rates of desertion, sometimes seasonal. A different patriotism, then, on each side guaranteed that once favored by war, it would prove a source not only of energy but also of ferocity. In that respect the Civil War resembled most wars: similar inward loyalty (to match the resemblances in facial appearance in the American Civil War) of armed men on opposite sides, but bodies clothed in different uniforms and flying different flags, each side trying to kill the other. Obviously, the war did not begin as a war between races, but as a war within one race over the fate of another race.

It is almost impossible now to summon up the appropriate gravity when writing about the ferocities and traumas of this period and Lincoln's place in it: especially his struggle during the war to combat or employ ferocities and to intensify or ameliorate traumas. Drew Gilpin Faust's tone and gaze are uncommon. For us this period is now a subject. All right, let it be a subject, but also let us acknowledge that it is not an ordinary subject; it is not even an extraordinary subject. The war has not ended. Will it ever? Will Southern aggression ever end? Henry James referred to the South's "undying rancor" (386) in *The American Scene,* a book published in 1907 about his trip as an expatriate through the United States a few years earlier. The daughters of the Confederacy, he said, "nurse the old wrongs and the old wounds" (385; both quotations are from the great chapter 12, "Richmond"). Yet undeniably James expressed a fair amount of pity toward the South in its perceived enervation. But we cannot be blind to the way in which the fury of former masters can be much worse than that of former slaves: Southern treatment of black prisoners of war was execrable. It is instructive to recall the exemplary figure of Dostoyevsky's landowner Gaganov in *The Possessed,* who felt personally insulted, not only disadvantaged, by the emancipation of the serfs.

———

I wish to make one last point about the peculiar nature of the period 1854–1865. Although we are likely to perceive the traumas and ferocities, the inexhaustible passions and immeasurable suffering, even if we find it hard to reproduce and represent and respond to them adequately, we are not likely, whatever our differences of feeling and judgment, to face a conceptual gap of the sort that existed between those who judged slavery to be unacceptable evil and those who either were indifferent to it, except as a source of trouble or turmoil in political life, or positively supported it as something good or approved by God, even when they had no direct personal interest in its maintenance. Not all who did have a personal interest in slavery and who supported it were merely rationalizing their interest. The goodness or sanctity of slavery had lodged itself so deeply in their psyches that after a while they could no longer understand how others could oppose slavery unless they were warped fanatics or rationalizing some interest of their own. At one point, Lincoln rather ingenuously reduced the reason for any possible Southern secession to a thwarted desire that the North consider slavery good, not unjust, let alone evil (Address at Cooper Institute, February 27, 1860, LA, 2:128). The South wanted admiration for its peculiar institution, not grudging acceptance or, even worse, condemnation. But I think that it would have accepted even condemnation as long as it got its way. It was too confident to be as thin-skinned as Lincoln said it was.

The believers in slavery usually did not envisage extending slavery to poor whites—they did not want to, or they knew better than to try—but George Fitzhugh was quite happy to claim that white workers in the North were already worse off than slaves, and Governor Hammond of South Carolina made his fame with the mudsill theory of society, which claimed that slaves or lower classes in general existed to make the high culture of privileged classes possible. But the tenacity of the South's ideological adherence to the institution of slavery finally rested not on what Fitzhugh or Hammond said but on racism, the dislike of the color and features of blacks and the often fantastical assumptions that Southerners permitted themselves, with male sexual envy thrown in, so as to saturate blackness with subhuman qualities. Correspondingly, those who felt the horror of slavery, the moral outrage of it, could not understand how anyone could be so blind or deceived as to find slavery either a matter of indifference or a good institution, even when—appallingly—it was religiously approved or sanctified. The conceptual gap was thus unbridgeable.

Some of the ferocities, North and South, arose, then, from mutual incomprehension, which aggravated mutual suspicion. Fellow citizens became hostile aliens, but asymmetrically: Northerners became alien (at least in the abstract) to Southerners, but not the other way around. For a time, Northern reluctance to kill was not shared as much by the South. In a number of letters, before the ascendance of Grant, we see

Lincoln struggling with his generals to be as ready to move and kill as the Southern leaders were. But the South was fighting against what it felt was a foreign invasion of what it conceived as its homeland; every place in America, in the Confederacy or not, where slaves were held was part of its homeland. After a while, Northerners killed as easily as Southerners. The mental condition of being at war descended on both sides equally. The frantic effort made by each side to win, and feared by both to be fruitless, meant that the war won, as Edmund Blunden said about the enthrallment that led warring nations to keep the struggle going in World War I. But Lincoln was at war from the start. In January 1861, when seven states had already seceded, he said, "Compromise is not the remedy, not the cure. . . . The system of compromise has no end" (F, 193). There would always be more Southern demands. Then when war came, Lincoln never accepted the finality of the overall asymmetry represented by Southern bellicosity and Northern defensiveness, even though he appeared to lack on most (not all) prewar occasions a right understanding of the South's ferocities and could scarcely believe, even right after his election, that the South was serious about secession.

The mutual incomprehension eventually led to ever deeper mutual animosity. Principals on each side came to think the worst of each other. In the North some believed that, given the impact of the Mexican War and the admission of Texas to the Union, the South would never freely give up its aim to make slavery legal in every state in the Union and to extend slavery as far south into the Americas as possible. The *Dred Scott* decision was the climactic episode of such fear. Lincoln, de-spite the prudence of his positions, was one who thought and said in his moments of truth that the South would never be satiated. In the South many thought that the antislavery elements in the North would not rest until they had abolished slavery in all states. These mutual sus-picions based themselves on the logic of the situation, as Lincoln formulated it in his House Divided speech in 1858: the Union would become all slave or all free. But it must be repeated that Southern extremism—the will to go to the end of the logic of the situation—far exceeded that of the North until the middle of the war, and where popular moderation meant containing but not abolishing slavery, and abolitionist sentiment was widely repudiated until well into the Civil War.

A curious episode that reflected the Northern reluctance to fight involved an officer in the Union army, Major John J. Key, in late September 1862. He was dismissed for having said that the Union army had deliberately failed to pursue the Southern army after the battle of Antietam (Maryland) in order to avoid capturing or killing their soldiers. Key is quoted as saying, "That is not the game. The object is that neither army shall get much advantage of the other; that both shall be kept in the field till they are exhausted, when we will make a compromise and save slavery" (LA, 2:373). Although Key did not say anything straightforwardly disloyal, Lincoln endorsed his dismissal. The report on the incident said, "The substance of the President's reply was that if there was a 'game' ever among Union men, to have our army not take an advantage of the enemy when it could, it was his object to break up that game" (374). Lincoln had seen by then (June to September 1862, the period of the preliminary draft of the Emancipation Proclamation) that whatever the sentiment of gamesmanship anywhere in the upper ranks of the Union army, the South had never thought that it was playing a game; it was fighting a war as hard as it could in order to be rid of the Union. Lincoln's disgust with General McClellan's unaggressive disposition—buttressed by an antipathy to emancipation—to let the Southern army get away rather than chasing and defeating it, was so strong that any apparent justification of it aroused Lincoln's fury. He later said, "I dismissed Major Key for his silly treasonable talk, and I wanted an example" (September 25, 1864, F, 231). In fairness we should notice that Key said he only meant that the rebels would not let the war be decided; they wanted to prolong the war and hoped after common exhaustion that a compromise could be reached, with presumably both the Union and slavery preserved (CW, 5:443, n. 1).

The Lincoln-Douglas debates of 1858 are a perfect introduction to the fateful conceptual gap between one representative speaker who thought slavery a monstrous injustice and another who did not care whether slavery was allowed or prohibited in new territories or anywhere else, provided disruption in or of the Union was avoided. For Douglas, a slave was just another piece of moveable property. I do not know which conceptual gap was greater: that between Lincoln and Douglas or that between Lincoln and Fitzhugh, though it is surely true that Douglas would never have defended or taken part in a war to preserve slavery for the sake of slavery, despite his expressed racism. Indeed, in his speech in the fifth debate, he said that though blacks were inferior to whites, and should not ever become equal citizens with whites, "it does not follow by any means that he should be a slave," but can be allowed "every right, every privilege, every immunity which he can safely exercise consistent with the safety of the society in which he lives" (October 7, 1858, LA, 1:698). Free blacks deserved limited guarantees, but black slaves did not deserve to be free unless their masters agreed. Indeed, conceptual gaps make study of the Lincoln period all the more disorienting.

———

Obviously, the worst conceptual gap between proslavery and antislavery people was the disagreement over the humanity of black people. For some later scholars, therefore, the temptation offered by cultural relativism has permeated the subject of slavery. By relativism I mean the view that something is wrong (not to be done or allowed) only by local standards. The upshot is that if there are no general standards of any type, then there are obviously no moral standards and hence no universal morality. In matters of conduct, there are only particular systems of mores or codes of life. But Lincoln said, "If slavery is not wrong, nothing is wrong" (letter to Albert G. Hodges, April 4, 1864, LA, 2:585). He also said, "Questions of abstract right and wrong cannot be questions of locality" (speech at Beloit, Wisconsin, October 1, 1859, CW, 3:484). But the issue was not relativism. People who thought slavery good or at least permissible did not argue that questions of abstract right and wrong were questions of locality. Rather, many of Lincoln's opponents just did not think that elementary morality applied to dark-skinned people who were inferior by nature; moral relations were obligatory only among whites. Dark skin infallibly indicated inferiority or was in itself sufficient proof of inferiority. For centuries, European imperialism all over the world certainly reflected that belief. Self-evident justice for all, irrespective of race based in color, was generally helpless against early social inculcation, daily confirmation, conformist mimesis, and un-subtle rationalization, which all worked to favor the whole system of slavery as well as other kinds of oppression. The impact of the system of enslavement was to degrade blacks and then justify whites in speaking and acting as if the degraded condition were innate and incorrigible. There was thus supposedly no inflicted degradation; enslavement was an appropriate response to what blacks were by nature.

Southern apologists for slavery and their widespread following did not answer their critics by claiming that there was no morality; they did not hold that nothing was wrong on both sides of a boundary or that within a boundary there was only correct or deviant adherence to local (state or regional) social and cultural mores. They did not deny that all white persons deserved basic legal protections of life, liberty, and property, even though they did not think there was anything wrong with established and perpetuated political and social inequality among whites. Calhoun, for one, did not believe in Jefferson's idea that equal rights derived from God's endowment, or in the social contract of equal participants, but he did not renounce justice for whites. The apologists did not claim that they obeyed a higher principle than morality, such as obedience to God's arbitrary will as revealed in the Bible, and certainly did not think that God's will sometimes coincided with morality and sometimes did not—an idea that Lincoln as president, not Southern apologists, seriously considered. They maintained instead that blacks and perhaps all nonwhites were not persons; as subhuman, blacks "had no rights which the white man was bound to respect," in the words of Chief Justice Taney in the *Dred Scott* decision when he summarized the contempt in which whites held blacks, as demonstrated by white behavior from the beginning. (Calhoun, the most resourceful thinker among the apologists, contented himself with saying that blacks were human beings but innately inferior to whites, and improved by being and staying slaves. Slavery was a positive good for the black slaves; freedom would be their undoing.)

Southern apologists did not say, despite all their separatist ferocities and all the cultural dissimilarities between South and North, that white Northerners were not full persons. Nor did Southern apologists hold that if there was general morality, the particular mores that constitute a way of life were supreme and exceeded morality in value; that is, the mores constituted a code of life that was sufficient to everyone in every sphere and detail, while morality had a subordinate place in the mores, if it needed to have a place at all, or became just one more custom, if it had a place. No, it was the passion of racism that transcended morality, and apologists and their following did not or could not candidly acknowledge that they believed it did. Instead they persuaded themselves that being inferior, blacks were not entitled to morality at the hands of whites, the elementary morality that whites, strengthened they supposed by their religion, aspired or aimed to use with one another.

The kind of relativist or pluralist proslavery outlook that I have reconstructively stated was not the stuff of public discussion, though I think it tacitly helped to supply some sentiments that fortified the

Southern will to believe they did no wrong. Not overtly claiming to establish a doctrine above morality, despite any inclination toward amoral or morally indifferent cultural pluralism that some people were likely to have harbored—this is our way, whatever anyone else believes, and nothing matters more to us than it does—apologists learned to think and act as if morality permitted the enslavement of blacks and perhaps religion demanded or at least encouraged it.

Racism is incomparably worse than relativism: a whole society can be organized around racism but not around relativism, which always has been a philosopher's idea. Relativism can be rebutted, but racism can withstand all argument. Children cannot be indoctrinated in relativism, let alone raised in a culture that practiced relativism in all the details of life, no matter how tolerant of difference it is; relativism is shallow, while racism is deep. Indeed, the fixation on relativism is, in some cases, a quite deliberate attempt to obscure the hold of racism or make it easier to practice. The paradox of racism is that the depth of its passion, the ferocity of its emotions, grows out of the most superficial differentiating characteristic, skin color. Such difference was made to engender boundless contempt, disgust, and aesthetic vanity. If one did not know better from experience, one's reason would say that there is a mystery in the attractive power of such superficiality. These emotions once implanted could not be uprooted, and could be restrained only with great difficulty; they spread over every aspect of life. The racist conviction was that blacks were not true people because they were not white; they were less than human; or, though human, innately inferior; or at most, they were cursed by God always to be servants because of the sin of Ham, Noah's prurient son and their alleged ancestor. Apart from the Bible, the claim sometimes was that slavery saved imported blacks and their descendants from unspeakable practices or reversion to them, but nothing could elevate them into full humanity, not even the perpetual apprenticeship of slavery.

I think it would be a bad mistake to say that racism was only an insincere rationalization of slavery, and that the real motive was greed. To work as a rationalization designed to satisfy a huge audience, racism would have had to be addressed to an audience already reflexively sympathetic to it. Of course there was greed, but its limitlessness, as shown in the determination to perpetuate and extend slavery, was made psychologically possible only because of racism. Of course other ideas or visions can make greed limitless, as industrialization after the Civil War made clear. But black slavery in its time was not a slightly different form of commercial profit-seeking, immensely profitable though it was for many slaveholders. To make a profit from slavery placed the slaveholders in a separate world from other entrepreneurs, no matter how greedy, when shrewdly responding to old needs or newly stimulated ones. No doubt, independent white farmers did not want millions of free blacks to compete for public lands, but that was racially defined selfishness, not limitless greed. Limitless greed seemed to partake of a passion made ferocious by its racial abstraction; it seemed malignant, the original American malignity.

Thus the essence of the struggle over the rightness of slavery was not between moral absolutism and cultural relativism, the obsessive theme of some of Leo Strauss's followers. How much easier the situation would have been if the conceptual gap between proslavery and antislavery and hence the contest had in fact been between absolutism and relativism, if one could imagine that there could ever have been such a cultural contest that consumed millions of people on a continental scale. (Nor was the founding revolution, when it was justified by the inalienable and absolute rights of the colonists, a struggle against the relativism of the mother country and its political establishment; it was in part a struggle of American whites for white status equality against prescriptive hierarchy.) Douglas's doctrine of popular sovereignty was not a relativist idea but a racist one; he never said or came close to saying that the basic rights of white people were to be determined by either popular sovereignty or routine majority vote. He would have rejected with indignation the idea that any white person should be a slave.

In any event you do not need moral absolutism to condemn slavery, because if slavery is not wrong, nothing is wrong. All you need is decency extended by enlightenment to include people not of your color. In other words the division over the rightness of slavery was between on the one hand the minority's strong opposition to slavery on moral grounds and on the other hand the majority's compound of an extreme racism that showed itself in keeping black slaves or unequivocally supporting those who did, and a mild to moderate and nearly ubiquitous racism sometimes joined to faint antislavery sentiment. The latter kind of less intense racism often showed itself in thoughtless indifference to slavery or to the determination not to see that abolition was the most urgent moral question in American life, and that therefore persons should try to do something about it within the system; or if they gave up, to do so in embittered resignation.

The historical vindication of antebellum abolitionists is that their agitation kept the question of slavery alive as more than an issue, as much more than a usefully acrimonious political issue, and thus prevented a sizable number of whites, especially if they were only vaguely antislavery, from falling asleep out of boredom, in disregard, precisely, of the most urgent moral question in American life.

To illustrate the point about the racism of the majority: in the election of 1860, 40 percent of the people (largely white) voted—and not only for antislavery reasons—for Lincoln, who did not run as an abolitionist, while 60 percent (surely almost all white) voted against him, and they were not only antiabolitionist but proslavery in intent or in effect. Without antiblack racism in whatever degree, strengthened by orthodox religion and pseudoscience, there would have been no slavery practiced by white Christians and its continuous augmentation or tolerance of it. The history of racial segregation after abolition, from reconstruction to Jim Crow and up to the present day, shows the deep, continuous, indelible racism that accounted for the very possibility of black slavery in the first place, and that kept it going after the Revolution in a so-called democracy that was populated by Christians who were said to worship God on a cross, who died like a slave.

The group ferocities were not mere ruthlessness; they were far in excess of the inflamed and at times brutal partisan and regional passions of ordinary American politics and made ordinary politics precarious and then impossible. I do not deny that there are always a few submerged ferocities waiting for their opportunities when unusual situations overtake ordinary politics, but the period 1854–1865 manifested several concentrated ferocities, a convergence of extreme or infinite passions. We must add that in the South exaggerated fear for the future of black slavery was joined to adventurism, a willingness to risk much and keep on risking for the sake of ever more future advantage or for the sake of impregnable superiority. The enormous country as a whole was barely held together institutionally, and the South wanted to break it at its strongest point, the seat of the federal government.

The striking thing is that Southern ferocities in the period of, say, 1854–1862 did not consistently register on Lincoln, or if they did, he did not usually allow himself to represent them in his speeches and other writings. One especially noteworthy example is found in the great speech at Peoria (October 16, 1854) after the passage of the Kansas-Nebraska Act. This speech is complex and full of passion against the act that repealed the Missouri Compromise. Yet Southern ferocities, the ferocities of Southern people, not only slaveholders, were made to disappear by an evenhandedness that was so contorted it was spurious. In the same part of the speech where Lincoln spoke of "the monstrous in-justice of slavery," he pulled back and began to talk about how theoreti-cal defenders of slavery in the South, usually slaveholders, were "really good men" even though they were openly renouncing the ideal of equal liberty in the Declaration of Independence. This imputation of good-ness did not point to the banality of the evildoer but, absurdly, the goodness of the evildoer, as if holding a slave were nothing personal, even if the slave was a person. Can a man who holds slaves be a "really good" man, even though he treats well everyone white around him and close to him? It appears that Lincoln was trying to be magnanimous toward what he chose to construe as weakness of will.

He showed a comparable attitude in another sphere of life. In a speech praising the campaign against the consumption of alcohol but warning against demonization, zealousness, and unremitting censori-ousness, he said "In my judgment, such of us as have never fallen vic-tims, have been spared more from the absence of appetite, than from any mental or moral superiority over those who have. Indeed, I believe, if we take habitual drunkards as a class, their heads and hearts will bear an advantageous comparison with those of any other class. There seems ever to have been a proneness in the brilliant and warm-blooded, to fall into this vice" (Address to the Washington Temperance Society of Springfield, Illinois, February 22, 1842, LA, 1:88). Lincoln here too ex-tended magnanimity to weakness of will, but upholding slavery did not stem from weakness of will but strength of will. The campaign against it should not have been magnanimous; the slaves would have been lost sight of; magnanimity would have been at their expense. The virtue of magnanimity would have produced the effects of serious vice by being misdirected.

The targets of Lincoln's wrath before the war were rather those in the North, like Douglas, who compromised on the issue of extending slav-ery into the territories, as if only these compromisers, not the delegates of the slave power, should have known better. Lincoln acted as though he was aware that no reasoning or rhetoric could persuade the South to end slavery, and therefore that no principle embracing all races as human equals could possibly penetrate massed Southern opinion. White people in the free states should be expected to know better about the nature of equality. Already sounding like a president, he wanted to insist, however, that he declared no prejudice against Southerners. "They are just what we would be in their situation. If slavery did not exist amongst them, they would not introduce it. If it did now exist amongst us, we should not instantly give it up. This I believe of the masses north and south." When Southerners said that slavery was "difficult to get rid of," Lincoln said he understood them. "I surely will not blame them for not doing what I should not know how to do myself." If Lincoln had all the power, he still would not know what to do about the institution of slavery. Lincoln went on to canvass various possibilities, all of which he rejected: deport all slaves; free them but keep them as underlings; free them and make them the political and social equals of whites (speech after the Kansas-Nebraska Act, Peoria, October 16, 1854, LA, 1:315–316). He thus made the situation hopeless and the South blameless. What Lincoln showed was not exactly empathy with those who held slaves or only supported slavery in their states, but an ability to substitute rationalization for understanding in order to give reassurance. The South, however, did not want empathy; it wanted admiration for building up its peculiar institution. It was not sorry it held slaves and was not asking to be forgiven. It did not want obstacles to its determination to proceed as it wished. But if slaveholding were spoken of as if it needed forgiveness and such forgiveness could be bestowed in the abstract as easily as Lincoln bestowed it in his gesture of appeasement, which makes us all alike and a lucky or unlucky condition everything, you might as well say that slavery was nothing and therefore blacks were nothing, and that there was no wrong.

It was one thing to hold that the North bore some, even a large responsibility, for the continuation of slavery because of its eager use of the products that slave labor made possible: "how unhesitatingly we all use cotton and sugar." It was quite another to hold that "it may not be quite safe to say, that the south has been more responsible than the north for its continuance" (Annual Message to Congress, December 1, 1862, LA, 2:408).

One moment of truth about the South's ferocities, however, appeared in the superabundant and hence heterogeneous Peoria speech—it was almost novelistic—in which he lamented the loss of the spirit of compromise and imagined what would take its place. He spoke prospectively and said, "The South flushed with triumph, and tempted to excesses; the North, betrayed as they believe, brooding on wrong and burning for revenge. One side [the South] will provoke; the other resent. The one [the South] will taunt, the other defy; one [the South] aggresses, the other retaliates" (LA, 1:335). I infer from the context that Lincoln did not mean that provoking, taunting, and aggressing could be done by either side; only the South would do those things. Whether I read the passage correctly or not, it is one of the keenest passages of abstract psychology in Lincoln's work; but if I read it right, it showed him capable of acknowledging the asymmetry of the situation: I think he meant the asymmetry created by the South's will to expand slavery and the North's to confine it but not abolish it (to leave aside abolitionists who did not hold many political offices and did not inspire much nationwide respect). (Symmetry would have meant that the South wanted to expand slavery beyond where it existed and the North to contract it where it existed. This was not the case.) In the middle of the war, right after great Union victories in July 1863, when Lincoln looked back to the war's beginnings, he could bring himself to say without hesitation that it was the South's "anger, which has produced, and so long sustained a needless and cruel rebellion" (Proclamation of Thanksgiving,

July 15, 1863, CW, 6:332). Still, anger is less than wrath, and is a kind of terminological domestication of ferocity.

Lincoln called secession a rebellion, refusing to allow that any state of the Union could legally or constitutionally secede without consent of the other states. He also called secession treason, and not only a rebellion but a revolution, and such language could only mean that the South would not be conciliated (Special Message to Congress, July 4, 1861, LA, 2:252, 254). In the last two years of war, Lincoln's response changed even more drastically; the nature of the South's ambition at last fully registered. In a counter-passion he not only wanted to destroy the armies of the South, he permitted the destruction of the land in parts of the South, especially Georgia and South Carolina. With composure, he spent and allowed Grant to spend Union lives. He could refer to human beings—young men in the North—as "national resources" for war; the Union could maintain a war "indefinitely" (Annual Message to Congress, December 6, 1864, LA, 2:660). At last, he crossed all bounds to win the war and save the Union. It took aroused group ferocity to defeat entrenched ferocity, with trauma for all. Then close to victory, Lincoln was unscrupulous in directing the process of ratification of the Thirteenth Amendment, so that the Civil War could not be un-won. As president, he showed growth not in moral enlightenment, which he did not need, but in determination, in the readiness to identify a section of the country as the enemy, not merely as a wayward region.

The moral outrage and shock to conscience in the North were also rarely represented in Lincoln's work, though on one private occasion, in a letter to his friend Joshua F. Speed, he said that he carried away from witnessing slaves "the power of making me miserable" and asked Speed to "appreciate how much the great body of the Northern people do crucify their feelings in order to maintain their loyalty to the constitution and the Union" (August 24, 1855, LA, 1:361). There were public occasions when he summoned his powers to convey the awfulness of the slaves' condition, and let the mere charged description do the work of commentary. However, despite his hatred of slavery, the moral outrage felt by him and others was usually kept at an antiabolitionist distance, and carefully controlled, for the most part, in its manner and infrequent occasion of utterance until late in the war.

In saying that the South's ferocities did not always register on Lincoln, I mean that his commitments were such as to induce in him a minimization of the trouble that the country was in before secession. As a midwestern Whig and then Republican politician, he tended to make the national situation appear more manageable than it was. He tended to underestimate the intensity of the South's unappeasable ambition; he did not perceive its immitigable ferocity. Such ambition was what I called the original American malignity (politely said: dynamism); abstractly put, it was a compound of rapacity (itself a combination of greed and abstract insatiability), some guilt, and acute paranoia, and was often permeated by racism; part of its instigation was racism. It was the model for later postslavery American maliginity, which was often but not always race-based; and it is still operative today.

Of course the word *malignity* may appear melodramatic, but only to the lucky ones who do not suffer its systematic atrocious effects and who are unable to sympathize with those who do. Some observers might say, however, that in the case of Southern slavery, it was only the imitation of malignity and could have come from the conviction that the tendency of American national politics was unfavorable to it, no matter how apparently favorable it seemed. The South would inevitably emerge as a constantly besieged permanent minority that the Constitution could not adequately protect. This was the underlying anxiety in Calhoun's *A Discourse on the Constitution and Government of the United States* (written 1845–1850), the detailed elaboration of Calhoun's theoretical *Disquisition on Government*. The future was against the South for

geographic and demographic reasons, not because of a concerted abolitionist or even merely antislavery conspiracy. Slavery would survive
in the Union, but just barely and hence too uncomfortably. After all,
the Republican Party platform of 1860 which Lincoln represented denied in Article VIII "the authority of Congress, of a territorial legislature, or of any individual, to give legal existence to slavery in any territory of the United States," and did so on the grounds that a slave was a
person and enslavement was a violation without due process of the
person's rights of liberty and property, as guaranteed by the Fifth
Amendment. Holding persons as slaves was not, as Taney said, an exercise by the slaveholder of his rights of liberty and property over blacks
who were not constitutional persons. The platform's implication was
that slavery wherever it existed in the United States violated the Constitution perhaps because the Bill of Rights, properly read, superseded
whatever ran counter to the Bill in the original and unamended Constitution, as for example the recognition of slavery, if not by name.

It is interesting that a year later, Taney would imply in *Ex Parte Merryman* (1861) that the suspension of the writ of habeas corpus by Lincoln
was void perhaps precisely because the Bill of Rights superseded whatever ran counter to the Bill in the original and unamended Constitution. After the Bill, and first of all, Congress lost whatever power it ever
had to prohibit slavery in the territories. In Taney's jurisprudence it
would appear that the Bill of Rights thus voided both the territorial re-
striction of slavery without the slave-owners' consent and the suspension of habeas corpus even when there was rebellion or invasion. Of
course, Taney could not have struck down new constitutional amendments that would have authorized both—not that either amendment
would ever have been likely to pass.

Whatever Lincoln hoped or said he hoped, it is hard to imagine a
sharper line of opposition than that between the platform and the
South's position. It could be said therefore that what looked like the

South's malignity or insatiable dynamism was instead long-range defensive strategic prudence. But malignity and prudence coiled themselves around each other in people's sentiments and impulses. The prudence did not originate the racist malignity but served it, and in such a way as to make people lose sight of the malignant reality that was being served by it. The election of 1860 further obscured the malignity by creating excitement in the South over the prospect of independence, and redefined and thus further energized strategic prudence. The result of the election portended disaster in the South's estimation; secession was the only adequate strategy for nullifying that result.

In any case, Lincoln wanted before secession to posit the Union as being in less explosive peril from itself than it was. Are we allowed to say that if he did not know better, he should have? The same holds for other important matters, as I will try to show. Lincoln was hiding the truth or hiding from it. Yet, recurrently, in speeches, messages, and letters, moments of truth burst through. There was a convergence between what you surmise Lincoln really thought and what the situation that he was describing really was. I want to highlight these moments, even as I believe that some of Lincoln's commitments were so deep that he was unable to permit the fuller truth about them to appear. In Chapter 3, I will take up Lincoln's commitments. I will also try throughout to examine some of those occasions when the truth burst through Lincoln's caution or unreadiness.

2

Lincoln as a Writer

LINCOLN WAS A GREAT WRITER, though he wrote for the most part in the immediate moment for a political audience and with a political purpose. I would emphasize the richness of his mind, such richness that it invites multiple interpretations; this is not a common effect of the utterances of political actors, where the usual obstacles to understanding them are secrecy, withholding, manipulation of the truth, and lying. Not to deny that Lincoln sometimes engaged in these practices, but he was unusual because they did not define his utterances, which were marked by complexity and subtlety of meaning. His works will last, even if he did not always write them to last. He had a strong appetite to convert his political experience into articulate reflection, because that way he believed he could make the experience more real; he could make what he was doing and what was happening less confusing, less obscure to himself and others. His genius lifted the occasional and topical language of political life into the realm of permanent value. His writings contain numerous noteworthy sentences and passages, sometimes magnificent, often powerful.

We can go to him for the beauty of his intelligence, comparatively unschooled as it was, and give him his proper place in the American renaissance, alongside Emerson, Thoreau, Whitman, Melville, and Dickinson. Each of them struggled to discover an object worthy of reverence. Each was haunted by the question, "If nothing is worthy of reverence, what then?" but could not bear to leave that question hanging and perhaps answered it with a mixture of original invention and painstaking or perhaps frustrated discovery. Like them he had a commanding intellect devoted to producing the best words on just about every occasion, no matter how slight. I do not refer to Lincoln's professional writing as a lawyer; the little of it I have read is as boring as you could want, though Herndon singled out for the highest praise Lincoln's unpreserved speeches in courts, especially the Supreme Court of Illinois (Herndon, 210, 356). And of course there were numerous straightforward communications that dealt with business transactions, political maneuvers, and military tactics. A lot is still left when all of these are put aside. Emerson, the prince and benefactor of the renaissance—actually it was a birth, not a rebirth—said in his powerful eulogy of Lincoln that "the weight and penetration of many passages in his letters, messages and speeches, hidden now by the very closeness of their application to the moment, are destined hereafter to wide fame" ("Abraham Lincoln" in Emerson, 919).

Lincoln was at least as profound an American political writer as Jefferson, Madison, or Calhoun (to give the devil his due), or the Justices of the Supreme Court in their accumulation of theoretically significant passages in their collaborative achievement in jurisprudence over two hundred years. We should not exaggerate Lincoln's debt to Jefferson. Even when writing, occasionally but rarely, on a nonpolitical matter like human technical ingenuity throughout history, his mind was fresh and energetic (lecture on Discoveries and Inventions, April 6, 1858,

CW, 2:437–442; another part of the same lecture, February 11, 1859, CW, 3:356–363; see editors' note of Herndon's Lincoln, 271, which corrects Basler). Even his verses are not embarrassing. It is fitting that Fred Kaplan's subtitle for his life of Lincoln is *The Biography of a Writer*. We call him a writer because he was unafraid—actually proud—to say that "he supposed his style was peculiar and had its earmarks, so that it could not be mistaken" (August 25, 1864, F, 483). A recognizable style lays claim to distinctiveness of mind. Lincoln's style is simple and averse to grandness or clutter, and is at the service of thought that is harder and more resourceful than that of his political contemporaries in the period of Lincoln, including Seward.

Almost all of Lincoln's preserved writings were political. Politics, far more than anything else, elicited from him the wish to set down his thoughts and made him a writer. This disposition was more true of him than it was even of Edmund Burke. Lincoln's responses to political developments seem also to be an expression of his character, not an impersonal literary wish to create in words another world. The most searching study of the qualities of that character was put forth, I think, by William Herndon, his law partner. The vindication of Herndon's magnificent analysis, as presented in a lecture in 1866 and inserted as chapter 20 (the last chapter) of his biography, comes from the assistance he gives to later readers who struggle to understand Lincoln's words. I single out Herndon's lecture not to disparage the rest of the book, co-authored with Jesse Weik, but because as Allen C. Guelzo points out, the publication of the whole biography was delayed until 1889: audiences who heard Herndon's several lectures in 1866 were repelled by their candor (Guelzo, 442–446). Reading Herndon's lecture after reading Lincoln's works and after whatever else one reads about Lincoln produces the impression that Herndon, in the concentrated utterance of one lecture, came as close as anyone can come to Lincoln, to his genuine idealism, his patient willingness to take the long view and persist in the delicate balance of his idealism, his personal kindness joined to remoteness, his complete lack of arrogance but his conservative blindness to certain features of the political situation he faced before the war, and above all, the nobility of his ingrained democratic stoicism. This is not to say that Herndon captured Lincoln's character, and hence the meaning of Lincoln's words, with complete accuracy; such an attempt must fail. You cannot pin Lincoln down; he did not want to be pinned down, especially about his aversions. Nor do I agree with Herndon's interpretation of every important matter. But acquaintance with Lincoln's writings authenticates Herndon's character study in the last chapter at least as well as any other study of Lincoln, by friends or critics; it is probably better. I propose that Herndon's lecture should lodge itself in the mind, and all the more so, if one comes to it late in one's initial study of Lincoln, having overcome the common prejudice against the whole book's accuracy or veracity; coming late, one is better prepared to appreciate Herndon's splendid combination of recklessness and subtlety and how it takes us closer to right understanding.

Our task, however, is to struggle against bewitchment. I mean that when we try to understand Lincoln's ideas and the sentences and passages that convey or suggest them, we should not find the effort easy or free of serious perplexity. It is not that he is a difficult writer in the sense of employing radically new stylistic or structural strategies like those who create innovative philosophy or poetry or fiction: he wrote to be understood without having to be reread. He does not have a reputation for difficulty, but rather for the utmost clarity. Yet some of his work must be reread often; when it is, the feeling begins to emerge that one had not really grasped his point before, and that perhaps we do not do so now, but at least we know we do not comprehend the text as we would wish. Alternatively, we could say that Lincoln wrote as carefully as if he would be reread but did not quite expect to be. In a Republican

Party rally on August 8, 1860, he went so far as to call himself a "representative of truth" (LA, 2:142). Indeed, we typically go to him for the transparency of his utterance. But the clarity of his style was sometimes at the service of withholding or otherwise not conveying the full significance of what he meant. We must keep coming back to his words to figure them out, if we can, and not give in too quickly to the temptation of sheltering ourselves in the comfort of the notion of negative capability. When we come to Lincoln's religious or metaphysical views and their bearing on politics, the problem of his opacity seems even worse.

Deliberately or not, Lincoln warned us about himself when he said that it is "impossible to determine the question of the motives that govern men or to gain absolute knowledge of their sympathies" (September 29, 1863, F, 216). On that occasion, he was lamenting the reign of suspicion of disloyalty to the Union in Missouri and the corrosive effect of such suspicion. Are we not allowed, however, to have certain suspicions about Lincoln? Yes, of course, he was a lawyer and quite regularly sounded argumentative like a lawyer, especially in the debates with Douglas. He was also a politician, with eventually tremendous ambition. As a lawyer and politician he could be counted on to withhold his full meaning, and to engage in other sorts of distortion. But the reasons for his distortion of some significant matters were not always or even often the worldly ones: to win an argument in court or an office in an election. He either was captivated by what he was saying or was afraid to look closely enough at it, or he did not want to insist on it. Or he wanted to leave it uncertain because he was uncertain, or certain but out of season.

What I have just said may seem unfair. A plausible mitigation, but one that applies only to his words as president, is to admit that like any wartime president, Lincoln had many things, too many things, to balance or reconcile. Their comparative weight had to be shifting, just as the reasons for acting had to be shifting because of tactical changes or the need to adjust both means and short-term ends in the light of the fortunes of war. The historical difference between Lincoln and any other wartime president, however, is that Lincoln was a leader who was at war with large numbers of his former countrymen, and that in addition he had to face the fact that his own side was divided not only between slave states and free states but also between Unionist citizens, whatever their state, who favored or opposed emancipation as a tactic of war and abolition as a war aim. Thus the complexity of Lincoln's endeavor had at times to be and to be thought unmanageable; and being unmanageable the endeavor made it inordinately hard and sometimes impossible for Lincoln to have a clear sense of priorities other than the highest priority, which was to preserve the Union against successful secession. It was also sometimes hard to have a clear sense of how to proceed and how to explain what he was intending or doing. Every group of supporters was differently motivated; every institutional support was fragile. All these uncommon or unprecedented complications increase the difficulty of understanding Lincoln's words. The nature of his predicament was such that he had to feel his way with a recurrent but always mastered sense of futility; he needed to alternate methods of decisiveness and methods of appeasement, and thus risk appearing headstrong or weak, devious or incompetent. Correspondingly, his record induces in us a response that can be and should be somewhat unstable, moving between admiration and occasional strong disappointment, and settling only at the end in admiration and even amazement. Such a response would repeat the sentiments of those who were closest to him.

In his rejoinder to Douglas in the second debate (August 27, 1858), Lincoln said, "I do not ask for the vote of any one who supposes that I have secret purposes or pledges that I dare not speak out" (LA, 1:575). I see no reason to challenge him generally on that point. That is, I am less sympathetic to the view than I once was that from 1854, Lincoln aimed at ending slavery in the whole country, and that every move he made along the way was guided by that aim and was the only (or the most effective) move that he could make. If that had been the case, the major part of his political career, when he sought high national office and then in the time of his presidency until the first draft of the Emancipation Proclamation (September 1862), would therefore have been a sustained practice of deceit, or playacting, or, if you will, of a heroic and successful guardedness. Ending slavery would have been his only aim and everything else either instrumental or of secondary importance. However, I have become persuaded that he had purposes that mattered more to him than ending slavery. Preserving the Union mattered more to him than ending slavery, and before the war so did the determination to avoid spending white lives in internecine struggle. I therefore cannot accept the view, though I am still drawn to it, that Lincoln systematically practiced deceit—forgivable deceit?—or something close to it, for eight years or so (1854–1862) on behalf of a secret plan to abolish slavery. But it was not only his enemies who suspected that Lincoln was often withholding his true opinions.

Herndon suggested that when Lincoln's constituents grew seriously dissatisfied with his opposition (1847–1848) to the war against Mexico, when Lincoln was in the House of Representatives, the experience "perhaps taught him that in order to succeed as a Congressman it is not always the most politic thing to tell the truth because it is the truth, or do right because it is right" (Herndon, 183). Thus, in other words, the motto of political office must be: say what is politic, true or not; do what is politic, right or wrong. I think that Lincoln's relation to the truth, leaving aside right and wrong, was governed by more than expedient calculation when his words appeared and still appear on important occasions distant from either his feelings or the reality of the situation. There was some profound alienation that made him move apart. He could not quite believe that the only democratic republic in the world was also the cruelest tyranny in the world. It was as if he had to keep reminding himself that the situation was not a bad dream, but a reality that kept falling out of everyone's grasp.

Yet I am still willing to think that there might have been at least one occasion on which he dared to give an indication of an abolitionist purpose beyond the containment of slavery, even if he had no strategy to achieve it. We could say perhaps that this purpose was lodged in the real but hidden meaning of the word *crisis* in the House Divided speech of June 16, 1858: only when "a crisis shall have been reached, and passed" will the House cease to be divided (LA, 1:426). That speech rightly caused a great deal of anxiety in those who feared abolitionism as disruptive of the Union or ruinous to the chances of Republican victory. When Herndon was shown the speech before its delivery, he said (true to his character) to Lincoln, "It is true, but is it wise or politic to say so?" Lincoln replied that the proposition about a divided house had been true for 6,000 years, and that he would rather be defeated with this expression than be victorious without it (Herndon, 243–244). Herndon reported further that the friends Lincoln called together to hear the speech beforehand were unanimous in calling on him not to give the speech and thought it foolish, or "ahead of its time," or would drive away "a good many voters fresh from the Democratic ranks." Lincoln replied to them, "let me die in the advocacy of what is just and right" (Herndon, 245). Lincoln was willing in this speech to have the truth as he saw it burst out.

Let us explore some of the ramifications of this speech. The metaphor of the House Divided speech, as employed by Lincoln, was that of a doctor who speaks of a bad fever: it gets worse and worse, reaches a crisis point, and then must break or the patient will die. In 1858 to pass the crisis meant that the divisive issue of slavery would be clearly and decisively resolved in favor of one side or the other, and the Union would no longer be perilously agitated; agitation would be futile. On its face, the metaphor seemed to give equal chances to both the slavery side and the opposition; it certainly did not predict the end of slavery as the near certain outcome. As well, it did not seem to predict the coming of war. Yet menace, perhaps ill-defined, was detected in the speech. He tried to reassure some friends afterward in the summer of 1859 that "you will see the day when you will consider it was the wisest thing I ever said" (F, 439). By *wise* he meant *prescient*. He would not yet disclose in so many words the hope he was hiding. The meaning of that word *crisis* when he first spoke it was not perhaps revealed until he became president and military prospects were decisively improving. In the Annual Message to Congress, December 8, 1863, he spoke of the "crisis of the conflict" as the point at which a military development might take place by which emancipation on an appreciable scale could begin to be effected (LA, 2:550). Now closer to victory, the crisis of slavery had been reached and would soon be passed, and the House that had been divided against itself would not only cease to be divided but become all free for the first time.

The speech was "wise" in its hopeful foresight. Did Lincoln therefore think, at the time of the House Divided speech, but not much before then, that war between the states would come and only a military victory over the slave states (almost guaranteed by the superior strength of the North) could abolish slavery completely in a series of steps, and end some of it, at least in a preliminary manner, on grounds of military necessity as defined by a Republican president exercising his war powers? Of course I am not saying that he assumed he would become president; rather he came to see perhaps that only the election of a Republican president would impel the South to initiate a war that would provide the chance for the stronger North to win and then abolish slavery, somehow. He had warned the South in a speech at Cincinnati, September 17, 1859, that if they "divided" the Union because a Republican had been elected president, there would be a struggle between equally brave men; by no means were Southerners braver than Northerners. The South "being inferior in numbers, you will make nothing by attempting to master us" (LA, 2:77). Less delicately put, you would be defeated by superior manpower, and lose what you wanted to keep, which was now protected by the Constitution and the obligations that antislavery people, like Lincoln, were ready to honor. Most harshly, Lincoln said a few months later that if the South attempted to break up the Union upon the election of a Republican president, "it will be our duty to deal with you as old John Brown has been dealt with" (speech at Leavenworth, Kansas, December 3, 1859, CW, 3:502). Anyone who makes war against the government of the United States for any reason will meet a bad end. How shocking to liken the South to John Brown, its worst nightmare. (It is all the more startling to us, when we learn that some Confederate prisoners of war were confined at Harpers Ferry; see Christopher Benfey, letter, citing Nathaniel Hawthorne in 1862, *New York Review of Books*, July 11, 2013, 62). Lincoln had already given a blunt warning against regional violence *before* the *Dred Scott* decision, when he urged the South to allow the Supreme Court to decide peacefully the issue of slavery in the territories; of course his assumption then was that the Court would as a matter of reasonable interpretation decide in favor of keeping slavery out (speech at Galena, Illinois, July 23, 1856, CW, 2:355).

Yet for all his blunt talk about defeating a Southern effort to break up the Union, Lincoln was keenly aware of the cost in human life that a war between the sections would exact. In several speeches in New England soon before he won nomination for president, Lincoln contemplated what a war to end slavery would entail. The issue that he took up in these speeches was not a war to undo Southern secession, but a Northern war initiated to abolish slavery. Perhaps he thought that no cost would be too great to save the Union, but an abolitionist war would certainly cost too much even if it cost a good deal less than a defensive war to save the Union. The direct abolitionist military cost of any size would amount to a greater wrong than the wrong of slavery; an abolitionist war would "do more hurt than good" (speech at Hartford, Connecticut, version 1, March 5, 1860, CW, 4:5; see also the speech at Dover, New Hampshire, March 2, 1860, CW, 3:553). To kill a snake in the bed of a sleeping child might inadvertently kill the child (speech at New Haven, March 6, 1860, LA, 2:137). Well before then, he said that to lance a wen on a man's body might cause him to bleed to death (Peoria speech, LA, 1:338). On another occasion he worriedly told a delegation opposed to moving Union troops through Kentucky that using force against Kentucky Confederate sympathizers who persecuted Unionists would strike the "children"; his word seems to refer to the Unionists, not to the slaves; yet, "he dared not let them die without an effort" (July 1861, F, 161). The point that there would be an exorbitant cost paid by innocent whites in a military process of ending slavery, because of the broad effects of violence, was made for the time being. In the background of these metaphors was perhaps the parable where Jesus warns that "while you gather up the tares, you root up also the wheat with them" (Matthew 13:29).

In sum, in the metaphor of the house divided much was compressed, waiting on time to release itself.

<hr>

If we do not accuse Lincoln of having "secret purposes or pledges," we should at least see that he sometimes withheld truth, or forced the evidence, in order to protect his deepest commitments, or sometimes remained deliberately opaque about the full significance of what he was saying. Nevertheless, it is not the case that he confided his real thought to a few and dissimulated to the rest; he confided in no one and had no secret doctrine. He wanted to be understood by everyone, if not always immediately; when the time came he would be understood. His purposes would be revealed, but only with time and luck. It is no wonder that General Grant, just like Stephen Douglas, originally thought that he could not share the view that a house divided could not stand, but after the war at last came to the conclusion that "the saying is quite true" (*Personal Memoirs*, 773). But by then, of course, the house was no longer divided. Have we, even now, really understood the House Divided speech?

Lincoln told William Herndon "many times" that one should not "shoot too high; shoot low down, and the common people will understand you.... The educated ones will understand you anyhow.... If you shoot too high, your bullets will go over the heads of the mass and only hit those who need no hitting" (Herndon, 203). The reverse might be closer to the truth. It appears that most people have usually found no trouble in believing that they understood Lincoln well enough to catch the tendency of his thinking, but the "high" were and are perplexed some part of the time. There is, however, good reason for some perplexity. I believe that Frederick Douglass was to an extent generously over-simple when he said in his great Oration of 1876 that "the image of the man went out with his words, and those who read him knew him" (Douglass, 3). A possible generalization from the start and almost to the end is that when Lincoln disguised his words, it was often to reassure opinion that was proslavery; or pro-Union and antiblack; or antislavery, but less passionately than he was. Politics dictated that he be far less anxious about the abolitionist side. But the wish to be politic was not the deepest cause of his opacity. Whatever his feelings or motives, his articulated views were nonetheless what they were, and their immediate influence, sometimes morally questionable, was spread by the power of his articulation.

Perhaps the greatest impediment to understanding him is the view of him we have grown up with. We want Lincoln to be a political leader who always acted with single-minded purpose to end slavery as rapidly as possible, and did so for the best moral reasons. After all, he died because he freed the slaves. What more could be asked? Perhaps nothing more. But imagine that Lincoln was not murdered. We would be able to see the obvious: his moral outrage before the war was not a dominating passion that made every other consideration secondary to abolishing slavery. He could accommodate himself to the thought that the course of ultimate peaceable extinction of slavery would only come "in God's good time" and that therefore it could exist an indefinitely long time (speech at Edwardsville, Illinois, September 11, 1858, LA, 1:582). It did not bother him that people could be rewarded ("compensated") if they stopped enslaving other human beings, as if they had a morally tolerable legal *right* to enslave, to begin with. Even if we see compensation as bribery, bribery to do the right thing is scarcely excusable. The moral odium of compensation remains, especially when joined to a total absence of the will to provide reparations to the emancipated slaves. Lincoln saw uncomplainingly that deportation of numerous blacks could be part of a deal or even a necessary condition for abolition. He also did not share the abolitionist desire that slavery end as rapidly as possible.

Lincoln was so far from being an abolitionist that he was antiabolitionist, or at least spoke like one, until deep into the war. Then he became an abolitionist, ruthlessly and reluctantly. (In general, his actions were often ruthless and reluctant.) Before then, his terms of emancipation were rather miserly, and were justified in a nonmoral and fully practical manner. He hated slavery with a deep hatred, as much as almost any abolitionist, but he had other commitments than acting on that hatred, and these commitments, or some of them, mattered more to him—he said, I think sincerely, that they mattered more to him— than the end of slavery. Only when in the middle of 1862 his deepest commitments required the end of slavery as its necessary instrument did the end of slavery begin to come. Then it must be said that when circumstances were most favorable to abolition—that is, after Lincoln's reelection and the growing likelihood of Northern victory—he seemed to have no passion but a constitutional amendment to abolish slavery.

When we immerse ourselves in Lincoln's writings, we find distortions of reality in the claims he made on important occasions. He sometimes seems to me to be hiding from himself, rather than always being manipulative. He loved Aesop, but he was not quite Aesopian in the systematic Leninist sense, which is defined in the preface to *Imperialism* (1917) as misshaping your thought by as it were pressing it into a vise out of fear of the censor. However, for all of Lincoln's contrivance—and this is part of his greatness—he erupted into moments of truth. In these moments the distortion vanished; the truth, as he knew it but did not always want it to be the truth or want to say it, came out. The moments of truth-telling occurred when they did. For us as readers, there is no predicting their appearance; they were not organic parts of his composition. He stopped hiding from himself for a moment, but then went on as if nothing had happened. He described the truth of the situation, but not steadily. However, he did not always manage to see the truth, or if he saw it, to say it. Lincoln's commitments mattered more to him than the truth about reality, and obscured it, if only incompletely, just as such commitments, certainly some of them, mattered more to him than ending slavery, deep as that commitment was, too. (Indeed it is possible to say that his hatred of slavery was deeper than his commitment to abolish it.) I do not deny that he sometimes distorted for the sake of political expediency, personal or public, but these distortions were mere blemishes. The important distortions, however, served to protect and further a higher purpose than speaking the full truth.

That higher purpose was quasi-religious—that is, religious only in a manner of speaking and not religious as most people understand that word, but nonetheless the higher purpose was, Lincoln thought, worthy of religious devotion. On the other hand, it is sufficiently clear that for Lincoln no organized religion—religion, properly speaking—was worthy of religious devotion. Or, at least, no organized religion mattered to Lincoln as much as the objects of his quasi-religious devotion. The Bible greatly affected Lincoln in every respect except the substance of his beliefs. For him it was a work of everyday wisdom, perhaps a supreme fiction, but certainly not a book of revelation or a guide to political principles. In his hands it could also be of political usefulness when he spoke to his Christian audience.

Disturbed by "outrages committed by mobs," outrages that "alike . . . spring up . . . among the pleasure hunting masters of Southern slaves, and the order loving citizens of the land of steady habits," he asserted the need of a "political religion" (Address to the Young Men's Lyceum of Springfield, Illinois, January 27, 1838, LA, 1:29, 31). (Notice how his sarcasm seemed evenly distributed; perhaps more of it was directed at the North than the South.) The very phrase, not only the idea of a political religion, was hence not foreign to Lincoln, and at the early age of twenty-nine. In this address the object of religious reverence was the laws, duly enacted and constitutionally valid. Citizens should feel devotion to the laws with a religious intensity. Lincoln dared to set up what genuinely religious people would call an idol, an object equated to divinity in fundamental importance, even if people continued to worship a divinity. It was a daring move, made all the easier by a thought I impute to Lincoln and that was constantly present in his responses, if not always articulated. This thought was that if there were a divinity we could scarcely speak about it, but we did not need a divinity to know what morality or justice is; and since laws enacted under the Constitution were political expressions of justice, then we must revere them, if we wish to be moral, which is equivalent to the wish to aspire to the highest active piety within our comprehension. Lincoln's political religion was thus in substance the religion of political morality; it was not state-worship. This was not Christianity, but perhaps Deism, with the deity needed to sanctify but not to define justice, but remaining for the most part otherwise inactive in human affairs. Then again, Deism did not turn out to be adequate for Lincoln's political purposes, or for his metaphysical intuitions.

Not quite two years after the Lyceum address, Lincoln closed a long speech on economic matters with a declaration of loyalty rather in excess of what the occasion needed. He accused the van Buren administration of every corruption and urged his listeners to keep up the fight against it and the deplorable effort to reelect van Buren for a second term. The young Lincoln's devotion to his country was expressed not as fear of the ambition of one man aspiring to be the single man at the top and suppressing the freedom of everyone else, but as readiness to stand alone in defense of "our country's freedom" even when the cause seemed hopeless. He said, "Without contemplating consequences . . . I swear eternal fidelity to the just cause as I deem it, of the land of my life, my liberty and my love" (speech on the Sub-Treasury at Springfield, Illinois, December 27, 1839, LA, 1:65).

Thus, within a short period of time in his young life, Lincoln expressed extreme but divergent fears for the safety of the laws, the object of his devotion. The danger came from ambitious people like himself and the rescue also came, if it came at all, from other ambitious people like himself. He might kill the established order or have to die for it; it turned out he did both. More accurately, he died because he re-established the order in a way to make it consistent with the promise he saw in it and thus killed the original order. Lincoln was not yet disposed, however, to insert providence as the cause of events with himself as its principal instrument.

One more initial point about Lincoln's commitments and the words he used to promote them. I would suggest that Rousseau's civil religion in *The Social Contract* is not interestingly compared to Lincoln's political religion. Rousseau's civil religion had an unmysterious and benign divinity; Lincoln's political religion had almost none; and when Lincoln does speak in hints about divinity in his properly religious utterances, the divinity is mysterious and therefore not reliably benign. What is equally important, Rousseau prescribed severe penalties for personal infidelity as such; Lincoln had no such thoughts. In any case Lincoln will eventually enroll the Republican Party in the long tradition of commitment to republican principles. He said that the Republican Party was republican not only in the partisan sense but as we hope "in the true, original, sense of the word republican" (Notes for Speeches at Columbus and Cincinnati, Ohio, September 16, 17, 1859, CW, 3:429).

3

Lincoln's Political Religion of Human Equality

THE LYCEUM ADDRESS was certainly not the last word about divinity in Lincoln's work. We will return to Lincoln's religious or quasi-religious views of divinity when we must. Let us observe for now that Lincoln's political religion, which he sincerely held, would justify in his mind giving orders to kill and die, when it was threatened by armed denial of it, whereas a religious war in the usual sense would have excited his disgust. On the other hand, the ferocities of race, regional patriotism, and cultural identity—the South's political religion—drove the South to denial of Lincoln's political religion and to secede, and kill and die to make that secession successful. In the Civil War many motives induced men to kill and die, on both sides; not all men were ferocious in their war-making adherence, but some were; and fear, duty, camaraderie, and conformity made up for any absence of ferocity in the others.

We must be clear that the abolition of slavery was not originally a tenet of Lincoln's political religion, despite the undeniable hatred of slavery he felt. John Burt says that the Republicans' core constituency "was people who disliked slavery but feared the consequences of abolition" (366). Lincoln always hated (not merely disliked) slavery but never lost his fear of the consequences of immediate abolition—though he finally achieved it; he had for the longest while thought that the slaves had to be gradually prepared for it. But until the war began he settled for the containment of slavery as a substitute absolute; he held containment to be constitutionally proper in spite of the *Dred Scott* decision in 1857. He would compromise on slavery to a significant extent, but only so far. He claimed in 1854 that he would have settled for repeal of the Kansas-Nebraska Act, but when *Dred Scott* came along three years later, Lincoln and his party and their sympathizers were left with profound uncertainty. However, in a startling aside he had unaccountably said beforehand that "no one would controvert its correctness" if the *Dred Scott* decision were to hold narrowly and simply that Dred Scott remained a slave, no matter what territory he was taken to (Fragment on the *Dred Scott* case, written between December 1856 and March 1857, CW, 2:388; for an ambiguous repetition of this view in public more than a year after the decision, which was issued on March 6, 1857, see also the speech at Carlinville, Illinois, August 31, 1858, CW, 3:78). Actually, in 1847, Lincoln had defended a Kentucky slave-owner's right to use his slaves seasonally not in a territory but in the free state of Illinois, without the automatic irrevocable emancipation that even temporary residence in a free state was thought to bestow; fortunately he lost his case. (Lincoln's bête noir, Roger Taney, who had manumitted his slaves, had before appointment as chief justice in 1836 served as a lawyer in 1829 in federal court for a freed black's right to inherit land but unfortunately lost his case.)

Shortly after the Carlinville speech, and still wrestling with himself in private, Lincoln said that if a state's own [fundamental] law prohibited slavery, that law should prevail over the national right of property in slavery (Fragment: Notes for Speeches, c. September 15, 1858, CW, 3:101). Lincoln appeared to imply thereby that the Constitution was not the supreme law of the land, "the laws of any State to the contrary notwithstanding" (Article VI). The Supreme Court had by this time already held in *Dred Scott*, however, that a slave could not become automatically free if his owner took him to labor in either a free state or a free territory. The slaveholder's right of property in slaves would be unconstitutionally violated if the slave were ordered to be freed, no matter where. This decision would seem to have allowed slavery on constitutional grounds everywhere in the United States, whatever federal law or state law said.

Once Lincoln became a war president he could act to erode slavery; but in the course of his actions he had to violate every tenet of his political religion, including at times (but only in the short run) even the commitment to human equality (as when he revoked early military proclamations of emancipation). He did not allow the Constitution to get in the way of preserving the Union; but we must remember that he saw the Union as the only polity in the world that the promise of human equality could call its own. Only there did the passion for equality (which he and others hoped could not remain forever racially selective to the extreme extent of slavery) already give direction to the long-term energies of the polity.

———

At what was Lincoln's devotion aimed? What were his deep commitments, so deep that they constituted a political religion and continuously inspired his actions as president, but also prompted him to remain guarded in his words, even as president, about the end of slavery until September 1862? These are easy questions. It is much harder to say what were or appeared to be Lincoln's religious beliefs, in the proper sense of religion, and what relation his political religion had to his religious beliefs, if we find that Deism actually did not fit what he said, as I will eventually discuss.

His deepest commitment was to human equality, to the equal humanity of all persons and races. That was his master principle; it was his religion; it was a moral principle from which his entire political thought derived. He was originally committed to the preservation of the US Constitution as the overall best statement of the implications and ramifications of that principle. In turn the Constitution would remain a document merely if there were not a political system that was created in conformity with it and its basic principle. For the Constitution to live, there had to be a structure of government; a specification of its powers to make laws and execute them, and limits on those powers; and a charter of rights. In turn the Constitution made a union of states, which for Lincoln meant a society of one people. Lincoln revered the principle of human equality and believed that he therefore should revere the US Constitution, the system of government created under it, and the Union that lived bound by it and obedient to the laws enacted under it. The Constitution, the system of government under it, and the Union formed by it all passed the test of making real the abstract principle of human equality. Each feature was necessary to the continuous enactment of that principle. All of them had to be preserved if the realization of the abstract principle were to be preserved. The Declaration of Independence and the Constitution were the scriptures of his political religion, his holiest scriptures.

Lincoln frequently and consistently defined the Northern aim of the war as the preservation of the Union. Compressed in that aim were two matters: first, the defense of the territorial integrity of the Union against attempted secession; second, and necessary to that end, the continued ability of the system of government as specified by the Constitution to use its powers, including violence against violence, not only to defend all the territory under its rightful jurisdiction, but to defend its legitimacy against assault. He felt obliged by his oath not to allow the Union to shrink in size and not to hand on to his successors in office a government compromised or humiliated in its authority. The integrity of the Constitution and therefore the integrity of the system of government, together with the integrity of the Union, are complexly entwined. Preserving the Union thus meant for Lincoln preserving not just the Union against secession but also the Constitution and its specified republican system of government. Each element helped to define and sustain the other two, and all were implicated in the aim of serving the highest principle, human equality.

However, more formally put, apart from any substantive principles, Lincoln said to John G. Nicolay, his private secretary, "The very existence of a general and national government implies the legal power, right, and duty of maintaining its own integrity. This, if not expressed, is at least implied in the Constitution. . . . He [Lincoln] cannot entertain any proposition for dissolution or dismemberment" (December 13, 1861, F, 342). He went so far as to say that the "paramount idea of the Constitution is the preservation of the Union. It may not be specified in so many words . . . for without the Union the Constitution would be worthless" (April 7, 1864, F, 83). He did not say that without the Constitution the Union would be worthless. The formalist reduction of Lincoln's claim is that there is no society of any kind that can hold together without a government of some form, and no government can function in the long run unless there is a society disposed to be law-abiding. The only question about the relation between government and society would be, which uses the other, or which is the end and which is the means? What saves Lincoln's view from mere formalism, which is political realism at its starkest, is that in the United States, clearly and forever, the substantive principle of human equality determines the fundamental law that establishes government as the means to the protection and advancement of a society that practices human equality. But I do not deny that at times, Lincoln resembled a formal realist; or at most and more substantively, a Hobbesian realist, in the sense that he thought that there could be no peacefully inclined society on any terms without a functioning government of some form or other. Lincoln's commitment to human equality was obviously not identical to

Hobbes's. I will return to this subject when Lincoln's presidency is discussed in Chapter 6.

If the United States disowned the principle of human equality, Lincoln would have turned around and disowned his country. His reverence was for the principle (the "proposition," as he called it in the Gettysburg Address) of human equality, and his protective reverence was then necessarily extended to cover what derived from the principle: the Constitution, the political system (essentially, limited and representative government; what Lincoln during wartime reconstruction regularly called a republican form of government, following the guaranty clause of the Constitution, Article IV, section 4), and the Union of people in states that had no right to secede and that owed their organized legal existence to the Constitution.

Lincoln made clear the comparative rank of the tenets of the political religion in the unpublished Fragment on the Constitution and the Union, written while he was president-elect (c. January 1861). In this fragment he used phraseology from the Book of Proverbs for his purpose. The verse says that "a word fitly spoken is like apples of gold in pictures of silver" (25:11). (The New English Bible says "like apples of gold set in silver filigree"; let us say: apples of gold put in an intricately designed silver piece to hold them together and keep them in place—to set them off or show them at their best—as if they were precious jewels.) For Lincoln the principle of the Declaration of Independence was the apple of gold and the Constitution and the Union formed together "the picture of silver subsequently framed around it." The picture is a setting, not a picture frame, and is the secondary part, "made not to conceal, or destroy the apple; but to adorn and preserve it" (quotations, CW, 4:169). If the metaphor was not quite under control, and the singular and plural were unsteady, the sense is clear enough.

He defined the principle of the Declaration as "liberty to all!" (CW, 4:169). What is liberty? Freedom from tyrants of every kind, for all people.

The Declaration affirmed the liberty of all; in context, Lincoln's meaning was that the Declaration was written to include blacks, free and slave, as he had said many times earlier, with particular vehemence in his debates with Douglas. The Constitution and the Union were silver and instrumental: precious but not as precious as the gold of the principle; neither thing of silver was an end in itself, as the golden principle was, as stated by the Declaration. The golden principle had I think an affinity in Lincoln's mind with the golden rule. Treat others as you would be treated by them; treat others as your equal, as you would be treated by them as their equal. Any free person would think it unjust to be enslaved; therefore he or she should not enslave another person because of any passion or under any pretext. As Lincoln put it, "for although volume upon volume is written to prove slavery a very good thing, we never hear of the man who wishes to take the good of it, *by being a slave himself*" (Fragments on Government, 1854?, LA, 1:302).

In amplification of Lincoln's point, we have seen that proslavery people, unlike many antislavery people, could not imagine that they would ever be chattel slaves and hence could not feel sympathy for slaves or take seriously the question of fairness when asked how they would have liked being treated as they treated blacks. Whiteness magically— we could say, *ontologically* in order to refer to a higher order of being— protected whites from having to practice elementary justice toward nonwhites, and they therefore could not be reasoned out of their commitment to slavery, or appealed to emotionally. Americans had attenuated the caste or class oppression that their forebears practiced or suffered in Britain, but they aggravated British racism, which had always worked as an invitation to use, subordinate, or oppress nonwhites. Or the defenders of slavery thought that the only people who deserved freedom were those who would have lost their lives in resistance to being enslaved or taken their own lives if they had to surrender; they would never have endured slavery. Live free or die, and in the meantime exploit those who chose life over freedom. The defenders of slavery could not lend themselves to the decent thought that no human being should ever have to make such a choice or that great care should always be taken to try to avoid the need to make such a choice.

Perhaps as long as the Constitution and the Union permitted slavery, they could not be golden and not only because as instruments they could not be ends in themselves. They would continue to be of diminished preciousness, even as instruments, as long as slavery existed. But they would still be worthy of reverence with undiminished intensity. For the time being, there was no alternative. The Constitution and the Union were silver in comparison to the tyranny that existed everywhere else.

Another metaphor that Lincoln used about the proposition that all men are created equal ("the father of all moral principle") was that it was "the electric cord" that linked the hearts of all those who love liberty (speech at Chicago, July 10, 1858, LA, 1:456). I guess that this cord must be a telegraph wire that sends the word of equal liberty everywhere.

It should also be noticed that though Lincoln did not waver (except rarely and tactically) in his deepest reverence, which was for the principle of human equality, he did vary his comparative estimation of its derivative (silver) emanations. Before the Civil War, the practical object of his reverence was the Constitution. Although it was silver, precious but not the most precious, partly because it was not yet perfect—it was a rather excellent and improvable vehicle of the principle of human equality. For a while he could believe that the system of representative government and the integrity of the Union were secure, whereas, in contrast, quarrels over the meaning of some parts of the Constitution jeopardized people's devotion to it. Then during the war, a war of secession and therefore a violent assault or revolution against the Constitution and its government, it was the integrity of the Union, understood as indispensable to the protection of the principle of human equality in the country and symbolically potent for human equality throughout the world, that took precedence over the Constitution. As a politician before the war he was prepared to compromise on the maintenance of slavery within limits, as the Constitution and expedient politics demanded, but it was clear he would never compromise on the integrity of the Union. As president, once the Union was close to defeating secession, and its integrity was safe, he at last would not compromise on the existence of slavery, as he showed when he helped push the Thirteenth Amendment through Congress and worked to secure ratification in several states before his death.

I have just said that Lincoln rarely wavered in his commitment to human equality. The wavering came when he twice revoked emancipation proclamations issued by military commanders when he doubted the legality of these acts or thought them politically premature. But suppose it were said that his long-lasting espousal of the policy of urging without compelling black people to settle outside the United States was a major deviation from his commitment? The best that could be said is that he sincerely thought that whites would never accept blacks as equal citizens and that it would be good for blacks to emigrate. When it became clear that blacks had little interest in leaving, he dropped his defense of colonization in his efforts to secure abolition of slavery through constitutional amendment. But there is more to say on this subject later on.

It is obvious that the South's violent revolution was not in the name of replacing the Constitution with a new Constitution for the whole country. It wanted a separate constitution for itself, one that enshrined and protected slavery. For that purpose the Confederate Constitution spoke of slavery by name and in the most matter-of-fact way, as if there could not have been any doubt that the institution would exist forever unquestioned. Its revolution was against the principle of the equality of all races. The South therefore did not seek to overthrow the US government but to create a new government for itself that was independent of the established one and apart from it. The South did not mount an internal revolutionary movement to rewrite the US Constitution in accordance with, say, the plan of Calhoun in the late 1840s to have two presidents and other new devices of concurrent majority; the effort would have been futile anyway.

Correspondingly, I think it might be said that Lincoln could not tolerate the idea that a new American polity would be founded that bordered on the United States and that was devoted to slavery. The South had to stay in the Union and not become a rival to it, especially a rival that practiced slavery uniformly throughout its domain and dedicated itself to the proud defiance of the proposition that all men, irrespective of race, are created equal in their entitlement to the status of freedom. It turned out that if the South wanted to secede in part to annex new territory for slavery, the Union would by counter-violence re-annex the South and end slavery. He certainly did not share the opinion held by some in the North that favored letting the slave states go and therefore ridding the Union of the stain of slavery and the constant dispute over it, and therefore also ridding it of further association with millions of blacks. He was always adamant in the will to defeat the slave states; but after a short while in office he decided that they would have to be reincorporated not only as states, but as states without slavery. I do not say, however, that his most important aim in preserving the Union was to end slavery, even though after a while he insisted that beginning to end slavery was indispensable to preserving the Union. Geopolitics, one nationality, and human equality were not to be pried apart. All these considerations worked together to make the idea of an independent Confederacy abhorrent.

———

The striking fact—which I touch on here and will return to recurrently in the rest of this book—is that, in effect, Lincoln suspended in time of war the Constitution of silver that he revered. Reverence did not stand in his way. He suspended not only the writ of habeas corpus, but most of the Bill of Rights, and did so with the explicit authorization or tacit approval of Congress. Through the suspension of habeas corpus, all other freedoms could be eroded; their exercise of First Amendment rights was blocked for some people and "chilled" by intimidation for others, and the procedural rights of the Bill were disregarded. In his determination to prevail on his terms, Lincoln destroyed the revered Constitution temporarily to save it, and replaced it with an executive system, under the direction of the president, and working by means of war powers and the powers of the commander-in chief of the armed forces. With no guaranteed habeas corpus, the US government was in an attenuated state of war with a nominally loyal population so that it could wage protracted war against its secessionist enemies. The fight for human equality necessitated the erosion of constitutional equality. Lincoln became something like a dictator, and to his foes a tyrant.

In Lincoln's effort to keep the loyalty of the slave-owning border states, they became the scene of greatest constitutional erosion; they were also the source of the stain of slavery on the Unionist cause, but their loyalty to the Union, no matter how resented or resisted by their own citizens, made the Union's victory much easier, or perhaps as Lincoln claimed, made its victory possible at all.

Then, as victory neared, Lincoln worked to amend the Constitution in order to abolish slavery. But the Thirteenth Amendment was not only another important amendment. It fundamentally rewrote, remade the

Constitution. Thus the original Constitution that Lincoln revered was shown to have been from the start, if not usually to Lincoln, except on one fleeting occasion before the war, unworthy of reverence just because it was a Constitution of slavery. On that one occasion, an inconvenient but imperfect truth burst out. He said that with the work of containing (not abolishing) slavery, the Constitution would be saved, and "we shall have so saved it, as to make, and to keep it, forever worthy of the saving" (Peoria speech, October 16, 1854, LA, 1:340). Let us emphasize the fact that he said the Constitution had to be made forever worthy of preserving, as if it were not yet worthy. Lincoln meant that if the Missouri Compromise could be restored by repeal of the Kansas-Nebraska Act, the Constitution would again be worthy of reverence. He thus at least entertained the idea that an object of his reverence could be or become, if only temporarily, unworthy of reverence.

As abolitionists insisted, however, only containing slavery, even if it could be contained legally (and this was highly doubtful after the *Dred Scott* decision), was never enough to make the Constitution worthy of reverence. That truth eventually was forced on Lincoln by becoming overpoweringly clear; there had to be imposed abolition to make the document consistent with its foundational principle of equal liberty as stated in the Declaration—even if we grant that equal liberty had been the foundational principle of either document. He thus had to destroy the old Constitution twice, in two different ways and for two different reasons: first by suspension and then by a transformative amendment. Both processes of destruction were necessary if there was to be a Constitution that really was silver, really stood for the principle of human equality, and thus would be worthy of reverence and hence unequivocally worth preserving. It took a successful war against domestic enemies—who saw themselves not as enemies within, not as rebels or revolutionaries, but as oppressed foreigners in search of national self-determination—to establish a Constitution that became legitimate for the first time in its existence. By one amendment it became legitimate; that was all that was needed, but it could never be gained peacefully. Only victorious war against secessionist slave states could achieve that amendment in a restored Union. The Constitution owed its prior existence to atrocious racism and therefore from the moral point of view it should never have been born, but once born it had to go under and be changed altogether by just one amendment, but one that could be added only in extraordinary and therefore unforeseeable circumstances.

For Lincoln, victory in civil war, despite all the war's horror, and all its ruin of the old revered Constitution, was the irreplaceable device first of emancipation and then of complete abolition. But well before the war he had his suspicions that war was the only answer to otherwise intractable abstract moral problems or to an untenable condition in which two antithetical systems shared one polity. I have already referred to his mention of fortunate crisis in the House Divided speech, and its possible hidden significance; the identity of that crisis was revealed to be war. We could add the letter to Erastus Corning (and other associated citizens) written in the midst of war for some indication that Lincoln had suspected for a long time that war would have to come: he said that the South had been preparing to rebel "for more than thirty years" (June 23, 1863, LA, 2:456). To refer to rebellion and then speak of "insurgents" indicated that in his mind secession should never be peacefully allowed; it was illicit and completely undesirable.

———

We must say that what Lincoln had revered in the period before the Civil War was a frozen Constitution, frozen because the Thirteenth Amendment could never have passed if the South had stayed in the Union without interruption; slavery could never have been abolished if the South had not made war on the Union—not merely to preserve but to extend slavery everywhere possible and maintain it indefinitely—and been defeated. Even if the number of slave states did not increase from fifteen, forty-five states would still have been needed to abolish slavery peacefully by constitutional amendment. We the people still do not live in sixty states. Not to say that all the free states would have voted for abolition, though it is more than likely that the fifteen slave states would have voted against it, even if done gradually, and even with compensation. Secession would have occurred with the passage of the amendment, if not before. It certainly did occur when the national and constitutional political situation was favorable to slavery.

Then too, the clause of the Fifth Amendment that permitted forced takings by congressional legislation of property (with compensation) in its possible national application to slaves as property would have been forcibly resisted in the slave states. Lincoln did think that if the due process clause provided at least prima facie protection of the preservation of slavery in the states against congressional legislation, despite the takings clause, emancipation would therefore have to be voluntary. In his restless thinking, however, he also wrote that although the due process clause protected slavery in *territories*, all that was needed for due process to be satisfied was prior notice in the constitution or law of a territory that slavery was prohibited and this would allow depriving a slaveholder, whether a migrant or temporary visitor, of his slaves (Fragment: Notes for Speeches, c. September 15, 1858, CW, 3:101).

Whichever way we turn, the words of Eric Foner in his masterly book *The Fiery Trial* (2010) ring true: "there was simply no constitutional way that this [ending slavery] could be accomplished [without the consent of the slave-owners]" (125). Yet before the war and at least a year into it, Lincoln accepted all the restraints on political efforts to emancipate the slaves; he knew the bald truth that the Constitution established slavery in the United States. Indeed, the frozen Constitution he revered was in most respects, in word and practical effect, little different from the Confederate Constitution (March 11, 1861), which borrowed almost everything from the US Constitution except the insistence on the sovereignty (a word not found in the US Constitution) of each state. In the seceded South, constitutional delicacy for roughly five and a half million whites coexisted with the utmost dehumanization of roughly three and a half million black slaves. Thus, by transatlantic standards of the time, in the 1860 census, in the states that were to form the Confederacy one year later, opposite extremes in the treatment of millions of human beings were reached solely on the basis of color. The difference from the North was in the numbers: not quite half a million black slaves in the loyal border states in 1860 and roughly twenty-three million whites in all the loyalist states.

Brushing aside reverence for anything but the principle of human equality, Lincoln felt driven, during the indispensable war, to destroy the Constitution he had revered; as I have said, he did so because he thought its guarantees against governmental interference with freedom made victory in civil war impossibly difficult, and because only by being remade utterly could it become a charter worthy of reverence at last. The Constitution would be at last the precious setting of the Declaration's proposition that freedom from personal tyrants and public systems of tyranny was a right of all persons and races. But before the abolitionist outcome dissolved the effects of Lincoln's reverence for a frozen Constitution, for an illegitimate Constitution, the fact of such reverence cannot be dissolved.

———

If we want to try to understand Lincoln's thinking about the founding documents of his political religion we must ask several questions. First, why did he revere the principle of human equality as it is formulated in the Declaration of Independence? Then there are certain questions about Lincoln's reverence for the Constitution before the Thirteenth Amendment. How could Lincoln have revered such a Constitution? How did he revere it? How did he countenance the presence of the rights of slavery in it? Why did Lincoln hate slavery so much? How did his reverence for the Constitution nevertheless survive his hatred of slavery?

Let us start with Lincoln's reverence for the principle of human equality as it was stated in the Declaration. There is of course not much that ought to be said: the Declaration holds its truths about equality to be self-evident. The Declaration also invokes the Creator and says he or it endows every human being with certain inalienable rights, among them life, liberty, and the pursuit of happiness. Lincoln thought that this view of the Creator showed a "lofty, wise, and noble understanding of the justice of the Creator to His creatures," as if God acknowledged and administered the requirements of justice rather than arbitrarily decreeing them (speech at Lewiston, Illinois, August 17, 1858, CW, 2:546). Now, Lincoln did not usually call human equality a self-evident principle; but in a near and usable synonymous phrase, he did once speak in a different context of the requirement enjoined on those who make a senseless war to pay its cost as "too obviously just, to be called into question" (message to the Senate and House of Representatives, July 17, 1862, CW, 5:329). In a phrase especially resonant to us, he said soon after the Emancipation Proclamation that the US government was built "on the foundation of human rights" (to the workingmen of Manchester, England, January 19, 1863, LA, 2:432).

Thomas Jefferson knew that the principle of natural rights, though self-evident, had been denied by every system of government in the world, even when the principle was known to exist by the authorities who denied them. The principle was a universal truth that had not been universally acknowledged; indeed it had been only occasionally acknowledged, even as late as Lincoln's lifetime. I suppose that "self-evident" implies a rhetorical question: what is the alternative to believing the proposition, if you are reasonable or disinterested? When Jefferson was George Washington's secretary of state, he said that to deny the proposition that ports of neutral countries should not be blockaded by a country at war was "so manifestly contrary to the law of nations, that nothing more would seem necessary than to observe that it is so" (quoted in Witt, 60). Similarly, all that would be needed to rebut a denial of equal inalienable rights would be to "observe that it is" contrary to the "Laws of Nature and Nature's God," as Jefferson said in the Declaration of Independence.

But unlike Jefferson, Lincoln rarely spoke of natural law, even though he considered human equality an abstract right. The only occurrence I can find is in a speech (right before the address at Peoria) in which he called slavery "a gross outrage on the law of nature" and rejected the proposal to accord slavery any right to exist by the law of nature on free soil because it "carries a rot and a murrain in it" (speech at Springfield, Illinois, October 4, 1854, CW, 2:245). He said, however, during the presidential campaign in 1860, "I agree with Seward in his 'Irrepressible Conflict,' but I do not endorse his 'Higher Law' doctrine," that is, Seward's doctrine that there is a higher law than the Constitution. Lincoln reasoned as if the Constitution embodied a philosophical but philosophically unelaborated commitment to human equality (Herndon, 278). Neither could we call the Declaration of Independence, which is the foundation of the Constitution, a philosophically elaborated text, although it was quite elaborate in its stated grievances. Lincoln usually, but not always, thought he could proceed more simply than Jefferson had. He emphasized the idea that the only alternative to human equality was the "tyrannical principle" (Lincoln's reply to Douglas, seventh debate, LA, 1:811); such a principle was so morally absurd that it was self-evidently false. As a republican, Lincoln would not countenance a distinction between monarchy and tyranny.

Lincoln did not hold that the idea of human equality was axiomatic in the technical sense, but firmly believed that its polemical denial by American citizens had to portend suicide by the polity or murder of the polity by antiegalitarian factions in it. Was there not "a common right of humanity" against all rulers and all races who act tyrannically—that is, who do "just as they please" with other people—a common right that surpassed in moral and philosophical significance all differences among people? (Lincoln's reply, seventh debate, October 15, 1858, LA, 1:811; also, earlier, in the speech on the Kansas-Nebraska Act, at Peoria, Illinois, October 16, 1854, LA, 1:342). Lincoln thus designated as tyranny any government, whatever its form or the nature of its ruler or composition of its ruling class, that in its workings did not adhere to the principle of human equality, with divine right often supplying the rationale for tyranny in the past and racism supplying the animating spirit of its rationale in the American present. The United States practiced a racial tyranny, even though Lincoln obviously did not extend the designation of tyranny to the American system in its entirety. In any event he surely espoused a radically republican position, and was therefore aghast that there were Americans, especially in the South, who not only denied the principle of human equality but went so far as to call it, rather than the defense of racial tyranny, a self-evident lie. Here were the seeds of a revolution against the American Revolution.

Nothing made him angrier than the denial of or contempt for the principle of human equality, just as the refusal by antislave adherents to call slavery a positive good, not merely a tolerable evil, made proslavery persons furious. Lincoln said that the thing the South wanted most before it seceded and never got was for Republicans and others in the North to stop calling slavery wrong and start calling it right, and act accordingly (speech at Cooper Institute [Union], February 27, 1860, LA, 2:128). Was the South, however, aggrieved most by moral disapproval? It would be nice to think so, but probably naive. The South feared that in moral disapproval there was lodged a hatred that would turn into hostile action. It was shocking in any case that there were Americans who would deny the validity of their own country's—or at least their ancestors'—foundational statement, or interpret it out of existence by interpreting it in a racially exclusive way.

⸻

The shock is amplified when we read the full extent of the authoritative rejection of the doctrine of human equality that is found in Chief Justice Taney's majority opinion in the *Dred Scott* decision in 1857 (*Dred Scott v. Sandford*, 60 U.S. 393, 1856). The opinion is unapologetic and unadorned. The racial basis for the institution of slavery is candidly described and its sentiment attributed to the whole country, past and present. Lincoln's speech about the decision is obviously angry but did not register the shock I think it called for. The most famous sentence in it is "A black man has no rights which a white man is obliged to respect" (406). This is not Taney's volunteered dictum but a summary of his historical analysis of American practice and was intended to shore up his conclusion. In a long and at times off-putting legalist opinion, but compressed and straightforward when it comes to its major points, Taney made it clear that not for himself but for white Americans during the Revolutionary period and the years before the Constitution was ratified, and most importantly, for the Framers of the Constitution and the whole country in its subsequent practice, the guiding assumption was that persons of African descent were not citizens and not part of the constituent or continuously sovereign people, and that was the case because the white people considered blacks a "subordinate and inferior class of beings who had been subjugated by the dominant race, and whether emancipated or not, yet remained subject to their authority, and had no rights or privileges but such as those who held the power and the government might choose to grant them" (404–405).

As Taney proceeded, he tried to establish the perfect constitutionality of two main ideas. First, Congress could not prohibit the introduction or maintenance of slavery in any US territory because a slave was the legal property of the slave-owner, whether migrant or visitor, and hence ownership was protected by the Fifth Amendment clause that said that the federal government could not take a person's property without due process of law. The Bill of Rights as a document for whites only was jurisprudentially supreme. Just as Congress could not abridge free speech in a territory, it could not prevent any person who held slaves or wanted to hold them from doing so (450). Second, not being a citizen, a black had no standing to sue in federal court for his freedom. If a black man claimed in court that when he was taken as a slave to labor in a free state this new residence automatically liberated him from slavery, he had no right to present his case; his suit must be dismissed and he must be returned to his owner. Along with these two main conclusions, Taney and his majority said nothing that would block the possibility that if a free black who traveled to a slave state was caught and enslaved, he or she would not have the right to sue for freedom. Furthermore, I see nothing in the decision that would prevent a white person traveling in a free state from claiming that a free black he saw was actually descended from the slaves of the white man and could be transported back to slavery without the right to sue for his freedom in a federal court. Free blacks were not citizens of the United States, whatever their status in a free state. A state could not define national citizenship and the protections such citizenship was entitled to. Doubtless there were oppressive black codes in some free states, including Illinois, which signified that blacks though free lived precariously, as if not quite free. Taney supported the supposition that when free blacks exercised rights of speech and assembly they would endanger the safety of the white population by "inevitably producing discontent and insubordination" among black slaves as well as other free blacks (417).

Such was the legal situation that the antislavery movement was up against from 1857. Taney authoritatively re-froze what had never been thawed: the Constitution in its proslavery form. Despite Lincoln's counterarguments it is hard to see how he and his party could peacefully dissolve Taney's decision for the Supreme Court. However, this decision was constitutionally plausible and perhaps even closer to being jurisprudentially correct than merely being plausible. In his debates with Lincoln, Douglas used some of Taney's arguments when he could, and just made light of Taney's nullification of any exercise of "popular sovereignty" that would prevent slavery in a territory; but he spoke as just one citizen running for office, not as head of the third branch of government.

I have already referred to the plank in the Republican platform of 1860 that defied Taney's holding about congressional power in the territories, and did so in the name of the Bill of Rights. We will also see that in 1861, Taney returned to the Bill of Rights in an attempt to void Lincoln's suspension of habeas corpus; and the Supreme Court in 1866, after Taney's death, declared not that the suspension of the writ of habeas corpus was unconstitutional, but that the use of military commissions to try detainees when civilian courts were functioning was unconstitutional on the grounds of the Bill of Rights. This legal game of leapfrog, with the Bill of Rights supplying the push, is one theoretically important part of the story of the period of Lincoln.

———

Lincoln's commitment to human equality sensitized him to the tyrannous nature of slavery. The democracy that harbored slavery contained as many actual tyrants as there were slaveholders (Peoria speech, October 16, 1854, LA, 1:342). Yet in the same speech, Lincoln took pains to go against himself and thus be conciliatory. He said that "only a small percentage are natural tyrants. That percentage is no larger in the slave

States than in the free" (326). Such conciliatory qualification, however, is no better than ingratiation. But we can extend Plato's scheme in Books 8 and 9 of the *Republic*—which Lincoln did all but literally on one occasion, even if he had not read Plato, but only keenly observed his own psyche and the slave democracy that was the American polity— and say that the underside, the hidden longing, of one's citizenship in a democracy of equals is not so much a wish to be mastered by a tyrant as to flee the discipline of being an equal citizen by exercising personal tyranny over some others, or at least, by being part of a group that exercised collective tyranny over another identifiable group, inside or outside the polity, as all whites did over black slaves inside the American polity.

In a letter to George Robertson almost a year after the Peoria speech he exploded in a moment of truth when he denounced the potential slavishness of a nominally free people whose appetite for mastery threatened to prepare them for their own enslavement. He said, "When we were the political slaves of King George, and wanted to be free, we called the maxim that 'all men are created equal' a self-evident truth; but now when we have grown fat, and have lost all dread of being slaves ourselves, we have become so greedy to be masters that we call the same maxim 'a self-evident lie'" (August 15, 1855, LA, 1:359). It is not merely or even primarily that democracy tends to engender a few ambitious souls who aspire to use class or race war as a vehicle on the way to their own personal tyrannical rule over the whole society. Rather, "we have become so greedy to become masters." Not "a small percentage of us" but "we" (all of us or almost all) have this greed. The theme of Lincoln and tyranny will return when we discuss his presidency.

Slavery had thus introduced so profound a distortion of character in human beings that they became almost not-human. The most extreme systematic and inherited denial of human equality—the institution of monstrous injustice—had produced such arrogance in the masters and such abjection in the slaves that common humanity was lost in an artificial creation of two species different only in natural color, but both of them lost to the possibility of moderation, the foundational virtue of civilization. The mere possession of slaves, even if they were treated nicely, and even if the owner was good to everybody white, deprived the owner of the right to be called moderate. Many whites could no more imagine, for the purpose of moral reasoning, putting themselves in the place of slaves than they could imagine putting themselves in the place of animals they domesticated or looked on as food or prey. The racist imagination could not leap what we would designate the species-distance between the human and the not fully human.

Racial aristocracy was tyrannous and hence the most abominable kind of aristocracy. The question arises, was it truly worse than ancient slavery and later sorts of serfdom? Yes, because these earlier systems did not emerge in societies that professed belief in human equality on earth and they were therefore free of the terrible stain of hypocrisy; and the chattel slave system emerged on a basis—color—that was even more arbitrary than the good fortune of victory in wars of conquest that often produced slaveholding in earlier societies. Actually the word *hypocrisy* is not good enough to describe the relation between the founding proposition and the actual practice: it was not merely a serious discrepancy of the sort that hypocrisy designates; it was a chasm, all the difference in the world. Cruelty for cruelty, degradation for degradation: can we estimate which historical system was the worst? To make a judgment we would have to know the numbers subjected to one or another kind of servitude and the extent of the misery and brutalization. Comparisons aside, these systems were all evil. What a scandal that the despotism of Czar Alexander II could by an edict abolish serfdom in Russia, while a supposedly democratic system required a long and bitter war to end slavery thanks to the power of racism to nullify the freedom of millions and to the chances of a war that the North did not originally intend to lead to abolition.

Then, too, the widespread effects of slavery on the character of those who were neither masters nor slaves in the United States depended of course on race, and were damaging—even if the damage was not felt. Both non-slave-owning whites (the majority of the population) and free blacks were damaged in their understanding and experience of freedom in at least nominal equality because in the peaceful course of events most blacks would never be free and no whites would ever be enslaved.

Lincoln did not produce or did not think he had to produce a lengthy treatise on the grounds of human equality. But there were a few recurrent points that he used to emphasize his commitment. One was the idea that all governments except constitutional democracies (there were none but the United States) degraded the masses of people and rode on them and over them for purposes that severely damaged the personhood and basic interests of the people; this was and is the essence of tyranny. In a "free society" the spirit of the laws is to persist in attachment to the "standard maxim" of human equality, so that the process unfolds of "augmenting the happiness and value of life to all people of all colors everywhere" (Peoria speech, June 26, 1857, LA, 1:398; see also Fragments on Government, 1854?, LA, 1:302). Another point was that no one should be ruled without his consent; there was a sacred right of individual and group self-government. Lincoln insisted that "no man was good enough to rule another without his consent. . . . Allow ALL the governed an equal voice in the government, and that only is self government" (Peoria speech, LA, 1:328). A people could not claim to be self-governing if some ruled others, if any or some of its members were denied an equal voice. A third main point was that since labor was the source of all wealth, every person had a right to the results of his or her own labor; that is, persons were made victims when their labor was systematically uncompensated, as in slavery (or Mexican peonage, which Lincoln condemned); or unfairly compensated when wages were too low. In "Fragment on Free Labor" Lincoln said that since labor was the common burden of our race, the effort of some people to shift the burden onto others was "the great durable curse of the race." By the practice of slavery, the original curse was "concentrated on a part [of the human race] only," and became "the double-refined curse of God upon his creatures" (September, 17, 1859?, CW, 3:462). Lincoln stops at Genesis 3:19 on the theme that human labor is a curse. But the South seemed to be guided tacitly by Matthew 13:12, where Jesus says with approval, "Whosoever hath not, from him shall be taken away even that he hath," though Jesus was not defending slavery but celebrating the luck of those to whom it was given to know the mysteries and not caring about those who were denied such knowledge. Lincoln did not approve of such arbitrariness. The strength of his commitment to these main points was not diminished by the comparatively few words he wrote to defend them. True to Lincoln, we could say that it was a shame to have to defend them at any length. Vivified recollection under the pressure of willful doubters should be enough.

———

The dispute that appeared recurrently in the eight Lincoln-Douglas debates is whether the Declaration meant to include nonwhites among the recipients of the Creator's endowment of the basic rights that serve to protect human equality. It is worth noticing that the Creator's intentions scarcely figured in the speeches of either orator, or in Lincoln's other speeches on the theme. Politicians knew that many or most good Christians accepted slavery and did not think, or did not like to think, that they were disobeying God by doing so. If for the most part the Creator had to be left out of the discussion and if people could quarrel over whether a proposition was self-evident, the question became why some Americans found it plausible to deny human equality to the extreme point at which slavery was practiced and defended, when in the founding and for a while after, the largely unchallenged assumption was "that all men are created equal."

Devout Christians found extreme denial of human equality plausible in part because, as Lincoln said, God did not speak "audably [sic]" on the subject, and his revelation in the Bible gave no certain instruction (On Pro-Slavery Theology, 1858?, LA, 1:685). Jefferson and Lincoln could not work for rights-based human equality in this life on a Christian basis, even cynically. Historically, Christian theology, Protestant and Catholic, had been more on the slavery side than on the opposite side. It is all the more striking that non-Christians like Jefferson and Lincoln could speak so effortlessly and without elaborated theology of any kind about God's endowment of all humanity with inalienable rights. (When discussing human equality, Locke at least tried to keep up Christian appearances, except in his most important passages.) Jefferson and Lincoln certainly did not speak biblically; the Declaration did not owe its religious teaching, such as it is, to scripture. The explanation is that only (but not always) when religion was heterodox and thus practiced only by minorities, if at all, was it on the side of equal rights. But the larger part of the plausibility of religious denial of equal rights was sanctified so to speak by skin color, by white racism—that is, from something that was made visceral by habitual reinforcement and was not inherently religious and that most of the time religion was not strong enough to combat, even if it wanted to. Conventional American religion gave no strong reasons to abolish slavery; it usually did not say that eternal punishment awaited those who enslaved others; such influence as it had, more often than not, abetted slavery, especially in the South, but not only there, and perhaps sometimes to protect itself against public opinion.

We have said more than once that racism, not universal human equality, was in fact the regnant assumption in the United States before the Civil War, and racism usually went the length of restricting equality of human status in white societies to whites. Furthermore, in the absence of unmistakable opposition to slavery in revelation and theology, the deemed inferiority of blacks led, in Christian circumstances, to white racist enslavement of blacks or other nonwhites, not merely racial subordination, and did so with little inhibition. There were forms of white near-enslavement of whites, like impressments and indentured servitude, but no whites were chattel slaves (people treated like cattle, or not as well), born into slavery—at least not in the Atlantic world. Not even white serfdom imposed by white rulers elsewhere, even at its worst, was chattel slavery, although in Russia it eventually came close before it was abolished.

Lincoln thought it would help his cause if he could wrest the question of equality away from orthodox religion, certainly in the North, so that the political religion of reverence for the principle of Jefferson's founding document could have a chance. The general question is, can a person be orthodox in religion and simultaneously subscribe to a political religion? Perhaps one could do so by some contrived arrangement of the two spheres, but the religiously orthodox Christian would probably not think it proper to have the intensity of devotion to any political religion that Lincoln showed for his declared political religion. The truth is that after the Enlightenment, people were willing to die for their country, but not their religion, despite having more devotion to their religion than to their country. Lincoln did not subordinate his political religion to any supernatural religion, but for himself and he hoped for others, political religion deserved to be supreme in conflicts between the two, as in the most important case, the absolute wrongness of slavery. What Lincoln tried to make salient was not the intentions of the Creator but the imputed intentions of Jefferson and the people who rallied to the cause of independence in the spirit of the Declaration, and turned the Revolutionary War into a war for universal equality. Nothing could shake Lincoln's devotion to this picture of the

Revolution, not even the fact that slave-owners took part in it and did not typically free their slaves as a result of it and of their supposed devotion to human equality. Where in the North slaves were far fewer, the spirit of the Revolution did encourage gradual, piecemeal abolition.

Lincoln's political religion needed the authority of the fathers and continuity with their teachings; he did his best to supply a lineage fit for reverence. But he seems to me to have forced the fathers into service by purifying their record. He helped to invent a political tradition, just as he helped to invent a political religion. Of course there was some unequivocally antislavery theory that preceded him. The most valuable were the writings of American abolitionists—Garrison, Parker, Phillips—but he was careful not to use them, certainly not to use them by name. In the founding generation there was Thomas Paine, whom he admired but did not press into explicit service, again perhaps out of caution. It was an American who wrote the Bill of Rights, but it was not an American who wrote *Rights of Man*.

There is a curiosity that we should notice in the view that the abstract idea of equal rights of all human beings was needed to condemn chattel slavery. What should have been the most obvious wrong had to get theoretical backing for the effort to condemn it. The reason for this anomaly was inveterate racism, which could countenance every wrong, no matter how great, and make it look both right or morally indifferent, and natural. Yet when we look at the Declaration of Independence we barely see theoretical backing for human equality; even though we see a few dramatic assertions about the divine endowment of human beings with certain inalienable rights. The extended work done in the Declaration turned out to be a denunciation of the colonists' political slavery, not black chattel slavery. The American colonies suffered under political slavery because they lacked a dependable political structure of consent and also suffered from various particular grievances, all of which amounted to some injustice and a fair amount of blocked opportunity, but not oppression, let alone evil. The grievous acts listed in the Declaration could have been condemned without invoking the idea of human equality, but instead could have been protested, some of them anyway, in the name of traditional British privileges. Lincoln said rather casually but arrestingly in his speech about the *Dred Scott* decision that the "assertion that 'all men are created equal' was of no practical use in effecting our separation from Great Britain, and it was placed in the Declaration, not for that, but for future use" (June 27, 1857, LA, 1:398–399).

We should notice that the discourse of the Declaration did not build up to the conclusion that all persons are created equal but rather to the conclusion that all peoples are equal and therefore the American people were equal to all other peoples, in the name of what we now call national self-determination. That point is clear from the first sentence of the Declaration, which refers to the necessity of dissolving the bands which have connected one people with another. The conceptual tie between the independent person and the independent group, if any, is hardly obvious. Common grievances had changed a group of colonists into a people organized in states. Furthermore, unaddressed grievances had given this people a supposed right to revolution when the old order inflicted numerous wrongs on it. The plain truth, however, was that the unaddressed grievances inflicted by the ruling system on the English people at home, including the exceedingly narrow extent of the franchise, were much worse than those inflicted on the American colonists, and could have made a stronger case for violent revolution against the English government than the Americans could make for themselves. Thomas Paine had to leave England and go to America and then to France to find revolutions that at least partly resembled the one he was looking for at home.

When therefore Lincoln made slavery the wrong that had to be condemned above all, he was joining those persons who saw that if resistance to political slavery was justified on the grounds of human equality, the grounds for resistance to chattel slavery—by the slaves or their sympathizers—were unconditional. Many people were impervious to perceiving what should have been obvious: the moral case for the end of slavery was altogether stronger—peacefully if possible, by violence if necessary—than the case for American violence to redress grievances or secure independence. Lincoln was not the heir of Jefferson because he transformed Jefferson's Declaration by identifying the unwanted true meaning of its abstract clauses—just as he re-created the Constitution just by struggling successfully to add the one sentence in the Thirteenth Amendment that abolished slavery.

I do not find any moment of truth—actually any moment of doubt—in Lincoln's advocacy of the idea that Jefferson meant, *with a whole heart,* to include all blacks in the sentence, "All men are created equal." He should have seen or even said that Jefferson had his hesitations about including blacks—if there were no other evidence than that Jefferson did not free his slaves. Yes, Jefferson surely intended to include all people, including blacks, in the scope of equal rights; but then kept blacks as slaves. How could he, as a man of principle, have done so theoretically?

Jefferson constructed a story in which the English monarch had forced chattel slavery on the colonists and blocked any effort to stop the slave trade ("this execrable commerce"). Slaveholders were thus forced to live as slaveholders. Jefferson then engaged in a partly plausible but basically paranoid thought-experiment in which the same monarch was now exciting slaves to rebel and thus forcing the slaveholders to act on behalf of preserving their right of life against vengeful slaves, who if freed, were likely to engage in "paying off" former crimes committed against them. Slaves had to be kept in slavery under a strict discipline, not freed and allowed to rampage.

Perhaps Jefferson could not imagine himself as a slave who would not try to kill his master before or after manumission. To him, slave-owners were not obliged to die at the hands of the smoldering slaves they might be forced to set free. The right of self-defense, justice to oneself, transcended the claims of justice to others. Jefferson described the clash as the lives of one people against the liberties of another. The clash was right against right. The slaves' right to liberty was undeniable, but the slave-owners' right to life was also undeniable (all references are in *Autobiography*, in Jefferson: *Writings*, 22). Only force could decide which of the two rights would prevail. Jefferson thus made it appear that it was not immoral to continue to hold slaves if freeing them would lead to massacres by the liberated mob. As Jefferson repeated many years after the Declaration, there is "justice in one scale, and self-preservation in the other" (*Writings*, letter to John Holmes, April 22, 1820, 1434). But it was perhaps not, or not only or mainly, literal self-preservation that worried him, but the preservation of white cultural identity and the habits of white superiority that were built on the exclusion of blacks from equal freedom. The necessity for maintaining slavery was not physical or not only physical but cultural.

Jefferson's reflections naturally lead to the question whether any free person, but not holding slaves, is morally obliged to risk or sacrifice his life for the sole purpose of ending slavery, which is arguably as high a duty as ending any other political evil or performing any other kind of political duty. I think that it is the case that a person cannot be morally obliged to risk or lose his life for the freedom (or lives) of others. I believe that Lincoln accepted that view. That is why he was adamant in claiming that emancipation was a military necessity that impelled his action, not his moral or legal duty, and that, correspondingly, a soldier had a civic or legal duty in time of war to obey the commander-in-chief. No self-sacrificing altruism would be asked. The trouble, in my judgment, is that most people thought and still do think that you can be legally obliged by the state to risk or lose your life to defend the state; the state does no moral wrong in exacting such a legal obligation, whether or not you have a moral obligation to comply with such a legal obligation. You cannot lose your right of self-preservation as a private person, but can be obliged, even legally coerced, to lose your right of self-preservation as a soldier. The case for conscripted self-sacrifice is worse than shaky.

Jefferson's discussion of the clash of rights was excised from the final version of the Declaration by his collaborators, but Jefferson recorded it and all the other excised parts in his *Autobiography* (written in 1821, and published posthumously in 1829). I do not know whether Lincoln could have had access to it. We must also notice that Jefferson had already speculated about apparently innate black inferiority in some respects in Section 14, Laws, in *Notes on the State of Virginia*, 1787 (in *Writings*, 264–270). On the other hand, he sometimes worked for emancipation in Virginia. (In his will, he emancipated a mere five.)

Then again, in private, he denounced the Missouri Compromise for confining slavery's extension, and thus supposedly concentrating the problem of emancipation in a minority of states rather than spreading slavery to many more states; the spread supposedly did not increase the number of blacks enslaved (*Writings*, letter to John Holmes, April 22, 1820, 1433–1435; and letter to Albert Gallatin, December 26, 1820, 1447–1450). Did Jefferson expect Southern slaveholders to reduce the number of their slaves and sell them in order to distribute slavery more evenly? I suppose his strategy was to give all states an interest in defending slavery; they would come to see slavery as the only way to handle significant numbers of black people in their midst. He did not mention the pressure to increase the slave population by restoring the slave trade by congressional statute—a perfectly constitutional measure—if the slavery interest were to exist in most states. He therefore did not stop to think that future slaves would be made all the more numerous by an ever-expanding right to hold slaves. In his letter to Gallatin, Jefferson went so far as to say that if Congress somehow presumed to legislate emancipation in all states, "all the whites South of the Patomak [*sic*] and Ohio [River] must evacuate their states" (*Writings*, 1449). They would leave black people behind. I assume he meant that whites simply could not live with a large number of blacks unless blacks were enslaved and kept under tight and profitable control. Large numbers of freed slaves would have to be deported to S. Domingo (1450). Jefferson claimed that if there were mass black deportation, then (and perhaps he meant only then) the gradual end of slavery ("that kind of property, for so it is misnamed") would be a "bagatelle" (*Writings*, letter to John Holmes, April 22, 1820, 1434).

In the United States and elsewhere in the western world, devotion to Christianity facilitated or did not retard the belief that a commitment to human equality actually permitted the institution of slavery, though some Christians resisted such theological complicity while still holding to their religious beliefs. At the same time, the equally important fact was that many people who were not devout Christians were not as troubled about slavery as Jefferson was; they did not think that their secular commitment to equality required them to condemn slavery. Religious doubt or vague agnosticism was hardly enough to condemn slavery in the face of orthodox commitment to it. Anyway, nonbelievers did not need their proslavery commitment facilitated by religion. As believers in human equality, they behaved as if slavery were at the least not immoral (though Jefferson was clear that it was unjust), even if they did not hold that black slavery was a positive good. Whatever they may have said or failed to say, their behavior demonstrated their morally untroubled attitude. The obvious reason for their acceptance of slavery was that racism was a sufficient religion; it still is. It is older than religion; its hold can be stronger than religious faith or philosophical adherence; it hardly needs but nevertheless could gain additional strength from such faith or adherence; it can and did organize a whole culture. (The same holds for ethnocentrism without difference in color.) A difference in color made black slavery possible and then made ending it within the normal workings of the political system impossible. Culturally instilled aestheticism of the surface, constantly reinforced in many ways by the ambient culture, can overcome all barriers of moral inhibition and will take advantage of what religion can offer, or do without it, as the case may be.

Lincoln had to have a stainless American source of devotion to human equality; the source had to be as old as the founding first steps of the Republic; it had to be the reason for the founding. If Jefferson's Declaration could not serve in this capacity, Lincoln would have had no object of devotion that was free of the stain of slavery—certainly not the Constitution, the policies of its government, or the Union as a whole. And he must have known that the only kind of American chattel slavery that could have existed had to have its basis in color. The distortion of truth came from Lincoln's insistence that the Declaration and the man who wrote it were single-minded in their commitment to the human equality of all persons and races and made that commitment uppermost. Lincoln had to mythologize in order to secure the tenets of his political religion. Thus, he wanted to feel and impart to other citizens a kind of religious devotion to a political principle and its derivative constitutional, governmental, and national expressions; he forced the evidence in a manner similar to that employed by propagators of all religions (in the proper sense). One of the meanings of the very word *religion* among Christians—not that Lincoln was one—is going beyond the evidence (that is, having faith) and turning away from evidence that might threaten the religion's solidity (that is, having faith). "Now faith is the substance of things hoped for, the evidence of things not seen" (Hebrews 11:1).

4

Race and Human Equality

HOW STAINLESS IN FACT was Lincoln's commitment to human equality before he issued the Emancipation Proclamation and did the later hard work to get the Thirteenth Amendment approved by Congress and ratified by the states? I think he was closer to Jefferson than to some other Republicans, like Seward (at least before the war) and Chase, not to mention devoted abolitionists in office and outside party competition for office. In the prewar period, when he was pushing the strategy by which slavery was to be contained, rather than abolished, Lincoln's commitment to human equality was seriously flawed. Of course the primary flaw was that Lincoln was not an abolitionist. Let us put that matter aside for the time being and say that Lincoln's commitment was flawed because what distressed Lincoln was black slavery, which could not be touched, while the radical political and social inequality of free blacks, which was open in theory to amelioration, seemed not to bother him. In addition one of his great concerns was to exclude slavery from the territories, where possible, in order to keep blacks out of them and therefore avoid having slave labor compete with free white labor. At two places in his Peoria speech he made it clear that the effect of the Northwest Ordinance of 1787 was that the territories were intended by Jefferson and others to be "the happy home of teeming millions of free, white, prosperous people, and no slave [and perhaps no black?] amongst them"; "New free states are the places for poor [that is, poor white] people to go to and better their condition" (October 16, 1854, LA, 1:309, 331).

Just as important, Lincoln's steady implication was that whatever he may have felt, the introduction of even a few slaves into a territory would of course lead to numbers large enough to make whites think that the only or the easiest way to live among blacks was to enslave them. Slavery as an institution would come to seem natural and most convenient, the best way to handle a profitable but distasteful presence. As he said in a speech at Cincinnati, about the absence of slavery in Ohio: "you made it a Free State, not with the embarrassment upon you of already having among you many slaves, which if they had been here, and you had sought to make a Free State, you would not know what to do with" (September 17, 1858, LA, 2:78). The meaning of "not know what to do with" was that though black slavery was unacceptable for moral reasons, emancipated blacks in large numbers were unacceptable as citizens able to mingle on equal or even decent terms with whites. You keep out slaves in order to keep out blacks, and you keep out blacks in order not to create the temptation or the felt social need to enslave them. To be sure, on one occasion Lincoln spelled out the process by which the political power and public influence at the disposal of those who owned slaves would always protect slavery, no matter what others thought or wanted (speech at Janesville, Wisconsin, October 1, 1859, CW, 3:485). He thus located, though not routinely, the source of the tenacity of slavery more in the interest of a few than in the racism of all.

On this major matter of knowing and accepting the situation in which whites did not want to live among numerous free blacks as fellows, much less as fellow citizens, Lincoln was Jefferson's heir. Lincoln easily understood the distaste felt by whites toward blacks; he shared it. I think that he found the proximity of even free blacks undesirable. As for Douglas's charge that Lincoln advocated black-white intermarriage, Lincoln had said complacently that there was a "natural disgust in the minds of nearly all white people to the idea of an indiscriminate amalgamation of the white and black races" (speech on the *Dred Scott* decision, June 26, 1857, LA, 1:397). Lincoln wanted a country where there was more equality between whites and only a minimal equality between whites and free blacks. He hated white degradation of blacks as ' much as he hated anything, but he was pleased by the thought of whites living apart from blacks, either by (voluntary) deportation of blacks or what appears to me to be some kind of domestic segregation. Soon before his debates with Douglas, he said in a speech in Springfield, "What I would most desire would be the separation of the white and black races" (July 17, 1858, LA, 1:478). He would do without blacks if only the South could do without slaves. He hated slavery but disliked blacks, not individually, but certainly as a group in the abstract. In the same speech he said, "All I ask for the negro is that if you do not like him, let him alone"—that is, do not enslave him; rather, let him lead his life (478). I believe that he thought that such dislike was quite understandable. This abstract dislike lost its potency, however, as his hatred of slavery shoved aside all other feelings when the time was propitious to abolish slavery by a constitutional amendment that victory in war made possible.

Although Frederick Douglass tried hard to see many of Lincoln's "unfriendly" (Douglass, 3) remarks as tactically necessary, it was with good reason that Douglass said in his celebratory "Oration in Memory of Abraham Lincoln," of April 14, 1876, "You [white people] are the children of Abraham Lincoln. We [black people] are at best only his stepchildren; children by adoption, children by forces of circumstances and necessity" (Douglass, 2). These words capture Lincoln's racial attitudes well.

Lincoln described himself as "a Southern man with Northern principles, with Abolitionist proclivities" (speech at Council Bluffs, Iowa, August 13, 1859, CW, 3:396). To call himself a Southern man is likely to imply invidious race consciousness, while the word *proclivities* falls short of an absolute commitment to abolish slavery. Late in the war, well after the Emancipation Proclamation, he did not mind saying to Sojourner Truth, "I'm not an abolitionist; I wouldn't free the slaves if I could save the Union in any other way. I'm obliged to do it" (October 29, 1864, F, 116). During the war he had to weigh his conviction that many blacks were culturally unready for economic self-reliance and hence for immediate emancipation against his wholehearted acceptance of their value as soldiers in the cause of the Union. Lincoln "thought it proper to put arms in their [blacks'] hands to save white lives" (July 1862, F, 162). The rather heartless meaning was that blacks, unjustly deprived of their liberty, were going to have to earn it with sacrifice of their lives. Yet undeniably the arming of blacks to kill whites was in itself a socially radical act, felt by many as the high crime of lèse majesté against the white race. It was inevitable that Southern soldiers would kill black prisoners of war; re-enslavement was too good for them. The other side of the coin was Northern white resentment of dying to free blacks from slavery, as one of Lincoln's correspondents, the Illinois friend and pro-Unionist James C. Conkling, made clear. Lincoln wrote back: "You say you will not fight to free negroes. Some of them seem willing to fight for you [that is, in your place]" (August 26, 1863, LA, 2:498). For a change, he uttered a friendly pro-black sentiment. More than that, he produced on this occasion an expression that accepted complete human reciprocity between the races on the individual level.

Lincoln made an infamous address on the benefits to both whites and blacks, if already free blacks joined together with black slaves once emancipated, to leave the United States and colonize some other country.

The presentation was made in the White House to a delegation of free blacks on August 14, 1862. It is perhaps as personally insulting a face-to-face presentation as has ever been made by an American president to a group of ordinary citizens. Blacks should leave this country because "you and we are different races. . . . Whether it is right or wrong I need not discuss, but this physical difference is a great disadvantage to us both, as I think your race suffer very greatly, many of them by living among us, while ours suffer from your presence" (LA, 2:353). To their faces, Lincoln calmly said that the white race suffered from the black presence—that is, from their mere presence, as a physically different group of people. What was he saying if not that their black color excited distaste, even loathing, in whites? Here is unadorned honesty; but coming from the president, and published almost immediately in New York and Washington, it was a slap on the face meant to resound through the country. The delegation, however, went away apparently persuaded, but reports of the meeting aroused disgust among many other free blacks. Yet, two months earlier he had drafted a confidential emancipation proclamation. What are we to make of this mixture of elements? Honesty and deviousness, sympathy and coldness are thrown together on this occasion, and perhaps characterize Lincoln much of the time.

It seems clear that Lincoln's devotion to human equality for blacks was not single-minded before the war or during it. Unless, of course, he always hid his true feelings in order to safeguard his determination to emancipate, and secretly awaited his chance to establish *full* political and social equality for blacks. To do him justice, imagine the outcry if he had been outspokenly committed to full equality and had expressed his true feelings at any time before he died. The need to express such feelings would have come only when he had to answer the question after the war as to whether he supported or opposed the Fourteenth and Fifteenth Amendments, which were required to complete the remaking

of the Constitution. He never faced the need. But what would he have
done in the face of widespread antipathy to the proposals, and not only
in the South? The signs were not good. Sentiment in the North was
mixed; witness the obtuse pragmatism of the great-hearted Melville
playing the statesman; he warned the North to be conciliatory to
Southern feelings, in order to reunite Southern citizens more easily
with the rest of the country (see the "Supplement" appended to his col-
lection of war poems, *Battle-Pieces and Aspects of the War*, 1866).

As for sentiment in the South, every indication was that only a
nearly free hand in dealing with blacks would be satisfactory. That
meant not that slavery could be restored but that the situation would be
to leave the blacks nominally free but utterly rejected and unwanted,
politically and socially, and exploited where possible; and thus the
South would succeed in establishing a system of subjection in large
part when secession had failed to preserve a complete system of subjection. The ruinous war had not served as a chastisement, as Generals
Grant and Sherman had wanted and expected from the devastation of
the South. Despite the Fourteenth and Fifteenth Amendments, and despite the efforts of Radical Republicans and President Grant, once the
Union military left the South in 1877, a condition in which blacks were
either second-class citizens or not citizens at all began to change only
in the 1950s amid fierce resistance. When has the South ever been reconciled? Racial ferocities, not merely political disputes, had originally
brought on the Civil War; such ferocities were exactly what could not
be conciliated, even though moderated in practice after defeat in
war. The conviction that blacks were innately inferior or even less than
human was not and has never been overcome.

A second miracle performed by Lincoln was inconceivable. The first
one, abolition in a restored Union, continuously made a second one,
full acceptance of blacks, impossible. He perhaps told Andrew Johnson,
his vice-president in 1865, that he favored only one more amendment

after the Thirteenth, and that would compel the states to send their representatives and senators to the Congress of the United States (Johnson's speech, February 22, 1866, F, 268). A very curious idea, indeed. In 1864 Lincoln did not object to the draft of a reconstruction constitution of Arkansas that excluded blacks from voting and holding office (1864, F, n. 438, p. 427). To a close associate, he said that he saw the justice of enfranchising all blacks in the South, but he did not support "unlimited social equality," and thought that a proposed law (the Ashley bill) granting universal suffrage was "of doubtful political policy" and could hurt the Republican Party, "the freedman himself," and the whole country (December 1864, F, 291).

Perhaps Lincoln would have changed his mind had he lived and would have worked hard for the Fourteenth and Fifteenth Amendments or something like them. Yet his passion for the Thirteenth Amendment, when he was certain the right time had come, overrode every other consideration. He might have once thought that the Emancipation Proclamation was his greatest political act, but as victory approached he saw that this militarily necessary act of executive power was only preliminary to a constitutional amendment abolishing slavery everywhere in the country forever. I attribute to him the sense that though the political and social condition after abolition would present tremendous problems, at least they would not involve appalling political compromise with and adjustment to monstrous evil. Perhaps the worst problem would continue to be racism, white dislike of or distaste for blacks, but now deprived of its most terrible manifestation.

———

If we go back to the time before the war, what do we see when we look at Lincoln's views on race? Consider his words right after the *Dred Scott* decision, and also when he campaigned the next year for the nomination to the Senate from Illinois and in the period that led to his Republican nomination to the presidency. Lincoln said more than once in the debates with Douglas, and elsewhere, that he wanted whites to be superior to blacks; perhaps he felt compelled to say so and would have preferred to leave it unsaid. Nonetheless, he said it: blacks should be free, but were not the physical and moral equals of whites and should not become the political or legal equals of whites. A little later and for the first time he publicly mentioned an incident in which at the age of nineteen, he and a companion who were hired hands on a flatboat to New Orleans were "attacked by seven negroes with intent to kill and rob them," but they succeeded, despite their hurt, in driving the blacks from the boat and went on their way. What makes this disclosure noteworthy is that this story was recounted in an autobiography written to promote his presidential electoral chances (c. June 1860, LA, 1:162; he was nominated by the Republican Party on May 18). Is it possible that this event on the flatboat marked the young Lincoln and left him with dislike of blacks, even if it did not affect his lifelong hatred of slavery? Or was it just another event that left no mark?

In his speech on the *Dred Scott* decision (June 26, 1857), he said with approval that the authors of the Declaration of Independence did not intend to "declare all men equal *in all respects*. They did not mean to say all were equal in color, size, intellect, moral developments or social capacity" (LA, 1:398). (What a heterogeneous assortment of traits.) In the debates with Douglas that came later, we have a fuller context for this statement. Speaking to audiences in various Illinois towns, Lincoln repeatedly said that he was not in favor of the political and legal equality of free blacks, and still would not be in favor, if slaves were emancipated. Although he did not put it this way but should have, Lincoln would thus allow newly freed chattel slaves and other blacks to be and remain "political slaves." This was a status intolerable to him as a white citizen and putatively to all whites. This status would be of course immeasurably better than chattel slavery; nevertheless it was once condemned as so deep an injustice to white colonists that it had justified in their eyes a violent revolution. Furthermore, if blacks did not participate in full citizenship, and would therefore be governed without their consent, their rights, such as they would be, would turn into unguaranteed privileges. I must add that if freed blacks and other blacks had only unguaranteed privileges, the whole polity would be back in a condition in which the guaranteed rights of the white people would once again turn into race-based privileges, and lose their nature as genuine rights because they were not held by all persons irrespective of race. (The same point perhaps applied to gender until women could vote, but maybe not.)

In the sixth debate, Lincoln said, "I agree with Judge Douglas that he [the black man] is not my equal in many respects, certainly not in color—perhaps not in mental and moral endowments" (October 13, 1858, LA, 1:734). (Is there any satire on white racism there as we go from *certainly* about color to *perhaps* about endowments?) He went so far as to say in the fourth debate with Douglas that since whites and blacks could not be equal, "there must be the position of superior and inferior," and he wanted the superior position assigned to the whites (September 18, 1858, LA, 1:636). He said a little later that if one race had to enslave another one, "I think I would go for enslaving the black man, in preference to being enslaved myself." If two men struggle for one plank to avoid drowning, "either of them can rightfully push the other off" (quoting from a judge's decision, speech at Hartford, Connecticut, March 5, 1860, version 1, CW, 4:5). (In "Civil Disobedience," Thoreau insisted that the moral man would yield the plank to the other.) A little later, however, the truth burst out. Lincoln said that there was "room for all races" and that therefore there was no necessary conflict between black and white; it was false that white freedom was insecure unless the blacks were reduced to a condition of abject slavery (speech at Janesville, Wisconsin, October 1, 1859, CW, 3:486).

He rarely spoke the truth about room for all races, but was happy to speak the truth freely about room for all whites, whatever their ethnicity. Although recent immigrants, perhaps "half our people" are not tied by blood to "that glorious epoch" when our ancestors declared their independence, they nevertheless could claim the idea of human equality in the Declaration of Independence as their own "as though they were blood of the blood, and flesh of the flesh of the men who wrote that Declaration" (speech at Chicago, July 17, 1858, LA, 1:456). Unlike many of his illustrious contemporaries, he was not an Anglo-Saxon (or British) supremacist. But his lack of ethnocentrism was not accompanied by a lack of color-consciousness.

In any event, the strong indication is that in the *Dred Scott* speech Lincoln was not referring primarily to morally allowable political and social inequalities among individuals irrespective of color, when he maintained that the Declaration did not intend to "declare all men equal *in all respects*," but was referring to morally allowable political and social inequalities between races, specifically the inequalities that rightly stemmed from the overall superiority of whites to blacks. Otherwise, why ever mention inequality of color? It was a rather arch way of saying that if you are white, white skin is more excellent to look at than black skin. On the other hand, Lincoln in fact said that the authors of the Declaration "did not at once, or ever afterwards, actually place all white men on an equality with one another." Part of Lincoln's political religion, however, was the expectation that if whites were not now equal in all the relevant respects, they would in time become less unequal (all quotations from *Dred Scott* speech, June 26, 1857, LA, 1:398). What is more, committed with a single mind to white equality, he hated any trace of an aristocratic-caste or fixed-class system among whites. Aside from the universal right of persons to be free, greatly reduced white social inequality (not white and black indiscriminately) was perhaps the most important kind of egalitarianism that he claimed was promised by the Declaration. The relevant sections in the *Dred Scott* speech perhaps provide the best (least pandering) summary of Lincoln's view of the not-quite-strict limits on desirable racial equality.

———

Given that Lincoln hated slavery, the question is why he did so, in the face of his expressed if abstract dislike of blacks and rather low opinion of their capacities. He held that slavery was "a moral, a social and a political wrong" (sixth debate, October 13, 1858, LA, 1:740). What is more, he thought that slavery was not only wrong in itself, "but a 'deadly poison' in a government like ours, professedly based on the equality of men" (draft of a speech, c. December 1857, LA, 1:414). We should spend a little time on this latter remark that slavery was a deadly poison in order to fill out the nature of Lincoln's hatred of slavery.

To allow slavery, Lincoln thought, "planted the seeds of despotism around your own doors. Familiarize yourselves with the chains of bondage, and you are preparing your own limbs to wear them" (speech at Edwardsville, Illinois, September 11, 1858, LA, 1:585). A little earlier he had said, "And then, the negro being doomed, and damned, and forgotten, to everlasting bondage, is the white man quite certain that the tyrant demon will not turn upon him too?" (draft of a speech, c. August 1858, LA, 1:494). Black slavery portended white slavery in perhaps a worse form than the political slavery white people endured under British rule. What is the nature of the portent? His answer was, "Accustomed to trample on the rights of others, you have lost the genius of your own independence, and become the fit subjects of the first cunning tyrant who rises" (speech at Edwardsville, LA, 1:585). Obviously he did not expect whites to become chattel slaves under a white tyrant, but rather perhaps create in a spasm, or drift toward, some condition more insidious or harsh than the political slavery that George III had been charged with imposing. I speculate that Lincoln perhaps envisaged

one-man rule more suitable to democratic America than European-style
kingship would be; he had already warned against such a development in
the Lyceum Address of 1838. Tyrants, whether kings or autocrats, enslaved "the people in all ages"; that is the nature of one-man rule (speech
at Chicago, July 10, 1858, LA, 1:457). If political slavery is only slavery
hyperbolically, and depending on the tyranny, it probably still would
have been hyperbolical to equate any new tyranny with the legal institution of chattel slavery. I grant that in the feelings of people with a republican sensitivity, the awfulness of diluted representative government
and abridged rights feels like tyranny, unless of course the people have
rushed to surrender themselves to the strongman. It is nevertheless
strange that in a slave society, as the United States was, the sharp difference between being a slave and being free could be so easily lost sight of
when free persons and groups felt their grievances as if they constituted slavery, when these grievances fell far short of slavery; many
privileges remained intact, and indeed removed free whites to an altogether different mode of being. To speak of political slavery or other
gross disadvantages in the same breath as literal enslavement, as Lincoln,
Jefferson's heir, seemed to do on occasion, was to encourage white people
to persist in their failure to imagine what being a slave meant. Lincoln
knew better, as his indictment of slavery as monstrous injustice showed.

Moderate disapproval of slavery, rather than hatred of it, would seem
more easily compatible with genuine dislike of black people—if my surmise is plausible that Lincoln truly felt dislike, if only because of an ingrained abstract preconception that was never truly overcome. In any
case, the portent of white slavery is but one element in Lincoln's hatred of
chattel slavery. What were yet more important elements? These elements
were conceptualized at different times and on different occasions, but
they add up. They were not discoveries that Lincoln made over time. He
knew at the beginning what should be said against slavery and only regretted that it had to be said and could not go without saying.

Violation of God's intentions for humanity when he endowed them with certain inalienable rights was not for a thinker like Lincoln a sufficient explanation of the evil of slavery or the fundamental reason to hate it; it was not even an adequate explanation of the evil, but rather occasionally the best usable trope. I have already said that Lincoln's commitment to equality of individual rights was based on these secular tenets: nontyranny, self-government, and self-ownership. In brief: a government is condemnable when it uses the people as it pleases without regard for their interests and purposes and thus treats them merely as indispensable resources for the government's ambitions; rule must be with one's consent, which is expressed through exercise of one's guaranteed political rights; and one must be preserved in the fruits of one's labor, rather than being exploited to the extent of dispossession or robbery. Slavery made a system of extreme violation of all these tenets, and on a hereditary basis that was meant to last generation after generation. All three tenets finally rest on the right to the most basic liberty, which Lincoln defined simply as the right of each man "to do as he pleases with himself, and the product of his labor," while of course rejecting "the right of some men to do as they please with other men, and the product of other men's labor" (Address at Sanitary Fair, Baltimore, April 18, 1864, LA, 2:589). In this speech Lincoln complained that the world had never had a good definition of the word *liberty*. From various comments Lincoln made, I would hazard the opinion that he thought liberty was not merely doing what you want for the sake of doing what you want, good as that was, but was especially being unimpeded in making the best of yourself, which primarily meant seizing opportunities for self-advancement and self-improvement, within the limits of decent respect for others and the requirements of valid law.

Although I would wish to emphasize the sufficiency of secularism for Lincoln's adherence to his tenets, I should notice that he invoked the deity especially when he talked about the right of persons not to be exploited. In a speech in 1859 he said that the right to dispose of one's earnings from labor with one's hands and the sweat of one's brow was "proved to be the will of God by external nature around us, without reference to revelation"; "this is the inherent right given to mankind directly by the Maker" (speech at Cincinnati, September 17, 1858, CW, 10:44–45). A little later he said more succinctly that if anything could be proved by "natural theology"—that is, not biblical religion—it is that slavery was wrong because all persons had a right to feed themselves from the production of their labor (speech at Hartford, Connecticut, version 1, March 5, 1860, CW, 4:3). But the theological references were for Lincoln, I think, redundant. What is noteworthy is that the absence of exploitation mattered to him as much as any other tenet, because exploitation was the worst category of *social* crime, and slavery was the worst form of exploitation. Although he enlisted the aid of theology, exploitation was for him a *self-evident evil*. (No theological claim can be self-evident.) The institution of slavery, however, practiced all evils, not only exploitation. It was comprehensive evil. If slavery was not wrong, nothing was wrong.

The three tenets were for Lincoln the core of equality in liberty, if not the entirety. Slavery was the worst conceivable violation of all three tenets. Obviously, slaves endured the ignominy of living only to be used and often cruelly and otherwise disregarded, and sustained the systematic loss of both self-government and self-ownership. There is a worse crime than any social crime, which is the crime of being reduced in humanity. Slaves were treated in certain deliberate or casual ways that stamped these losses on the self of the slave and dehumanized and degraded him or her with a depth that poor free white people did not have to experience, and that people of decent means who were able to exercise their explicitly guaranteed rights against government managed to escape—at least to some extent. Slavery was a qualitatively different kind of oppression, not to be classed with the exploitation of free white labor, as Lincoln was at pains to emphasize, or with the over-looked, when not always intended, attenuation of the exercise of rights. of citizenship that poverty entailed. These latter circumstances were bad enough, but no poor person who was free wanted to be a slave on a full stomach. Slavery was thus monstrous injustice, not simple and sometimes correctable but still unacceptable injustice. It was in the class of worst evils, and it was a system, not an aberrant episode. Slavery was a destruction of personhood; robbing someone of his belongings was bad enough, but worst of all was "robbing one of himself, and all that was his" (to George B. Ide and others, May 30, 1864, LA, 2:597). American slavery kept "one-sixth of the population of the whole nation in a state of oppression and tyranny unequalled in the world" (speech at Chicago, July 10, 1858, LA, 1:449).

On a number of occasions Lincoln spoke of the loss of personhood, the deliberate dehumanization of blacks, that the institution of chattel slavery aimed to establish. I am tempted to say that the strongest words are found in a speech at Lewiston, Illinois, August 17, 1858, before the debates with Douglas began on August 21. My hesitation stems from the fact that the only record was supplied by a reporter, Horace White, who failed to take notes because he was so moved he just wanted to listen. He then re-created the speech shortly afterward, and read it to Lincoln to make sure he got it right. Lincoln said, "Well, those are my views, and if I said anything on the subject I must have said substantially that, but not nearly so well as that I said" (Herndon, 255). Fehernbacher has strong doubts, but Basler who tells the whole story, including the reporter's mistakes, prints the speech as part of the canon in the *Collected Works* (2:544–547). I want to believe that this reporter, who attended all the debates with Douglas and many other speeches by Lincoln, was "substantially" accurate because the Lewiston speech produced a public defense of the equal humanity of black people that was so strong that we can read it as an extenuation of many other statements he made, especially in the subsequent debates, when he derided the very idea of full black equality. Equally important, there are other passages that uphold the equal humanity of blacks with vigor, but the Lewiston statement might have a rhetorical edge. It sounds like Lincoln at his best or at least most sincerely impassioned.

Lincoln in Horace White's reconstruction held that the authors of the Declaration of Independence understood that the justice of the Creator reached to all humanity, "to the whole great family of man. In their enlightened belief nothing stamped with the divine image and likeness was sent into the world to be trodden on, and degraded, and imbruted by its fellows. They grasped not only the whole race of man then living, but they reached forward and seized upon the farthest posterity" (CW, 2:546). The only possible cause for doubting the authenticity of these words is the reference to "divine image," but if authentic, the phrase at last did some radical political work; it was not indispensable, but helpful. Whatever the case may be, such a statement made it impossible to accept slavery, but it would also appear to have made it nearly impossible to accept any denial of full citizenship to blacks. Meagerly selective and variable privileges, recognized as privileges, extended or withheld arbitrarily by the will of some people or of a majority, are hardly compatible with the human status, let alone with being stamped with the divine stamp, especially when people of one race enjoy all the supposedly irrevocable rights and immunities that they for the most part deny to another race. How could members of a common humanity, a status that far transcended all distinctions of color, not be granted equal citizenship?

The contrast is sharp with Douglas, who had already proudly said in his campaign before the debates, "I do not think that the negro is any kin of mine at all" (July 17, 1858, A, 62). Then Lincoln capped his speech at Lewiston with a plea to the audience to hold the issue of human equality high above partisanship: "Think nothing of me—take no thought for the political fate of any man whomsoever. . . . You may do anything with me you choose. . . . You may not only defeat me for the Senate, but you may take me and put me to death. . . . I charge you to drop every paltry and insignificant thought for any man's success. It is nothing; I am nothing; Judge Douglas is nothing. But do not destroy that immortal emblem of humanity—The Declaration of American Independence" (CW, 2:547). Here is a rare personal eruption in Lincoln's speeches. I grant that the rarity might suggest that the words are Horatio White's, not Lincoln's, and that Lincoln might not have said these great words; typically avoiding self-congratulation, he certainly praised them as if he had not written them; he was given to constant self-depreciation.

Not long after the Lewiston speech Lincoln reinforced his commitment to black equality in a most vigorous address at Edwardsville, Illinois, on September 11, 1858, between the second and third debates. In a tone much like that of White's reconstruction, he described the damage to the body and spirit inflicted on slaves and that Douglas regularly defended and encouraged by advocacy of the idea that rights under the Constitution were for whites only, and that the government "was established by white men for the benefit of white men," as Douglas often put it; one example is found in the seventh debate (October 15, 1858, LA, 1:789). Lincoln tallied the effects of a sustained political policy that was indifferent to slavery in the name of popular sovereignty (as Douglas proposed) or claimed that slavery was a positive good (as Calhoun did): "by all these means you have succeeded in dehumanizing the negro; when you have put him down, and made it impossible for him to be but as the beasts of the field; when you have extinguished his soul, and placed him where the ray of hope is blown out in darkness like that which broods over the spirits of the damned" (speech at Edwardsville, LA, 1:584). (But the damned are not only the slaves but also those who condemn others to damnation.) In the Peoria speech in 1854 he had already expressed a similar and literarily inflected horror at the institution of slavery; it was not only moral indignation: "Like the 'bloody hand' you may wash it, the red witness of guilt still sticks, and stares horribly at you" (LA, 1:340). He meant to remind his audience of the perfidy of usurpation and tyranny in *Macbeth* and arouse people to think that slavery was bloodstained, a usurpation of humanity and a tyranny over human beings.

Let us say that Lincoln was correct to hold that the Declaration of Independence meant to include all persons and races in the principle of human equality. Despite their fears and disparagement of blacks, and despite the retention of slavery in the face of the very words they had written, Jefferson and the signers of the Declaration did not think that the white race alone had rights and that slaves were only a form of property and not persons at all.

For a concentrated time as a candidate for the Senate, Lincoln exceeded Jefferson in his espousal of human equality, while pretending that he was repeating not only Jefferson's ideas but also Jefferson's sentiments, so as to cloak his (studiously qualified) radicalism in venerable authority.

5

Lincoln and the Constitution

HAVING CONSIDERED THE VIEW of human equality that Lincoln attributed to the Declaration of Independence, we turn our attention next to the Constitution, one of the great derivative objects of reverence in Lincoln's political religion. I wish to make two claims about the Constitution as Lincoln knew it. The first claim is that it was a constitution of slavery as well as a constitution of freedom; it was not a constitution of freedom and only incidentally a constitution of slavery. Even so, it was a constitution of freedom as racial privilege and hence only prima facie a constitution of freedom. My second claim is that the defense of the compromise by which the Framers accepted the incorporation of slavery in order to be able to get a constitution approved and then ratified must be subjected to moral questioning.

The first point is obvious. If a constitution is understood to deny a whole identifiable group of people the protection of the laws and entrenches their systematic oppression, we would say that this constitution was not merely a faulty constitution but an illegitimate one, made all the worse in the American case by the fact that the US Constitution owed its creation to a people whose revolutionary theorists, it was thought, claimed they believed in equal rights of all human beings within its boundaries and possibly some day everywhere else in the world. The illegitimacy of the US Constitution was masked by a gross deception that became so habitual as to operate pervasively as self-deception; the deceived confirmed deception in one another. The tremendous opportunities for the large majority to live a decent life under the protection of the laws cannot be thought to outweigh the systematic oppression of a whole identifiable minority group of people who were denied the most elementary protection of the laws. When self-deception did not cloud perception, we say that the clear-eyed chose to live a lie contentedly, unless they made some effort to oppose slavery.

Where systematic oppression was the worst kind, as chattel slavery was, and where the Constitution owing to structural and procedural features froze that oppression beyond remedy by any constitutional or political process, we cannot say merely that the oppression was a bad spot on an otherwise morally admirable constitution. We must say that the US Constitution was unworthy of obedience, even though it was prudent to obey it; much more, it was unworthy of the reverence that Lincoln wanted to instill. From the moral point of view, and hence as defined by its worst major feature, it was a constitution of slavery. And because Lincoln (and any white American) would not have countenanced the chattel slavery of any white minority for any purpose, his revered Constitution was fundamentally a constitution of black slavery. He would not have revered for a moment a constitution that kept white people like him in any number as chattel slaves. That is the first thing to say and the most important. Then we add but only secondly that it was a constitution of freedom. But even to say that much is to say too much because it was only apparently a constitution of freedom.

I have no wish to deny that the individual rights specified in the Constitution before the Thirteenth Amendment were prima facie and in the abstract, safeguards of freedom. But only potentially could these rights show their real nature or intrinsic greatness as standing for the equal status of all human beings in the polity. Only when blacks were acknowledged as fully human and recognized in their equal rights did whites have genuine rights. I mean that when placed in a constitution of slavery—a constitution that enshrined and protected the enslavement of black people—declared rights were mocked and denatured by their context. Ideally, in a slave society, free persons would have exercised their presumed rights while knowing that their rights were not rights, but rather the privileges of race. The so-called rights were not universal, did not apply "to all men," and hence were not rights at all. Unconstitutional abridgement of the rights of white people, under any pretext, would actually have been, therefore, erosions of racial privilege, a serious breach but perhaps not serious in the way that whites could have thought, not serious as it would have been if the rights had been genuine. What are my rights if they are denied to fellow creatures in my society? I won't give them up, but I will hold them in an altered spirit. The views of some abolitionists were at least compatible with what I have just said.

A further major point, which I will refer to later in this chapter and discuss more fully in the next chapter, is that systematic (even if temporary) abridgements by government would show that rights were not rights because they were not recognized by government as absolute, but were instead treated as revocable privileges bestowed by government, whether on one race or all people. A right is a right only if it is both universal and absolute. But assume that the declared rights of whites were never abridged; all their rights would still be privileges, not rights. To call them privileges, however, is not to make light of them: to those persons who were able to exercise them they had all the force of true rights and surely felt like rights. People were aggrieved when their declared rights were abridged; they were also injured in their legitimate interests. Yet it was also true that often when white people exercised

their unfettered privileges under the Constitution they were contributing as a matter of course to the perpetuation of slavery, first of all, by
being so attached to their privileges and wanting nothing to disturb
them and hence contributing to the perpetuation of slavery. Whites as-
saulted not only the interests but the humanity of black slaves just by
living as if slavery did not exist or did not matter in their society. Secondly, the rights of free speech, free press, and free assembly and association, not to mention the right to hold chattel slaves as lawful property, were all exercised (but of course First Amendment rights were not
only exercised) to promote the entrenchment and acceptance of slavery. Racial privileges naturally symbolized and strengthened the institutions and practices of racism in its worst form.

When rights work with such an intentionally or obliviously inhuman effect, we can say that the society did not deserve to have rights, if
rights, to begin with, derive from the claims of equal human status. Society was too barbarous because of its racism; the majority of its people
did not even have the will to understand what rights meant to those
who launched the discourse of rights in Europe and America. Nevertheless, no government would have the rightful authority to act on the
premise that the people did not deserve to have rights because of their
complicity in the denial of rights to others. A newly abolitionist state,
for example, would not be justified in abridging the declared rights of
the majority solely for the sake of punishing the majority for having
participated willingly in the system of slavery, directly or indirectly,
even apart from whether that majority exercised its rights at the expense of others without rights. Compensation would be due from the
free, but not in the form of suspended or abridged rights. A newly abolitionist state would ideally stand for the rights of all, not for the inversion of the previous state.

To complicate matters further, if wartime abridgements of rights are
justifiable only on grounds of military necessity—a significant concept

that Lincoln employed—the abridgements, no matter how justifiable, convert rights into privileges. Lincoln's suspension of what were claimed, no matter how mistakenly, to be rights, in time of war, set precedents for future suspensions in conditions in which rights had become true rights and hence were unjustly violated. Later generations after the abolition of slavery could take only cold comfort in believing that people in a society that protected slavery had misunderstood (but by their own documents should have understood) their rights, and had misused, if not forfeited their rights, when we see that people who afterward deserved that their rights be honored experienced suspension of their rights under the cover or in the shadow of Civil War precedents.

There is yet one more complication. In his opposition to President Polk's war against Mexico, Lincoln made much of the insistence by his colleagues in the House that the war against Mexico "was unnecessarily and unconstitutionally commenced" and that Polk had shifted the grounds for the war so many times that "the President is, in no wise, satisfied with his own positions" (speech in the US House of Representatives on the War with Mexico, January 12, 1848, LA, 1:161, 170). I do not say that Polk set a precedent for Lincoln, or that Polk's real reasons for acting against the Constitution by making war without a congressional declaration had anything to do with the later military necessity caused by armed rebellion against the United States. I only want to point to the fact that some Unionists in the North would use arguments to oppose Lincoln's assumption of extraordinary wartime powers that resemble Lincoln's own earlier attack on an American president, and that he too did not seem quite "satisfied with his own positions" (as we will see in the next chapter).

———

Those white people, like the abolitionists, who went along, and lived decent protected lives but with a seriously bad conscience or even a traumatized one, and thus led contaminated lives, because they felt that they could not but continue to live in the polity, and were powerless to change it to make it self-consistent, deserve our sympathy, hoping as we must that we are not living in a comparable situation. The abolitionists knew that they could not change the situation by themselves, yet they did what they could. Their protests, when they were permitted to make them, would not let white Americans forget the lie the society was living.

My second claim in regard to the constitution of slavery—to go with the first point that the US Constitution was actually a constitution of slavery—is that Lincoln before the war strained his mind to the limit to make the case that the US Constitution was worthy of obedience and reverence. Our earlier discussion of Lincoln and the Declaration of Independence is continuous with our discussion of this second claim that we are about to undertake. The issue is still slavery, and how Lincoln thought about it. This has been our principal theme: how he managed to maintain his reverence for the founding documents and their practical results. I am not absurdly trying to hold Lincoln up to denunciation. His murder by itself makes this gesture look indecent. I mean only to examine what formal argument joined to a skewed interpretation of history made it possible for Lincoln, who hated slavery, to hold that the original entrenchment of slavery in the Constitution did not invalidate the legitimacy of the Constitution and made it instead a precious silver setting for the even more precious golden principle of the equal rights of all persons and races. The key to Lincoln's position is found in his idea of *political* necessity, which played a significant role in his speeches in the period of 1854–1860.

Necessity means of course that we had no choice but to do as we did, either by action or abstention. Although, strictly speaking, it lay in our capacity to do otherwise, anyone in our place would have done the same as we did. We would have been foolish to do otherwise because it would

have been too injurious. When we look back, having acted out of felt necessity still appears right to us, and we continue to endorse our decision.

Another main form of necessity in Lincoln's thought is *military* necessity in time of war; this was the reason that Lincoln gave for two
tremendous policies: emancipating slaves from mid-1862 to 1865 and
suspending the Constitution in time of war. We will come to these issues when we discuss the war. We are concerned here with political necessity, because Lincoln maintained that the men who framed the Constitution had no choice but to acquiesce in the entrenchment of slavery
in the document they were offering the people for ratification. The necessity, political necessity, justified their decision.

Lincoln was candid in describing and praising the calculation that
the Framers made during the constitutional convention. In a speech in
Chicago before the debates with Douglas, he said that "there are certain
conditions that make necessities and impose them upon us, and to the
extent that a necessity is imposed upon a man he must submit to it. I
think that was the condition in which we found ourselves when we established the government. We had slavery among us, we could not get
our constitution unless we permitted them to remain in slavery, we
could not secure the good we did secure if we grasped for more, and
having by necessity submitted to that much, it does not destroy the
principle that is the charter of our liberties" (July 10, 1858, LA, 1:457).
(He then used this passage again in his reply to Douglas in the seventh
debate, October 15, 1858, LA, 1:793.) In a speech in Springfield, Illinois,
one week after this Chicago speech, Lincoln said, "When our Government was established, we had the institution of slavery among us. We
were in a certain sense compelled to tolerate its existence. It was a sort
of necessity. . . . The Framers of the Constitution found the institution
of slavery amongst other institutions at the time. They found that by an
effort to eradicate it, they might lose much of what they had already
gained. They were obliged to bow to the necessity" (July 17, 1858, LA,

1:478). There are certain aspects of these two remarkable passages that should be looked at.

Like Jefferson, Lincoln said that he thought that in 1789 whites *found* themselves in a society that held slaves. That seemed true for those who held no slaves; they found themselves linked to those who did hold slaves; the necessity they faced was to incorporate slavery into the Constitution or do without a Union. Slavery was not nearly as important as Union. The same necessity did not of course hold for the slave states, which were creating a condition in which all the states would cooperate in the preservation of slavery. In a context like this the expression "finding oneself in a situation" indicates that we had no conscious share in creating or sustaining the situation and that it came upon us as an unhappy surprise and left us rather dejected and at a loss over what to do about it. It is true that slavery was not introduced in 1789 and that many of the slaveholders inherited slaves. But the free states knew that the slave states were not going to abolish slavery in order to create a Union. That was no surprise. The slave-owners would keep their slaves, encourage their reproduction, and buy new slaves by importing them or otherwise. Every effort to protect the institution from opposition was made, if there was opposition; and the defenders of slavery would not agree to the Union unless the Constitution not only allowed them to keep their slaves, but gave them various guarantees, including a fugitive slave provision, an option to maintain the slave trade indefinitely, and the three-fifths clause for the purpose of increasing their representation in the House. If all this was the "condition," then "we" (the free states) did not find themselves in it. There was willing compromise on the main details, as if slavery was just one more issue, important but not overriding. We must say that the Constitution once ratified would re-create slavery every day, and do so with determination.

It is noteworthy that in the Springfield speech just quoted, Lincoln somewhat diluted his concept of political necessity. First he spoke of how "we were in a certain sense compelled to tolerate" the existence of slavery—that is, only in a certain sense compelled, not absolutely compelled—and then he spoke of "a sort of necessity" that had compelled in a certain sense, a necessity that falls short of grim necessity. Perhaps we are here given hints of Lincoln's discomfort or caginess. But a moment of truth did come in early 1862, when Lincoln told Moncure D. Conway that "at an early day" Southerners felt a "feeble conscience" about slavery, and feeble as it was, it had given way to the corrupting commercial and social benefits of the slave system (F, 119). The implication was that the South's conscience was never more than feeble. One can infer the feebleness from the steady effort to strengthen slavery from the start. Lincoln aimed to be candid, but what he was routinely candid about was not the institution of slavery in the founding period, but his own feelings, including pity toward Southerners for having allowed themselves to be corrupted. He misapplied the otherwise defensible generalization that conditions can produce necessities for us against our wishes and then force us to try to respond to them, leaving us little choice but to do what we did, if we did not want to suffer grievously. And his pity turned into charity toward all whites in the Second Inaugural.

There was another moment of truth, but in an unsent letter, written not long before he was elected president on November 6, 1860. The US minister to Britain had said that slavery had been, in Lincoln's paraphrase, "a necessity imposed on us by the negro race." Such an assertion infuriated Lincoln, even though he had made remarks not sufficiently unlike this. He interpreted the words of the minister to mean that the whole effort of going thousands of miles to round up "savages" to enslave them here was "imposed on us by them," and denounced the idea as illogical (letter to Charles H. Fisher, August 27, 1860, LA, 2:178). If Lincoln interpreted the minister correctly, then indeed the statement was not only illogical but absurd. But suppose Lincoln's moment of truth was not quite a moment of truth. Suppose all that the minister meant was that once the slaves were here, "we" found them here, and there was no way of handling them except as slaves; numerous free blacks would be intolerable. He would have been stupid if he meant what Lincoln claimed he meant, but perhaps all that the minister meant was only what Lincoln, following Jefferson, had said or implied more than once.

But the morally worse part of Lincoln's speech in Chicago on July 10, 1858, was a calculation he made and then repeated in his seventh debate with Douglas. Lincoln reasoned that incorporating slavery into the Constitution was a necessary price to pay to secure the great good of the Constitution. If actual slavery was a tremendous evil, as Lincoln thought, how can one balance that evil against any good, which in this case is a future speculative good—namely, the superiority of the proposed Constitution to the existing Articles of Confederation? Was the condition so terrible under the Articles? Slavery was incalculably evil to the slaves, and the evil would grow with the numbers enslaved. The avoidance of doing such evil or supporting it by complicity must always take priority over the attainment of something good, even if one said that the Constitution was incalculably good. What is involved here is not doing the lesser evil for the sake of preventing or remedying a greater evil, but doing evil to achieve good, or at best perhaps doing the much greater evil for the sake of remedying the much lesser evil. Lincoln himself, much earlier, had said that "not to do evil that good may come" as a "general proposition is doubtless correct" (letter to Williamson Durley, October 3, 1845, LA, 1:112).

On the other hand, preventing the established Union under the Constitution (no longer a future speculative good) from breaking up could be seen, as Lincoln saw it, as an evil. The trouble is that he saw it as a greater evil than allowing slavery to be extended into the territories. Lincoln was explicit in the Peoria speech: he said, "Much as I hate slavery,

I would consent to the extension of it rather than see the Union dissolved, just as I would consent to any GREAT evil, to avoid a GREATER one" (October 16, 1854, LA, 1:333). When couched in these terms, the question then becomes whether disunion was a greater evil than slavery, especially if disunion were peacefully accomplished. The moral answer is no, and that answer is supported by the thought that slaves had a right of revolution against the Union and on good Lockean-Jeffersonian grounds. The Union had built into it from the start a condition that would justify a violent slave revolution against it—a justifiable revolution that never came, unless you want to say that Lincoln's presidency produced such a revolution from the top. The right of revolution signifies the existence of such degrading oppression that the oppressed, whether a minority or a majority, and their allies may use violence to end it. How can such a constitution of oppression be legitimate and hence theoretically invulnerable to justified revolution? Lincoln would have had to deny that slaves had such a right of revolution, but then any abolitionist, except a pacifist (say, Garrison until the war), would have charged him with the most obvious inconsistency and moral error. His false position would have been that what is right for whites is not right for blacks. Not even Jefferson swallowed the racism of this view. Lincoln's only plausible grounds could have been that peaceful disunion would inevitably lead to terrible wars between two neighboring countries with distinct and opposing interests. That again is speculative. From the moral point of view, slavery was a greater evil than (peaceful) disunion, even though there were many fewer black slaves than free whites.

If it could be shown that the Framers expected that slavery was on its way to *early certain* extinction, then Lincoln's acceptance of their calculation in their time was perhaps morally "tolerable" (to use his word in the Springfield speech of July 17, 1858). Just before, in the speech in Chicago of July 10, 1858, just referred to, he said that the Framers "intended and expected" that slavery was in the course of ultimate extinction (LA, 1:448). But there was little evidence for that belief; almost all the evidence went in the other direction. In Federalist No. 54 for example, Madison undertook to defend the three-fifths clause in the Constitution (Article I, section 2). For purposes of representation the whole (mostly white) population in every slave state was increased by three-fifths of the total slave population ("all other persons"), and the number of the state's delegation to the House of Representatives and the Electoral College augmented accordingly. He presented the argument initially as it might have been made by "one of our Southern brethren" but then had to confess that though "a little strained in some points," his invented argument "fully reconciles me to the scale of representation which the convention have established" (*The Federalist Papers* 354, 358). In the defense, putatively Madison's own, there appeared a terrible sentence that carried no expectation that the extinction of slavery was intended or expected. His imagined but all too actual Southerner said: "Let the compromising expedient of the Constitution be mutually adopted, which regards them [slaves] as inhabitants, but as debased by servitude below the equal level of free inhabitants; which regards the *slave* as divested of two fifths of the *man*" (357). The Homeric allusion is obvious: on the day a man becomes a slave he loses half his soul, as the common rendering goes (*The Odyssey*, Book 17, lines 320–324); in Robert Fitzgerald's translation: "without a master / they have no will to labor, or excel"; "Zeus takes away / half the manhood of a man" (p. 332). I cannot believe, however, that Homer's Zeus was behind the decision to make the white voter in a slave state count for more than one—how much more than one depended on the percentages of whites and slaves—while every voter in a free state counted for only one. Madison was a bit more—shall we say—generous to the slave in his estimate of the loss of manhood at only 40 percent not 50. The logic of Madison's position was that slavery could never be abolished because its degradation would be transmitted from generation to generation. (All the children would have to be taken from their parents and carried into freedom so as to break the cycle; Plato would recommend the age of ten at the latest.) It is also worth noting that when in Federalist No. 10 Madison discussed the real or trivial differences of interest or situation that create the will to divide into factions and engage in dispute or strife, he did not so much as mention difference of color as an instigation to rabid group behavior.

In Lincoln's time when, as he said, one-sixth of the population endured the worst oppression in the world, Lincoln's continued acceptance of the constitutional calculation looks poor. The 1860 census showed that there were more than four million slaves in a total population of thirty-one million people. The point is that the guilt of the North in cooperating with slavery and benefiting from its products was not its greatest guilt. Agreement to sustain slavery by incorporating it into the Constitution and protecting it thereafter as a constitutional and legal practice, and even as a fundamental right of property held by slaveholders, was the worst criminal offense. Union was preferred to the most elementary justice.

It is casuistry to justify the incorporation of slavery into the US Constitution by saying that only if there were a Union made by the Constitution could slavery eventually be abolished. Supposedly, in a looser confederation the possibility of coordinated action and the requisite resources needed to destroy slavery in fifteen states would not have existed, nor perhaps the force to resist its concerted expansion. The argument goes that the Union thus strengthened but contained slavery and then had a basis eventually to abolish it. Such a calculation, however, was not part of the Framers' original reasoning or even tacit speculation. Abolition was rather a gigantic historical contingency that, by definition, no one could have foreseen, for all the shallow or insincere talk about inevitable extinction. It was against the odds because all the arrangements were devoted to preserving slavery. Undeniably, only the truncated Union could and did abolish American slavery, but that fact cannot grant a retrospective legitimacy to the Constitution; the Framers deserve no credit for abolishing slavery, even though it turned out that the broken-up Union could begin to abolish it by war, and then abolish it altogether by a constitutional amendment that only victory in war made possible. There was nothing inevitable about such a sequence leading to abolition, which could have been derailed by events along the way. What is more, the Framers did not share Lincoln's espousal of the omnipotence of providence that as president he inserted into his reflections on the origins and destruction of slavery in the United States, most famously in the Second Inaugural Address.

In contrast to the original constitutional calculation, the cost in great evil of the war that ended the great evil of slavery is a case perhaps of the morally allowable lesser evil, if we believe that slavery was a larger evil than the war that ended it. But then we must remember that the war was initiated by the South to defend slavery, and the North responded, at the beginning, not to end slavery but to preserve the Union. However, if Americans knew *per impossible* that more than 750,000 men on both sides would die in the Civil War, would they have engaged in the war? Who can say? Early in the war, speaking to a company from Kansas, the Frontier Guard, in charge of the safety of the capital, Lincoln made a calculation he never abandoned: "If the alternative is presented, whether the Union is to be broken in fragments and the liberties of the people lost, or blood be shed, you will probably make the choice, with which I shall not be dissatisfied" (CW, 4:345). His language is more complicated than need be, as if to avoid bloodthirstiness, but it is unmistakable. But left unexplained is how the liberties of the people would be lost if the secession succeeded. At the start, while talking with a peace delegation, Lincoln was reported as having said that "in a choice of evils, war may not always be the worst" (April 23, 1861, F, 100). Toward the middle of the war, however, he told William Wyndham Malet, an English clergyman, that "if he could have foreseen it [presumably the scale of the war, or its duration, early as it was], he would not have accepted the office of president" (May 31, 1862, F, 309).

Lincoln's perspective was that the cost in lives lost in the war had to include the lives on both sides; both sides were American. It is not usual for the leader of one side to think that the losses of the other side morally mattered, even though his side, like the other side, made an effort to kill as many as had to be killed and sometimes more. However, Lincoln conceived of the soldiers of the secessionist states as once and future fellow citizens, not as foreign enemies. If they survived, these fellow citizens at war with their own country would one day be its citizens again, in more than name. Lincoln's perspective thus coincided with, even if it was not dictated by, the highest moral principle. In contrast, the leadership of the South thought only of its own deaths, and thought the deaths it inflicted as killing foreign enemies and hence as morally negligible, in accordance with the idea and rules of war.

Nevertheless, when it was all over, Lincoln never said that the carnage was not worth it; but, to be sure, not only was the Union saved but slavery was about to be abolished. What Lincoln did instead was to think about the carnage in two different ways; the second way supported if it did not replace the first way. First, from start to finish he refused to end the war on the South's secessionist terms. He thereby showed that he thought that the cost in human life (whether counting only the Northern dead, or the North's combined with the South's) was worth paying on the basis of the political calculation that the immense loss of life was a hallowed sacrifice necessary to preserve the Union, and exacted from both sides. Second, he conceived all those deaths,

North and South, as God's infliction of deserved retaliatory punishment to avenge the crime of slavery, as if the war was not in human hands. It was too hard for Lincoln, for everybody, to do without some metaphysical assistance. The cost would have been far too exorbitant for Lincoln, at least some of the time, if conceived *solely* as a sacrifice that resulted from human political purposes rather than also and perhaps primarily as an exaction that resulted from divine purposes. It is also true that Lincoln was susceptible up to a point to the abstract moral idea that every life was sacred and that a person may kill another person only in self-defense, and even then the act is perhaps no better than the lesser evil; otherwise killing is a greater evil than anything else. By this idea only the slaves could kill their masters and the supporters of their masters. But of course once any war is underway, any soldier is morally allowed to kill in personal self-defense, no matter what side he is on.

We must insist on the historical fact that the great evil of the war was initiated by the South to defend slavery, and waged by the North, whatever Lincoln may have secretly hoped, not to end the greater evil of slavery, but to preserve the Union and with it, slavery in the South and border states, if need be. Lincoln expressly said and perhaps truly believed and many people in the North truly believed that the dissolution of the Union was a greater evil than the perpetuation of slavery (and many in the North did not believe that slavery was evil at all), just as at the foundation of the Republic, many people thought that not to have a national constitution would be a greater evil than the perpetuation of slavery, if slavery were an evil at all. It is grim to say that probably a larger combined number of white troops on both sides in the Civil War died to preserve slavery, directly or indirectly, than to abolish it; to preserve slavery by destroying the Union; or preserve slavery by a possible and desirable compromise that would also preserve the Union.

It is also true that if early in Lincoln's presidency the South would have rejoined the Union with guarantees for slavery, Lincoln would have accepted the compromise, as the First Inaugural Address stated; but soon after hostilities began he knew that the South would not accept a Unionist compromise, and as this belief was recurrently confirmed, his actions indicated that he found the South's refusal liberating. Many white soldiers on the Northern side, however, came to see that their efforts would contribute to the end of slavery, even if their wish still was to preserve slavery, or at least not to die for the sake of freeing blacks. But the cause of the Union became inseparable from the cause of preserving the Union. Lincoln was sophistical when he told a Unionist unsympathetic to black freedom: "You say you will not fight to free negroes. . . . Fight you, then, exclusively to save the Union" (letter to James C. Conkling, August 26, 1863, LA, 2:498). The sophistry persuaded no one. According to James P. McPherson, the chances for the South's effort to secede "appeared brightest during the months after the Emancipation Proclamation [but before Union victories at Gettysburg and Vicksburg], partly because this measure divided the Northern people and intensified a morale crisis in Union armies" (108). By 1863, whatever the motive, when a soldier fought to save the Union he was perforce fighting to free the slaves, thanks to Lincoln's patience, shrewdness, and resolve, and thanks also to the South's intransigence.

The Confederacy mattered to the South because of slavery; the Union mattered to the North, with or without slavery. The generalization holds: the evil of war is rarely incurred for a moral purpose, as distinct from a patriotic one. It is as if the majority of men are willing to kill and die for almost any purpose except moral right. Perhaps a moral purpose can be *self-consistently* fulfilled only by nonviolent means, anyway. It is still the case that Lincoln and some others eventually stood apart in pursuing a violent war for moral reasons (to some extent) that would have a directly valuable moral consequence, however alloyed the motives of the North were and however much evil it did in the pursuit of victory.

———

The brute fact is that in the period before the war, Lincoln revered a frozen Constitution. He thought, however, that it would perfect itself by accommodating the end of slavery gradually and peacefully. Like almost everyone else in political life who was opposed to slavery, he clung to the fiction that if only slavery could be contained, if the Missouri Compromise were restored and the Kansas-Nebraska Act repealed, if slavery were prohibited by congressional action from spreading to new territories, if no new slave states were admitted to the Union, if the *Dred Scott* decision could be circumvented, then the public mind could rest in the belief that slavery was on the way to ultimate extinction. Lincoln frequently repeated this formula, and as late as the debates with Douglas in the fall of 1858. He did not spell out the process of extinction; he put his trust in sketchy ideas of gradual voluntary emancipation with compensation to the slave states and to individual slaveholders, and with vigorously advocated policies of voluntary deportation of blacks from the United States.

Douglas attributed to Lincoln the view that soil exhaustion would imperil slaveholders' profit unless they could move their slaves to ever new land; he added jokingly that the slaveholders, if slavery were to be confined to the states where it now existed, would eventually have to forsake their slaves, who would then perish from hunger and end the problem of slavery by killing off all the slaves (seventh debate, October 15, 1858, LA, 1:820). In an earlier speech in Springfield, Douglas had a much less crudely fanciful idea, which was that the logic of Lincoln's position was that there would have to be an abolitionist "political organization" that would destroy all slave state governments and by its power in Congress impose a centralized emancipation. The end of slavery required "a uniformity of despotism" (July 17, 1858, A, 51–52). That turned out to be not far from the truth. Douglas conceded, however, that Lincoln was not in favor of initiating a war against the slave states as the only way to end slavery (52). That was true, but trivially so. There was never a chance that Lincoln would ever advocate or initiate a war of liberation in a Union at peace. Not to say that any elected politician in the North would have done so, either.

Containment within the boundaries of the Missouri Compromise was a strategy that had no chance of abolishing slavery because slave states wanted to keep slavery, even if for freeing their slaves slave-owners could receive compensation determined by the market equivalent in money of their slaves—say, $400 a slave. Lincoln therefore admitted in effect that containment was a strategy to keep slavery, not to extinguish it—to keep it until, in Jefferson's words (quoted in the Cooper Institute [Union] speech), it became possible "to direct the process of emancipation, and deportation, peaceably, and in such slow degrees, as that the evil will wear off insensibly" (February 27, 1860, LA, 2:124). Slavery was to die, then, from the erosive workings of time. Bad enough that Jefferson said it, but for Lincoln to repeat it is appalling. Lincoln calmly said in his debates with Douglas that he was reconciled to the likelihood that he would not see abolition in his lifetime, and even said that slavery in the most peaceful circumstances could exist for another hundred years (fourth debate, September 18, 1858, LA, 1:677–678). (As president, Lincoln proposed, perhaps disingenuously, that Congress consider an amendment to the Constitution that would have allowed some slavery to last until 1900 in a restored Union [Annual Message to Congress, December 1, 1862, LA, 2:406].)

As we have said, there was no peaceful, gradual, and constitutional method of ending slavery. Yet Lincoln could not have stayed in politics if he had not believed there was such a method, or if he did not at least say that he believed there was such a method. The agitation about slavery would continue; he would go on contributing to the antislavery side and to the Republican Party. But like everyone active in politics on the antislavery side, he had no strategy that could work within the system. You stayed in the system if you did not feel that the most urgent task in public life was to see slavery abolished. Douglas and the Democrats had a strategy that appeared to work: popular sovereignty. Let the majority in all the territories decide whether or not they will allow slavery. Because Douglas thought that blacks had no rights, he could make their human status subject to popular will. He was not deterred by the *Dred Scott* decision, which held that slavery was only a form of property and could not be kept out of any territory, whatever Congress had said or would say, and which thus invalidated popular sovereignty when it encroached not on the human status of blacks but on the right of whites to hold blacks as pieces of moveable property.

Lincoln held firmly to his insistence that "the right of property in a slave *is not* distinctly and expressly affirmed in the Constitution," even though his conduct as president showed that he sometimes had to act as if it were (fifth debate, October 7, 1858, LA, 1:714). If another Court decision, based on the right of property, part of the grounds of the majority in the *Dred Scott* decision, extended the right to hold slaves to include the free states, Douglas at least promised armed resistance in Illinois to such a hypothetical Supreme Court decision (speech at Springfield, Illinois July 17, 1858, A, 62). But Douglas never promised the end of slavery. In sum the containment strategy was a substitute for a strategy. There was no constitutional way out of slavery and no political way to end the agitation over it. If containment was a strategy for any purpose, it was to keep as many blacks as possible out of the North and confine them to the South. Black codes that restricted the privileges of free blacks in the North abetted that strategy. Perhaps Lincoln gave intimations of adopting that purpose in his speeches at Peoria and to the Ohio legislature to which I have referred.

If we look at the House Divided speech again, we find Lincoln's famous prediction that the Union "cannot endure, permanently half slave and half free," because a "house divided against itself cannot stand" (Matthew 12:25). "It will become all one thing, or all the other," added Lincoln. The agitation over slavery will not cease "until a crisis shall have been reached, and passed" (already quoted, June 16, 1858, LA, 1:426). Lincoln claimed that one side must win completely and therefore the other side must surrender completely. Did he really think that either side could win total victory peacefully, even though the whole law was on one side, the side of slavery? He seemed to rule out the possibility of compromise, which had been destroyed by the passage of the Kansas-Nebraska Act and the *Dred Scott* decision and by continued Southern pressure on behalf of proslavery interests. Perhaps Lincoln was saying that the agitation would inevitably lead to a crisis worse than raucous political agitation, like, say, a test of political wills brought on by inconclusive outbursts of violence that were serious but only sporadic, but not to outright dissolution of the Union. But I do not really see what Lincoln could have meant by *crisis* anything but a test of arms.

There is an indication that even during his period of relative political inattention, Lincoln's mind was fixed in a certain direction. He said to his first law partner, his wife's cousin John T. Stuart, that if, as Stuart claimed, the time would come when "we shall have to be all either Abolitionists or Democrats," his mind was made up: "for I believe the slavery question can never be successfully compromised" (Herndon, 224–225, and the editors' note, 441). Clearly he was not on Stuart's proslavery side, but he continued to profess willingness to compromise, while strongly suspecting it was impossible.

In any case, the noteworthy feature of the House Divided speech was that its largest portion was given to describing the continuous energy behind the Southern effort to strengthen and spread slavery. The preponderant tendency of events, as Lincoln saw it, was to make the Union all slave and forever. In fact he was clear in notes he made before the House Divided speech that "whether this shall be an entire slave nation, *is* the issue before us" (Fragment of a Speech, c. May 18, 1858, CW, 2:453). The issue was really all slave or half slave, with all slave more likely. Douglas kept saying in the debates with Lincoln that the Union had already stood half slave and half free: why couldn't it go on doing so? Only fanatical abolitionism would try to block the way. Much closer to the truth, however, was that fanatical adherence to the institution of slavery would try to block the way to continued peaceful union. Such adherence was active while antislavery resistance to it was almost wholly reactive.

What little Lincoln said in the House Divided speech about how the Union could become all free is a mere closing flourish of exhortation. He still said he thought that arresting the further spread of slavery would "place it where the public mind shall rest in the belief that it [slavery] is in course of ultimate extinction" (LA, 1:426); but he said nothing to persuade his audience that containing slavery in the territories would lead the Union anywhere near total abolition, even in the short or middle term. "Ultimate" meant indefinitely long. But permanent total extinction of slavery was what he prophesied as the only alternative to slavery in all states of the Union. He had no plan to achieve it by the political process. If a Republican were elected president in 1860 or later, how much difference would that make to the project of *peaceful* abolition? Contain slavery and otherwise leave it standing, and thus keep the House divided with all its turmoil and threat of violence? The Union would be a permanently divided house that stood ever more precariously, requiring a nearly impossible ingenuity to keep it one house that was divided more or less peacefully. In fact after the debates were over, Lincoln accused Douglas precisely of ingenuity in espousing popular sovereignty over the slave issue, but mocked it. He said that Douglas "had the ingenuity to be supported in the late contest both as the best means to *break down,* and to *uphold* the Slave interest. No ingenuity can keep those antagonistic elements in harmony long" (letter to Henry Asbury, November 19, 1858, LA, 1:831). Although both Lincoln and Douglas refused in their debate to acknowledge the South's remorseless determination, if they understood it, Lincoln at least expressed the precariousness of the situation better than Douglas. Nevertheless Lincoln did say before the third debate that "whether it [slavery] ever becomes extinct or not, he was in favor of living up to all the guarantees of the Constitution" (speech at Greenville, Illinois, September 13, 1858, CW, 3:96). In this instant Lincoln wanted the Constitution to last forever even if it preserved slavery forever, though he once expressed the wan hope that the Constitution would outlast slavery.

Were there moments of truth that burst through the rhetoric of ultimate peaceful extinction? Yes, there were, and these moments were both public and private. In a letter written to George Robertson, August 15, 1855, after the Kansas-Nebraska Act was enacted and in a mood of despair but before the even worse *Dred Scott* decision had been handed down, Lincoln wrote that there was now "no peaceful extinction of slavery in prospect for us." Experience since the Missouri Compromise demonstrated this truth. For instance, Clay failed to achieve compensated emancipation in Kentucky in 1849 (LA, 1:359). The spirit that desired peaceful extinction died with the men of the revolutionary generation. The condition of the slave was "now as fixed, and hopeless of change for the better, as that of the lost souls of the finally impenitent" (360). The condition of the slaves thus reminded him of those who are condemned to damnation, but of course it was all those who were proslavery, not the slaves, who could be described as "finally impenitent." Perhaps some thought that blacks should be penitent for their skin color.

In his speech on the *Dred Scott* decision, Lincoln's pessimism had grown deeper than in the letter to Robertson. Lincoln questioned an assertion made by Chief Justice Taney that people at the present time could plausibly believe that the words of the Declaration of Independence, if written for the first time now, would mean that blacks were included in the words "all men are created equal" but in Jefferson's time, could not possibly have meant to include blacks. Lincoln attributed to Taney the view that white people's estimate of blacks had risen since the early days, and he found such a view "grossly incorrect" (June 26, 1857, LA, 1:397). Lincoln's point was that in any case the original meaning was not dependent on changes in public mood or opinion, whether more favorable to blacks or less. What mattered was that the aim of the slave power, now buttressed by the Supreme Court majority of 7–2, was to make slavery "universal and eternal" (LA, 1:396). Lincoln then rose to one of his powerful passages on the hopelessness of peaceful ultimate extinction of slavery. He said, "All the powers of the earth seem rapidly combining against him [the slave]. Mammon is after him; ambition follows, and philosophy follows, and the Theology of the day is fast joining the cry. They have him in his prison house. . . . One after another they have closed the heavy iron doors upon him, and now they have him, as it were, bolted in with a lock of a hundred keys, which can never be unlocked without the concurrence of every key" (396–397). (Lincoln was apparently referring to Calhoun's design, which had been to restore the Constitution by revising it structurally so as to produce rule by "concurrent majority," that is, unanimity of majorities in all the states, not constitutional national majority rule.) I do not see how Lincoln could have spoken these words and thereafter adhered until secession to the idea of ultimate peaceful extinction. It was not reasonable. In two speeches he said, casually but strikingly, that popular sovereignty— the majority vote of the people, apart from congressional legislation— had not produced one free state since the original thirteen (speech at Indianapolis, September 19, 1859, CW, 3:468; speech at Beloit, Wisconsin, October 1, 1859, CW, 3:483). He knew the worst, and still recurrently spoke as if he did not.

In the debates with Douglas in October 1858 he chided Douglas for being a conspirator with President Pierce, President Buchanan, and Chief Justice Taney to make slavery national and perpetual, but said he hoped to work to defeat the plot. But he did not say how the plot—a metonymy for the not-so-tacit cooperation of larger forces—could be stopped. "When he saw a number of men engaged in pursuing similar work, when he saw that their efforts all tended in the same direction, that each was performing a necessary part, and that the combined labors of all had the effect of building an edifice, he did not believe that the coincidence occurred by chance, but that there was a preconceived plan, a common design running through the whole of it" (speech at Clinton, Illinois, July 27, 1858, CW, 2:525–526). Lincoln believed, even if he could not claim certain knowledge, that there was a plot or "tendency" (first debate, August 21, 1858, LA, 1:516, 519). But though he knew the worst, the fruitless idea of peaceful ultimate extinction seemed to become an idée fixe in Lincoln's rhetoric, which moments of the greatest lucidity interrupted but did not uproot. In the period 1854–1860 Lincoln knew that the worst was the truth but could not allow it to be his whole message. His commitment to his political religion—his reverence for the derivative documents and institutions that he pictured as following from the basic principle of human equality—fought the truth he knew and usually triumphed over it, but could not obliterate it.

———

I have said that the appeal to political necessity in the period 1854–1860 figured importantly in Lincoln's effort to extenuate the acceptance of slavery in the great documents that he saw as dedicated to human equality. The extenuation carried over to both the representative political system and the Union of states that were created in the spirit of those documents, even though fewer than a third of the states when the Constitution was written were free states. Lincoln's appeal to necessity had a number of difficulties, which he was aware of, but thought he could surmount. I have tried to indicate why I believe that he did not surmount them. Necessity, as he invoked it politically, was actually not an irresistible pressure but a cluster of obstacles to some good—achieving and keeping a constitution, a system of government, and a Union of states—that mattered more to the Founders and their most distinguished successors than the effort to eliminate or isolate slavery in a timely fashion. If you accept reluctantly something that you could have rejected, though at some cost, then you are not caught up in necessity. Actually, it is not always clear that conforming to necessity was done reluctantly. Such conformity might be more like seizing an opportunity while talking oneself into thinking that one has no choice but to do what one is doing. We do not want to abolish slavery because we like having it so much, but we talk ourselves into thinking that we have no choice but to keep it; believe it or not, we would much rather not keep it, if only we could get rid of it. In lucid moments, however, some people can always see through the fog they and others have emitted.

It did not take much perception to understand that the true motive to keep slavery was not fear of what liberated slaves would do to their masters—the culture of slavery was the culture of manufactured slave docility—but the desire to keep the system of a racially defined group's superiority at any cost. Before the war and emancipation Lincoln spelled out the impossibility of a general or even extensive slave insurrection. In the Cooper Institute speech he said, "The indispensable concert of action cannot be attained. The slaves have no means of rapid communication; nor can incendiary freemen, black or white, supply it. The explosive materials are everywhere in parcels; but there neither are, nor can be supplied, the indispensable connecting trains" (February 27, 1860, LA, 2:124). ("Explosive materials" and "connecting trains" are obviously both literal and metaphorical.) Lincoln deserved to feel vindicated when he remarked to Congress in his annual message, December 8, 1863, "No servile insurrection, or tendency to violence or cruelty, has marked the measures of emancipation and arming the blacks" (LA, 2:551). Yet before the war Lincoln often seemed to accept at face value the South's contention that it was socially necessary, not a matter of Southern white self-preservation, and not only economically profitable, to maintain slavery.

6

Lincoln's Doctrine of Military Necessity in the Civil War

I HAVE REFERRED to military necessity, which is distinct from political or social necessity but often tied to it. I now wish to turn to Lincoln's appeal to considerations of military necessity to justify certain policies that he pursued while he was president, from 1861 to 1865. I do not refer to strategic and tactical battlefield policies or the precepts of military science that would be necessary for the decisive victory of Union armies. Nor do I refer to the effect of claimed military necessity on battlefield conduct and the treatment of prisoners of war and conquered civilians in the wake of victory in a battle. In a book of instructions that was distributed to Union forces, Francis Lieber treated permissible and prohibited battlefield conduct, and lawful military conduct in the aftermath of victory, founded in the idea of military necessity. But in general, I do not have in mind his pioneering work on what constituted military necessity in light of the laws of war. For a treatment of that subject, see John Fabian Witt's invaluable book *Lincoln's Code*. Rather, the subject is Lincoln's independently developed idea of military necessity as it applied to policies that affected especially white civilians in loyal states and runaway slaves and that aimed to make victory possible or much more likely.

Before he became president, Lincoln had used the argument of constitutional necessity to preserve slavery within limits, and even suggested that he perfectly understood the Southern claim that the institution of slavery might be a social necessity in the midst of a large population of blacks. In a radical reversal when he was eventually war president, he found the appeal to another kind of necessity, military necessity, indispensable to seizing the opportunity to begin freeing the slaves and thus dismantling the institution of slavery. (Lieber's codification helped to sustain Lincoln's emancipation policies but did not, I think, originate them.) The South's appeal to social necessity was finally countered by Lincoln's appeal to military necessity, even as secession had made the idea of constitutional necessity otiose for both sides. There is rigidity in Lincoln's dictum that "when an end is lawful and obligatory, the indispensable means to it, are also lawful and obligatory" (Special Message to Congress, July 4, 1861, LA, 2:261).

Necessity, now in military form, once again turned out to carry with it a great benefit. We are glad when, to win a war, we are forced to pursue a policy that we want, apart from any necessity, but could not promote by itself and for its own sake. The necessity that we feel—genuinely feel from the start or eventually—makes us glad, or at least glad in part, not only feel constrained, even though we cannot express our gladness directly. In Lincoln's case critics and friends thought he was glad that Union military necessity could be used to justify forcible emancipation *solely* on the grounds that to win the war the North had to deprive the South of some of its slave labor and transform the newly emancipated slaves into new power for the armed forces of the Union. But did he sincerely believe that without emancipation he could not win the war or win it only at a much greater cost in money and white

lives? Was reducing the number of Northern white deaths by substitut-
ing black deaths the real aim? I certainly do not think that it was the
only aim. Indeed, who could figure out whether his calculation was exactly correct, whatever his feelings may have been?

This justification of emancipation, however, was probably no mere
rationalization of expedience; it had perhaps at worst an alloyed genu-
ineness. Similarly, none of the battlefield violence was optional if the
Union was to be saved, but all that violence, in spite of the wishes of
many in the North, had to effect emancipation, if black soldiers helped
make the violence successful. Lincoln would never have used more violence than was necessary to subdue the secession; he would have preferred by far not to have had to use violence at all. I therefore tend to
doubt John Fabian Witt's contrary view that Lincoln was ready to use
violence when it was unnecessary but merely "helpful," and that he pro-
claimed emancipation only because it was "rationally connected" and
not indispensable to the advance of the war effort (239). It is quite possible that the Union did not strictly need black manpower to defeat the
South, but, as we shall see, Lincoln thought it politically or psychologically necessary to spend as few white lives as possible so that the war
could continue to be waged in the name of defeating secession. The differences among kinds of necessity have never been as sharp as perhaps
we would like.

Nevertheless, we must acknowledge that when victory was likely in
1864–1865, Lincoln did countenance the surplus violence of Sherman's
march through Georgia and South Carolina to the sea. Sherman himself called the much larger portion of the devastation and confiscation
"waste and destruction," not so much on the battlefield as off it (quoted
in Witt, 277). Indeed, in his memoirs, Sherman said that the march to
the sea was not "an essential act of war," but was a kind of stepping
stone to the principal end, which was to move from Savannah north to
Richmond and help defeat Lee's army. The forced civilian evacuation of

Atlanta was justified on the grounds that "we are not only fighting hostile armies, but a hostile people, and must make old and young, rich and poor, feel the hard hand of war, as well as their organized armies" (705). It is therefore far from clear that genuine military necessity lay behind the ravage, which we could say was inflicted from a compound motivation: to punish, to show symbolic mastery, and to serve tactical considerations. In turn, the punishment was not only vengeance, but also deterrence: an attempt to teach the South the lesson that it should never again attempt to break up the Union. Mixed in was Sherman's further belief that you reduce suffering in the long term by increasing it in the short term, a common belief that supplies nice comfort to the unscrupulous. For Sherman, the great crime was not slavery but the assault on the government and territorial integrity of the Union. As a man of war he was more purely a man of state than Lincoln. His memoirs are a great education in the nature of political realism. In any event we can find in Sherman's phrase about waste and destruction what might be an uncanny but one-sided and hence misdirected anticipation of a certain sentence in Lincoln's Second Inaugural Address on the indefinitely large debt of punishment owed by those who benefited from the slave system, as I try to indicate toward the end of this work.

Lincoln explained at some length the link between military necessity and emancipation and black recruitment in a careful letter (which I have already mentioned) to an anti-emancipation Unionist, James C. Conkling (August 26, 1863, LA, 2:495–499). The upshot of the letter was that the Union could be preserved only through military victory, and military victory could not be achieved without emancipation. Military necessity constituted a sufficient case for emancipation. If emancipation was an evil, as some people in the North believed, was it not surely a lesser evil than the destruction of the Union? Before the war, in contrast, Lincoln had maintained in the Peoria speech of 1854 that incorporating slavery into the Constitution was a lesser evil than the failure to create a Union under the Constitution. In the war his effort to end slavery in the secessionist states should be seen by people like Conkling as a lesser evil, if they insisted on seeing it as an evil at all, than the failure to restore the Union in its totality.

No doubt the use of the word *necessity* should often arouse hesitation in the observer, if not suspicion. In a startling moment of truth when the issue was buying foreign territory in which to settle liberated blacks, rather than strict military necessity, Lincoln asked rhetorically, "Does not the expedience amount to absolute necessity?" By ingenious alchemy, expedience (which usually has the connotation of self-interested and perhaps morally indifferent choice when precisely no necessity presses on the agent) is turned by resistible but unresisted desire into dire necessity. A month after his election, Lincoln went so far as to assert that colonization was such a necessity that the government of the Union could not be perpetuated without it and what is more, without colonization, the insurrection of the South could turn into "a violent and remorseless revolutionary struggle" (Annual Message to Congress, December 3, 1861, LA, 2:292). (Was he referring uncharacteristically to the possibility of a revengeful black insurgency, in the earlier manner of Jefferson? The words are not clear.)

If a policy is, speculatively, extremely useful or tempting, no matter how morally questionable, it has to be presented as necessary for it to be made morally respectable or permissible, usually in the form of the necessary and lesser evil. There is a warning to us in the moment of truth in the Annual Message about how elastic the term necessity can be; it can become synonymous with extreme expedience, a total lack of necessity. Necessity can be used to absolve many deeds that are not necessary at all but only expedient, nearly the antonym of necessary, and even productive of enormous advantage. It turned out that the North did not need colonization to attain victory; it never did; rather, much more plausibly, the military necessity, if it was such, was to recruit blacks to serve in the Union army.

On an important occasion, Lincoln was careful to use the word *expedience* untendentiously: to mean what was constitutionally questionable yet highly useful, though not indispensable. He did not instantly translate expediency into necessity, tempting though it might have been. He drafted an opinion on whether counties in northwestern Virginia that seceded from secessionist Virginia could form an independent state, called West Virginia; it would be admitted to the Union in 1862. Good practical reasons were cited for allowing the plan, but Lincoln had to overcome qualms about countenancing any secession, even on behalf of the Union, when the war from one perspective was about the right of states, even though not parts of states, to secede. He said that the "division of a State is dreaded as a precedent. But a measure made expedient by a war, is no precedent for times of peace" (opinion on admission of West Virginia, late December 1862, LA, 2:422). The structure of the reasoning about expedience followed the structure of reasoning about military necessity (which I will discuss further), but at least expediency was not transformed into necessity; valuable distinctions were preserved.

———

The claim of military necessity was Lincoln's source of emancipation. Now, I do not intend to suggest that Lincoln wanted to save the Union in order to abolish slavery. Rather, as he put it when he looked back, "the moment came when I felt that slavery must die that the nation might live" (April 7, 1864, F, 83). Until that moment came in 1862, he valued the Union so much that he would have done everything necessary to save it, half slave and half free, even if slavery were not on the course of ultimate extinction, as long as slavery stopped being the source of incessant and intermittently violent agitation for and against the maintenance or containment of slavery. But intransigent secession with the preservation of slavery at its core made it clear, if nothing else had before then been able to do, that slavery had never been in the course of ultimate extinction and therefore was likely to remain the source of incessant agitation.

Even before the claim of military necessity became the source of freedom for many slaves, it had been from early in the war the source of Lincoln's suspension of guarantees in the Constitution. Here the subject of military necessity acquires a new fascination, certainly for political theorists.

Before taking up the link between military necessity and emancipation in some detail, I would like to attend to Lincoln's treatment of what he and the rest of the country understood as constitutional rights. Lincoln's greatest aim was to preserve the Union, but to preserve it by a difficult and chancy war meant, he believed, that the Constitution had to give way under the pressure of military necessity. As president he had to disregard the Constitution, which he understood as a charter of freedom in spite of its incorporation of black slavery, when he thought that upholding the Constitution stood in the way of the effective unity of loyalist states in a time of war. The imperative of military success depended on unity: the Union could be preserved only at the expense of the Constitution. In order to fight the war for the Union successfully in the face of the South's intransigence, the Constitution had to be disregarded. Just as the frozen Constitution of slavery had to be unfrozen by the Union's victory in war, so constitutional rights in their strict guarantees had to be bent or broken in order to attain the victory. But victory was not the end of the process of unfreezing the Constitution. Slavery had to be abolished absolutely, rather than by piecemeal acts of emancipation ordained by military necessity. Slavery could not be restored, whether for reasons of morality, honor, political pressure, partisanship, or prudence. From the claim of military necessity came the opportunity to make a constitution of freedom, which meant not a "new birth of freedom" but simply the (first) birth of freedom, because freedom would now be at last a universal status, not a racial privilege. With the Thirteenth Amendment, the old constitutional guarantees of freedom could be maintained to the letter, but now transformed into genuine rights rather than the racial privileges that the earlier tireless rhetorical invocation of abstract freedom misidentified.

———

Both slavery and the Constitution had to be weakened if the struggle of the North was to be strengthened. The struggle against the Constitution was on two fronts—against Northern racist opposition to emancipation and against constitutional limitations on executive power—waged under the banner of military necessity.

Perhaps to say that Lincoln disregarded the Constitution is too polite a way of putting it. One should say instead that he seriously violated it; or even that he destroyed it, by working on the conviction that the rights guaranteed by the Constitution and the limits it placed on governmental action could not be honored in an emergency as awful as secession and civil war. Much injury had to be done to the ideal of constitutionalism. To be sure, elections in the North were never canceled. The structure of the government was not touched. Lincoln was firm on that point; after his reelection, Lincoln said that "we cannot have free government without elections" (Response to a Serenade, November 10, 1864, CW, 8:101). Of course the story of elections in the conquered and hence politically enslaved states is another matter because there cannot be free government unless elections are free.

But there is the common view that elections matter above everything else, and even define constitutionalism. That is, in my opinion, too convenient an exaggeration, despite the salience of elections for democratic politics, and despite the incredibly edifying spectacle of contested elections in the midst of a civil war in, yes, a truncated but nevertheless bitterly partisan Union not of one mind on whether the war should go on until secession was defeated. It is true in theory that unless there are elections for the highest offices, the people do not regularly reconstitute the government and thus give their continuous consent to be governed. Without elections, government would be imposed on the people by officials and emerge as superior to the people rather than being subordinate to them as their creation. But even with elections intact, with structure intact, the US Constitution (or any constitutionalism) was nothing without its guaranteed individual rights, or at least those racial privileges that had been conceived and then honored in theory and practice as if they were rights. These privileges were perhaps a promise that one day they would undergo a fundamental change by turning into rights for all persons irrespective of color or ethnicity, and do so without any change in their wording.

If the party system could not handle slavery before the war in a way that left all factions tolerably reconciled to the outcomes of this or that compromise, the Constitution itself could not handle the irrepressible war that slavery had brought on. Thus, the frozen Constitution in its structure and procedures could neither abolish slavery nor appease the slaveholders, and then in wartime it could not withstand the claims of military necessity in the violent struggle to save it. The Constitution was made for one country at peace, not two at war. For it to be the Constitution of one country again, it had first to go under. And when the North won the war, the Thirteenth Amendment was pushed through the states—some of them after Lincoln's murder—by sometimes dubiously constitutional methods in order to abolish slavery for good and with absolutely no compensation to slaveholders or deportation of blacks. Thus, first suspension and then transformation marked the fate of the Founders' Constitution in time of war in the period of Lincoln. But of course the frozen Constitution was not good enough for the

South, and they therefore renounced it and wrote a new one. Lincoln's espousal of a political religion had surely been premature.

Shortly after the Emancipation Proclamation, Lincoln wrote a letter in which he reproached Major General Joseph Hooker for saying, as Lincoln put it, that "both the Army and the Government needed a Dictator. Of course it was not *for* this, but in spite of it, that I have given you the command." Lincoln then added that only "those generals who gain successes, can set up dictators. What I now ask of you is military success, and I will risk the dictatorship" (January 16, 1863, LA, 2:434). He would happily risk the attempt by victors on the battlefield to usurp his power. Even before the battlefield successes of mid-1863, however, Lincoln himself had been embarked on dictatorial measures on the grounds of military necessity. He became a dictator in his dealings with some citizens; succeeded in his efforts to win, in part because of some of these dictatorial efforts; kept his office through defeats and victories; and paid not by a loss of power but with his life for his success, one death among so many.

The greatest part of dictatorial power was exercised over the conquered Southern civilians during the war. The military occupation suspended or controlled civilian rule. (Military rule then went on for another ten years or so after Lincoln's death.) This subject is a large one and not for this work, but is relevant because military rule over the South gave it an experience of *political* slavery and thereby vindicated in a comparatively mild form Lincoln's belief that those who enslave others (and then make war to defend the system) do not deserve to be free. In any case we cannot expect that military occupation, no matter how constrained by rules it might be, will follow constitutional practices and procedures in spirit, let alone the letter. This subject will not be pursued here. The profound injury to the Constitution that concerns us was inflicted by Lincoln's measures in loyalist states, not all of them slaveholding; people in some free states were simply antiblack and in such a way as to be seen as interfering with the prosecution of the war, though of course there were many personal motives for not wanting to contribute.

Then, too, my interest in this book cannot be all the ways in which Lincoln as president abridged certain rights of civilians in the loyalist states of the Union, especially those who acted against the war or against the Union side, or publicly were against the war, or publicly sympathized with the South's position on secession or slavery. He usually imposed abridgements with congressional encouragement, approval, or acquiescence, and acted under his executive powers, war powers, and position as commander-in-chief of the armed forces. He would not allow the South acting through its Northern sympathizers to take advantage of the Constitution against which it had rebelled, so as to restrain his effort to subdue the rebellion (letter to Erastus Corning and others, June 12, 1863, LA, 2:456). The abridged rights included the right of habeas corpus, the protections of due process of law in civilian courts (rather than military justice in military courts), free speech, free press, and the right of assembly. Furthermore, conscription is arguably an abridgement of freedom; the assumption that men could be conscripted for war came too easily to Lincoln, who rather breezily claimed that the power of Congress to conscript inhered in the Constitution's authorization of Congress "to raise and support armies" (opinion on the draft, c. mid-September 1863, LA, 2:505).

Additionally, when emancipating the slaves during the war wherever the North had control of secessionist land or of runaway slaves, Lincoln said, "In a certain sense, the liberation of slaves is the destruction of [the right of] property" (Annual Message to Congress, December 1, 1862, LA, 2:408). If we want to be legalist, we could therefore add the right of property (in the form of slaves) to the list of rights that Lincoln abridged, though clearly in this case with the direct authorization of Congress. I realize that the Bill of Rights specifically prohibits only

Congress from abridging First Amendment freedoms; I suppose that it did not occur to Madison when he was drafting the Bill of Rights that presidents of the proposed Union had to be named as possible sources of First Amendment abridgement by executive decree and subsequent action. Of course, the rights of due process found in the Fourth, Fifth, Sixth, and Eighth Amendments would have to apply not only to the maker of the laws but also to their executors.

The question is, did Lincoln usually make a well-founded claim of military necessity when he violated constitutional rights, or did he instead significantly stretch the term to cover numerous exercises of power that were merely expedient or, even worse, partisan? My short answer is that his suspension of certain fundamental rights in the loyalist states mostly answered to the demands of the situation he faced. That situation was defined by his overriding aim, which was to preserve the Union for the sake of the Union and for the sake of defending the principle of human equality, and by his judgment that the overriding aim of the South was to succeed in secession for the sake of preserving and extending the practice and culture of slavery on its own terms exclusively. It became obvious to Lincoln after some months that the South meant what it said at the start, and it should be obvious to us that these two sets of aims offered no possibility of compromise.

We could say that whatever opposition there was in the South to its professed aim was muted and lacked effective strength among the white people. They would fight to win their independence until they could not fight anymore. In contrast the North prosecuted a war that was driven by the president's instigating and tireless passion for the Union. Was it a one-man war, a presidential war? It came as close to that as could be in a democratic polity. It is hard to imagine any other Northern leader who would have had Lincoln's tenacity. Tens of thousands volunteered in the North, once the South began to wage war against the North; their reflexive patriotism was undeniable. But opinion in the

North did not have the solidity of that in the South. Some in the North were lukewarm toward the idea that the Union had to retain all the states that belonged to it in 1860; many more did not want the issue of emancipation to bedevil any opportunity to come to terms with the South, at the beginning of the war and throughout its course until very near the end.

For those who shared antiwar sentiment to one degree or another, Lincoln appeared as an extremist, especially when the cause of emancipation was fastened tightly to preserving the Union; they did not want to see, they did not even care, that his extremism was an answer to Southern extremism. Perhaps many people believed, perhaps plausibly, that only a few electable politicians in Lincoln's place, if any, and perhaps no one in his cabinet, would have answered extremism with extremism. It was hard not to feel shock at Lincoln's determination, as many Northerners did; it was easier to feel, as I suppose many Northerners felt, that the South did only what was expected of it. So, why not go more than halfway and end the war as the South wanted it to end and thus preserve slavery in a restored Union? But the South wanted more than guarantees that slavery would be unmolested in a restored Union; its distinctive culture had made a new and sovereign country, and the sovereign country never deviated from the purpose of defending its culture and its state as long as possible.

As I have said, the house of the loyal North (including the slaveholding border states) was to an extent a house divided against itself; it was mostly free, but partly slave. The border states unapologetically held onto their slaves and consequently barely held onto the Union. But Lincoln would go on in the struggle to restore the territorial Union of 1860, until he too, like the South, could not fight any longer. It was precisely this divided condition of Northern opinion that Lincoln had to face. His suspension of constitutional rights (though they were in truth racial privileges) was directed at preventing antiwar feeling, often reinforced by anti-emancipation sentiment, from making the conduct of war intolerably more difficult. If Northern opinion had been as solid for Lincoln's aim as Southern opinion was for the Confederate aim, the North would have obviously won the war more easily. The suspension of rights was in large part intended to control the expression in words and actions of antiwar opinion. The trouble was (and is still today in retrospect) that the ostensibly loyalist people he was trying to control by reducing their freedom had constitutional expectations. How did you fight those expectations, especially when the war was defined in large part as an attempt to defend the Constitution and hence constitutionalism?

Lincoln chose to override the Constitution and then to justify what he did. He had to offer justification of what he acknowledged would ordinarily be unconstitutional action. Constitutional expectations would not dispose people to accept such radical policies unless accompanied by the explicit attempt to defend them, if then. Silent commission of prima facie unconstitutional deeds, as if they were either routine and hence did not need mention or too sinister to be mentioned, might have been attractive but would have been unthinkable. Justification was as politically necessary as disregard of constitutional protections was militarily necessary. Lincoln could not do what he had secretly hoped General Hunter would do in May 1862, emancipate slaves under his military control "but not say it" (F, 393). He had to remain sensitive to constitutional expectations in the North, yet not be bound by them. The least he could do was to try, with the help of Congress, to mollify public opinion.

I do not detect much regret in Lincoln, however, for having to suspend the rights of those who were against going on with the war and tried to interfere with the war's prosecution. Mark E. Neely's judicious book *The Fate of Liberty* confirms that suspicion. This absence of regret has to be noticed. Reason of state has always ignored or dampened scruples, but more was involved. Perhaps Lincoln thought that active opponents of the war were misusing their rights in a way that threatened these rights in the long run by eroding the system that was needed to preserve them. Above all he strove to keep abundant antiwar feeling in the slaveholding border states in check; the suspension of rights was most frequent in these states. But suspensions took place not only there: after all, the suspension of the writ of habeas corpus applied from 1862 to the whole loyalist country, which was loyal only nominally in some places. (Technically, the suspension of certain rights applied prospectively to the whole country, North and South, even when the North did not yet control secessionist territory.) Lincoln was sure that if somehow any of the four slaveholding border states had seceded, the war to defeat the original secession could not be won, or would be won with an exorbitantly needless cost. The fear was not that the free North would be conquered and occupied—the South had no such ambition, except to create diversion and symbolic triumphs, as in the invasion of Pennsylvania, but that ended in the great Union victory at Gettysburg. And if the South ever contemplated more, the North would successfully resist any substantial invasion of its territory, and not only north of the slaveholding border states. How could the South have swallowed the North? The North conquered parts of the Confederacy during the war and finally had all of it by the end. But it is unimaginable that the South could have done the same to the North. The Northern fear was rather that if the border states seceded, the war would change its character substantially and perhaps the whole Union would fall to pieces irretrievably.

The writ of habeas corpus was the key right that had to be suspended; it made possible the abridgement of citizens' exercise of political rights. Only when the writ of habeas corpus is in effect can citizens be certain or more certain of their rights. The Constitution (Article I, section 9) permits its suspension "when in cases of rebellion or invasion the public safety may require it." Without this authorized departure from constitutionalism, I suppose that the common practice of martial law would have served as a substitute rationalization, though many would have considered martial law merely a naked assertion of power; the time of war against a declared armed foe would also be a muted state of war between the government and its ostensibly loyal people. In any case Lincoln believed that Northern victory would become too precarious unless the writ was suspended, because without prolonged military detentions of civilian "prisoners of state" (Neely, 45) and the subsequent trial and punishment of some of them by military commissions (tribunals), their use of the rights of free speech and free assembly would block or otherwise damage the Unionist war effort. (In violent acts of war against the Union by Southern sympathizers in loyalist states such as Missouri and Maryland, in particular, Unionist military countermeasures and martial law of course entailed the suspension of habeas corpus.) Lincoln's worst worry, though not the only one, about judicial recognition of habeas corpus was that it would be used in civil courts by Northern opponents of the war to press for release of conscripted soldiers and the Union's prisoners of war (September 14, 1863, F, 28). I repeat that I confine my attention to the states that never seceded.

Following a period of local authorization to military officers to suspend habeas corpus, which Lincoln justified in his Special Message to Congress, July 4, 1861 (LA, 2:252–253), Lincoln's first main comprehensive proclamation suspending the writ of habeas corpus was issued on September 24, 1862, after the military draft was introduced. It voiced the complaint that "the ordinary processes of law" hindered the working of the draft by not restraining "disloyal persons" from such activities as discouraging volunteer enlistments and encouraging personal resistance to militia drafts. Courts martial and military commissions superseded civil courts in all cases where military arrests had been made in nonsecessionist states (LA, 2:371). The second proclamation suspending the writ of habeas corpus made it explicit that the suspension applied "throughout the United States" (September 15, 1863, LA, 2:511). Between the two proclamations, Congress passed a bill in March 1863, finally authorizing the suspension of habeas corpus wherever necessary in the United States. But it stipulated that although there could be military arrests (and hence detentions) of civilians, trials by military commissions should not take place if the regular court system was functioning, and it made provision for the release from military prison of all civilians who were indicted by military courts when regular courts were functioning. Two years earlier, Chief Justice Taney had said unavailingly in *Ex parte Merryman* in an opinion without a vote in the Supreme Court, but pursuant to Taney's role as a district court judge, that only Congress had the constitutional right to suspend it.

Taney's decision in the *Merryman* case, to which Lincoln paid no attention, turned on the view that the provision that habeas corpus could be suspended was in Article I of the Constitution, on legislative powers, which meant that only Congress could suspend it. Lincoln had defended his action by pointing to the emergency created by the periodic absence of Congress from Washington; implicit was the view that only the executive branch was in permanent session and could always act (Message to Congress in Special Session, July 4, 1861, LA, 2:253). But Taney's larger point, made but not quite made, left perhaps for his readers to make, was that suspension of habeas corpus as such violated constitutionally mandated legal procedures and hence basic personal rights that not even Congress could suspend: due process of law, the right of people to be secure in their persons, and the right to a speedy trial, among other rights. Merryman should not have been arrested and detained by soldiers and therefore denied protection by the writ of habeas corpus. In denying him such protection he was improperly denied various procedural protections in the Bill of Rights. It seems to me that Taney meant, even if he did not say so, that the Bill of Rights superseded the provision in the original Constitution that permitted the suspension of habeas corpus. Taney's opinion was not perhaps correct jurisprudence, but it certainly registered the constitutional costs of suspending basic rights for any reason.

In *Ex parte Milligan,* a case decided after the war in 1866 that dealt with a military arrest made during the war in 1864, a closely divided Supreme Court held that though it was allowable that certain persons could be arrested by the military and therefore that the writ of habeas corpus could be suspended during a rebellion, a person in a state that was not at war with the US government and where civilian courts were functioning could not be tried by a military commission. The procedural guarantees of the Fourth, Fifth, and Sixth Amendments, already cited by Taney in the *Merryman* case to denounce military arrests of civilians, could not be abridged, but now these amendments applied not to arrest and detention but to subsequent trials. In regard to trials the decision in the *Milligan* case in fact followed the terms that Congress set down as part of its suspension of habeas corpus in March 1863.

Mark E. Neely's painstaking estimate is that "far more than 13,535 civilians were arrested" (p. 130); how many more is uncertain, but no exact number can be discovered owing to faulty and scattered records. Lincoln authorized cabinet members and any commanding officer where the military had control to suspend the writ and disregard civilian courts and thus engage in constitutionally unconstitutional conduct. The irregular arrests that concern us are those in which the military acted against nonviolent civilians who thought that in their public peaceful opposition to the war, they were acting under the protection of the Constitution. (I have no theoretical interest here in guerrillas, contractors, and civilian employees of the military; these categories are separate issues.) A typical suspension in a particular case worked through the refusal of a military officer to obey a civilian judge's order to release a person from detention or conscription. Frequently, detention

was not followed by a military trial; there were nevertheless several
hundred military trials of persons who did not use violence against the
government and lived in states that had not seceded. All these actions
showed that the revered Constitution, powerless to abolish slavery,
would also be powerless in the face of civil war, unless the one element
in it that was alien to constitutionalism yet explicitly incorporated in it
was employed to suspend constitutionalism almost in its entirety.

For persons detained as well as those tried by the military, constitutionalism was suspended in its entirety; perhaps for the conscripted,
too. Should we say that persons in these two categories were all "prisoners of state"? Or was the whole population in that condition owing
to apprehension that their least stray remark or well-meant gesture
would endanger them? Not quite: the methods of surveillance and control were often feeble, and the devotion to freedom was still too strong,
no matter how desirous the executive appetite for the people's docility
might have been. Yet even if the numbers were small of people arrested
and then detained without trial or tried by military commissions, when
it comes to abridgement of basic rights, small numbers count, not only
large numbers. But numbers, from another perspective, do not count: a
violation of even one person's rights is an absolute loss to that person,
an assault on that person's dignity that cannot be figured into a calculation of benefits. More impersonally we could say that when suspension
of habeas corpus kept someone detained because of a speech he had
given, the lesson was that persuasive speech against the government
was met not by counterpersuasive speech but by coercion. Holmes's
analogy between antiwar speech in wartime and shouting fire falsely in
a crowded theater is very poor and not persuasive at all; it is amazing
that he ever got away with it. The premise of silencing someone out-
spoken is that the speaker is dangerous because people are crude and
easily seduced, too stupid or impressionable to think for themselves.
The real thought behind the coercion was that secular blasphemy was

outrageous: certain thoughts were not to be uttered, even peacefully and no matter how minor the effect they might have.

I nevertheless think that it is defensible to conclude that Lincoln, given his aim, faced genuine military necessity and that for the most part he did not overreach. There was perhaps a somewhat tighter fit between military necessity and suspension of rights than between military necessity and emancipation. He did not subject more thousands of people in unsecessionist states to full political slavery, whether briefly or for a longer term, than his reading of the situation told him he had to. But it cannot be denied that there were mistakes in the administration of policies that suspended rights, and some reckless imprecision in identifying the disloyal. Lincoln or his military officers erred on the side of repression, but not by much. However, there were long-lasting costs that these policies exacted. Lincoln had to do what he did, but the damage done to constitutionalism was great, then and for the future.

I suppose that despite claimed military necessity, as it was or might have been, the suspension of habeas corpus, rights of due process when the regular system of justice was functioning, and First Amendment rights was felt as shocking, novel, and inexcusable, even when authorized by Congress. The shock was felt by many more people than those who were arrested. The shocked surprise was not the same as fear for oneself and others, though that existed, too; it was shock at the apparent disappearance of the Constitution, in spite of the possibly or probably true necessity of its disappearance in an unprecedented emergency. The disappearance was also unprecedented. The writ of habeas corpus had never before been suspended in American history. We should try to imagine the shock: the unimaginable had materialized. This was probably a greater shock than secession, or at least a greater surprise.

Whether or not one agrees that Lincoln did the right thing—call it the necessary and lesser evil of sacrificing the highest practical end, constitutional freedom of whites, for the sake of using constitutionally unobstructed means deemed needed to preserve it—his decisions to suspend or otherwise abridge certain rights meant that the Constitution he revered was grossly injured and endured the further injury of having precedents set for future presidents, who, we know, have acted not only in some approximation of good faith but also and more abundantly in bad faith. The injury of injuries that the Constitution experienced was that it was shown up as inadequate to the unprecedented emergency in which the Union faced destruction, and since that time has been treated, under such cover, as inadequate for much lesser emergencies or for spurious ones. Since that time, the need to produce justifications of unconstitutional actions has tended to produce all sorts of contrived rationalizations with the frequent result that innocent or unoffending people have been more readily seriously harmed and that accused people have been treated despotically. The pattern continues.

———

Lincoln was sure that the wartime abridgement of rights would have no lasting effects, and he likened anxiety over such abridgements to worrying that "a man could contract so strong an appetite for emetics during a temporary illness as to persist in feeding upon them during the remainder of his healthful life" (letter to Corning, June 12, 1863, LA, 2:460). The analogy was glib even for a lawyer, and was the worse for coming from a lawyer who was certain to know about the power of precedents. In any case in the same letter to Corning, Lincoln showed anxiety himself. He could not quite pin down the formula he wanted to justify his suspension and abridgements of rights (all of which he had the scruples to list). I suppose the difficulty he apparently experienced was and is to his credit. But we should acknowledge that an abridgement recurrently imposed now here, now there, is in effect not much different from an outright suspension.

Lincoln said that "public safety" made "certain proceedings" constitutional that would "not be constitutional" in the absence of rebellion or invasion; "the Constitution is not, in its application, in all respects the same, in cases of rebellion or invasion . . . as it is in time of profound peace and public security." He added that "the Constitution itself makes the distinction" between when it applies and when it cannot, and that "strong measures" were "within the exceptions of the Constitution" (LA, 2:460, 457). In a later formulation Lincoln said that he felt that "measures otherwise unconstitutional, might become lawful, by becoming indispensable to the preservation of the constitution, through the preservation of the nation." Unconstitutional measures to preserve a constitution, unlawful measures to preserve the fundamental law? Better to make a distinction and say only that they were meant to preserve the Union or public safety at the expense of the Constitution. (Compare Lincoln's dexterous conversion of expedience into necessity.)

"Indispensable necessity" marked not only his revocation of earlier military emancipations but also his later plan to enroll black soldiers in the army (letter to Albert G. Hodges, April 4, 1864, LA, 2:585). Right after the Emancipation Proclamation, he said to Major General John McClernand that he "struggled nearly a year and a half to get along without touching the 'institution' [of slavery]" (January 8, 1863, LA, 2:428), but then determined he had to do more than touch it; he had to start to end it, if the war was to be won.

Thus, in time of war, the president becomes sovereign and may wield powers that suspend or abridge basic rights, the soul of the fundamental law. The pernicious idea of the sovereignty of a branch of government (unlimited political will within national boundaries), which is the contamination of all constitutionalism, is thus imposed on the polity. Lincoln said to a Radical Republican senator on July 4, 1864, "I conceive that I may in an emergency do things on military grounds which cannot be done constitutionally by Congress" (F, 228). He told

Carl Schurz that "the executive could do many things by virtue of the war power which Congress could not do in the way of ordinary legislation" (quoted in Guelzo, 282). Lincoln's general point was that in some situations, the president's discretion must become lawless: the rule of law would never permit the actions he claimed the authority to do. The distinction of the chief executive lies in his claimed right to be above the law and all sources of law, including Congress, if need be.

When the Constitution is not in its application "in all respects the same" Constitution, is it not the case that the Constitution has been replaced while its text has not been altered? The upshot is that the Constitution is and is not the Constitution; it is itself only in periods of peace. When the integrity of the Union mattered most, the Constitution became much less itself; the terms on which the Union was founded receded for the sake of preserving the Union on whatever terms conduced to its survival. Lincoln bluntly said that "without the Union, the Constitution would be worthless" (April 7, 1864, F, 83). But without the Constitution in its fullness, the Union was still invaluable for Lincoln. Without incorporating slavery into the Constitution there would have been no Constitution, without slavery there would have been no war, and without war slavery would have continued indefinitely.

In his remarkable inventiveness, Lincoln seems to satisfy one's queasiness about suspending the Constitution, but then the queasiness returns. In his response to Lincoln's answer to his original letter, Erastus Corning had expressed his queasiness—more, his revulsion—for several reasons and had taken issue with Lincoln's formulations. For the sake of argument, Corning was willing to entertain the thought that Lincoln had not violated the Constitution by going outside it and resorting to a general idea of military necessity, even though Corning thought that by Lincoln's reasoning the "Constitution itself disappears in a total eclipse." For Corning there was something just as bad as a total (necessarily transient) eclipse: Lincoln had found within the Constitution itself "a principle or germ of arbitrary power, which in time of war expands at once into an absolute sovereignty, wielded by one man" (June 30, 1863, CW, 6:261, n. 1; see also the correspondence between Lincoln and Matthew Birchard and others on the case of Clement Vallandigham, an Ohio "Copperhead" opponent of the war, June 29, 1863, CW, 6:300–306).

I do not know which is more troubling: to think that the Constitution allows its own suspension or that the Constitution in an emergency needs to be supplemented by a doctrine external to it and contradictory to it. Compare Lincoln's statements with General Grant's considered judgment found years later in his memoirs. He said that "the right to resist or suppress the rebellion is as inherent as the right of self-defense, and as natural as the right of an individual to preserve his life when in jeopardy. The Constitution was therefore in abeyance for the time being, so far as it in any way affected the progress and termination of the war." The Constitution was in abeyance because it "was not framed with a view to any such rebellion as that of 1861–1865. While it did not authorize rebellion it made no provision against it" (all quotations, 749). Let us leave aside the untroubled way in which Grant assimilated the rights of a state to the rights of an individual, and hence presupposed that the continued existence of a state is analogous to the continued existence of an individual, and notice instead that Grant employed a doctrine external to the Constitution in order to justify placing it "in abeyance," when he believed that the secession of one-third of a nation was not conceivable to the Framers, even though they had severed their ties to the imperial overlord. I suppose that Corning would have been therefore troubled more by Grant's construal of the Framers' silence than by Lincoln's explicit appeal to allowable suspension of habeas corpus for the sake of suspending other rights.

Lincoln's formulation that what is "otherwise unconstitutional becomes lawful" becomes ever more troubling the more you think about it. The process of violation becoming lawful sounds like some sort of downward transubstantiation or like a whirligig in which opposites keep turning into each other. Can the law become unlawful? No, but discretionary authority can change from putatively lawful to putatively unlawful and still claim rightful authority. But at least Lincoln dared to use the word *unconstitutional* about his acts, even if he tried to take it away in the next breath.

If one generalizes Lincoln's position, and with much subsequent history in mind, we can say that the Constitution or any similar charter of constitutional democracy, when it was or will be made, is offered to a people as only provisional, and the people living under it must expect it to become in hard times the opposite of what it says: for example, depending on the interpretation of circumstances, speech and press cannot be abridged authoritatively, but they really can be. How can any such provisional document be worthy of reverence? Fittingly, slavery, which had originally made the US Constitution both possible and illegitimate, would make it provisional in the course of the violent emancipation and eventual abolition that made it legitimate. The underlying idea behind suspending major provisions of the Constitution must be that there are no absolute guarantees, no absolute prohibitions of any governmental action, whatever the language of the law. Any right can therefore be made to give way in exceptional circumstances, but "exceptional" is what the authorities say it is.

Such allowable suspensions, on suspiciously numerous grounds, are notoriously explicit and broad in, say, the Universal Declaration of Human Rights (1948), and look almost like invitations to authorities to suspend the enumerated rights when and how they please, whenever they can come up with a plausible rationalization that appears to fall into one of the broad categories of allowable suspension that are identified. The categories of limitations on rights include "just requirements of morality, public order and the general welfare in a democratic society" (Article 29). At least we could say about the US Constitution that only one right specified in it—"the privilege of the writ of habeas corpus" in cases of rebellion or invasion—could be suspended and only when "public safety may require it" (Article I, section 9). By the way, it is best not to make too much of the word *privilege* in this provision; people thought it was a right, not a mere privilege, even though perhaps some of the Framers thought it was only a privilege. How could it not be a right if it made the exercise of all other rights possible? Not to deny of course that each of the enumerated rights in Amendments One, Four, Five, Six, and Eight is required for the proper existence of all the other rights, while the spirit of Amendments Nine and Ten could be highly beneficial.

My conceptual claim is that if rights are treated as provisional entitlements, they cease being rights and become mere privileges. So too rights are not rights but privileges when they are selectively extended to only one race in a society and denied to the other race, or extended to some groups and not others. The conceptual difference between the two kinds of privilege masquerading as rights is that so-called rights were not intended by the Framers of the Constitution to be made amenable to suspension and thus changed in their nature by being made into provisional privileges, whereas the same rights were hypocritically intended or allowed to be racially selective.

In destroying its slave system by failed secession, the South helped in spite of itself to undo and remake the antebellum constitutional system. The Southern failure meant the end of race-based privileges masquerading as rights in the whole Union. As well, to ensure the failure of its attempted secession, the South provided the first and most decisive occasion in American history on which rights became provisional because of the claim of military necessity, and hence ceased being rights. For the future, the Thirteenth Amendment changed the Constitution forever for good, while the claim of military necessity on the way to the

Thirteenth Amendment changed it forever for the bad (the permanent
appeal to the alleged imperatives of national security).

———

On race-based privileges, I have no wish to deny that they were put forth
as absolute rights, felt like rights to those who enjoyed them, functioned
like rights, and provided the protections of rights (until their suspension). For the beneficiaries, the explicit existence of privileges masquerading as rights is immeasurably better than their absence. The difference between a right and a privilege appears insubstantial (metaphysical
in the bad sense) only until we remind ourselves of the excluded: their
right-less condition and the use that free whites made of their claimed
rights to maintain and strengthen the right-less condition of the excluded. There is surely a deep difference between a legal standing that is
universal and one that is radically selective. Notwithstanding that difference, a society with the privileges that masquerade as rights is morally better than a society without such privileges; the majority's privileged enjoyment of rights is much better than no privileges for anyone,
which is the absolute, arbitrary rule of the state over the whole population, despite the delusion that is perpetrated with the constant use of
each privilege. Before the abolition of slavery, there would have been no
altruism in refusing to take advantage of one's privileges; the only way
that such altruism could have operated would have been to try to avoid
using one's rights when they had the purpose or effect of strengthening
slavery. One can accept the critiques of race-based rights and still worry
about their suspension. Harm is done to constitutionalism, the very idea
of restrained government, even when racial privileges, understood as
rights, are suspended, even in emergency conditions.

   One further point is that my argument in the abstract is not that
we should conceive of the suspension of racial privileges (masquer-

ading as rights) as meting out to the holders of such privileges an appropriate punishment for holding them. No, the white people would be paying back in the wrong coin what they morally owed. It is a misdirected thought to hold that if some are not free, no one should be. That is a sentiment fit only for encouraging a power-hungry state or church, and is too feeble to placate an angry god. When acts of suspension are seen as morally appropriate apart from any military necessity, they would resemble the conduct of a warden in charge of a society-wide prison, instead of being understood as the response of the chief executive exercising claimed war powers in a time of emergency.

Lincoln did not see himself as a warden; he did not conceive of himself as the principal administrator of a political system that existed in order to punish. He certainly did not think, in an inversion of Taney's opinion in *Dred Scott,* that whites—certainly whites in loyalist states—had no rights which a government that opposed chattel slavery was bound to respect. Lincoln did not look on the whole white population in the North as deserving to receive some mild form of retaliation inflicted by human agency; specifically, the experience of a stretch of political slavery so that they could feel what it was like to be deprived of freedom. Lincoln might have suspended basic rights without much regret, but he did not do so with a metaphysically punitive intent. He acted out of military necessity to ensure that rights were not used to promote severe harm to a war effort that was in the course of ending the monstrous injustice done to others by their enslavement. If Lincoln's aim had been to punish people for their racially exclusive privileges, and deny them as much of the benefits of their privileged position as possible, he would have sought out every opportunity to suspend or abridge a right in order to rebuke culpable moral ignorance, and teach the lesson of "see how you like it" to everyone who did not seriously interfere with the war effort, not just those who did. These latter people he certainly wished to hold in check. It turned out that Lincoln entertained the idea that in God's eyes, it was possible that the entire white population deserved destruction, but this was not a political or secular idea, and Lincoln would never have deliberately striven to realize it. If God could in right destroy the whole people, Lincoln's suspension of rights was so minor in comparison to total destruction that no one could complain. Merely suspending or abridging constitutional rights would have been too paltry a sacrifice to stay the hand of a vengeful God in his retribution.

The plain fact is that Lincoln never perceived constitutional freedoms as racial privileges, whatever we in retrospect might have wanted him to say or whatever conceptual truth we believe he and others could have seen but did not see; or if they saw it, did not say they did. We could not have wanted him to act on this conceptual point, even if *per impossibile* he had accepted it. He thought along with everyone else that he was suspending or abridging rights, and whatever some of his opponents claimed, he sincerely believed that military necessity required him to do so. Lincoln's purpose was not vengeance.

To say it once more, Lincoln revered the prewar Constitution as a Constitution of freedom. He therefore knowingly did harm to what he considered a constitutional system; he believed it was harm he had to do. He did not think that it was an open-and-shut case that he could legally do what he did; he did not waver in making his decision but he struggled to justify it; his effort was not to be as artful as possible but to formulate a novel point. Let me add that on a metaphysical plane what the whole country owed as a matter of right for having practiced and prospered from slavery for more than two centuries is a separate question, and we will come back to it at the end. For the moment, I just wish to say that hatred of slavery and the wish to denounce race-based recognition of fundamental rights should not lead us to make light of Lincoln's suspension of those so-called rights. If he did so without too much regret it was because his eye was on what he took to be the highest possible political purpose, saving the Union while starting to end slavery, if necessary—or if possible. Everything else mattered less.

We must remind ourselves, however, not only of those whites excluded from protection of their rights but also of the fate of the included. It can happen, it did happen, it is happening now: if the privileges that people habitually think of as rights are suspended or abridged, the pained realization grows that there actually had not been rights before, only undependable privileges, illusory rights that gave way under pressure. If that sequence keeps on happening, directly affecting this group now, another group next, and therefore indirectly affecting everybody, people will learn the truth that dispels or weakens the delusion that they enjoy rights and behave accordingly; they become full of doubts, hesitations, inhibitions, apprehensions, and suspicions, enduring the "chilling effect" of intimidation that absolute rights in the proper sense are meant to reduce drastically, if not eliminate altogether. We surely live in such a society of intimidation today, even though the legal racial basis of supposed rights no longer exists. (Undeniably, ethnicity has become a new basis for selective exclusion from protection.) During the Civil War, not only were the rights actually racial privileges to begin with, the privileges of whites turned out under the idea of military necessity to be revocable or eroded privileges at best, and so no one had rights as they thought they had. This was the condition of the loyalist states during the Civil War. We should face the situation, and properly characterize it if we can, before we excuse or extenuate it.

Despite the designation of slaves as *persons* (held to service) in the original Constitution, the rights mandated for whites, but legally denied to slaves, were not recognized by the Framers as racial privileges, but disingenuously put forth as rights, in spite of the state court system of Massachusetts, which before ratification of the US Constitution had

abolished slavery in its state precisely on the grounds of the state's constitution's enumerated rights, properly understood as rights only when
and because slavery was prohibited and all inhabitants protected. Of
course the disfranchisement of women must also be taken into account, but there was nothing in the Constitution that prohibited any
state, if the men chose, from giving the vote to women—or to freed
blacks, for that matter, whatever Chief Justice Taney said in the *Dred
Scott* decision about rights being only for whites. A victorious war
fought by armed women against armed men was not needed for enlightened men to enfranchise women. Actually, the original Constitution guaranteed the franchise to no one in particular, despite the fact
that it did guarantee "a republican form of government," to every state,
which had to connote that some people had to have the right to vote to
fill some of the offices of state government. The same point holds as
well, most obviously, for the House of Representatives "chosen . . . by
the people of the several States" (Article I, section 2); "chosen" here
means elected on the basis of "the qualifications [greatly variable] requisite for electors of the most numerous branch of the State legislature,"
not inherited by birth or selected by democratic lottery.

———

War or its threat creates chaos within the fundamental law, because it
is at the mercy of the will of the political authorities. It is not suitable
to call this setup constitutional government; perhaps constitutional
government is truly possible only in geographical isolation or in Kant's
federation of republics. It would be better to call what the United States
has had an intermittent and selective (though not always racially selective) constitutionalism, with the intermissions of constitutionalism
since World War I getting shorter because of the claims of national security and the selectivity of constitutional protection fluctuating with
the political interpretation of international circumstances, even though

only a minority at any given time has had the direct experience of an abridged right. However, what touches a few should be felt by all; those spared for the time being might one day feel it in more than their imagination. Constitutionalism becomes the exception and near-absolute government (though always with elections) the rule. This is not merely "imperfect legitimacy." For all his scruples, Lincoln's presidency showed that constitutionalism and war (and threats of war) are not compatible. At his most direct, he said, "Was it possible to lose the nation, and yet preserve the constitution? By general law life *and* limb must be protected; yet often a limb must be amputated to save a life; but a life is never wisely given to save a limb" (letter to Albert G. Hodges, April 4, 1864, LA, 2:585). But you can save a life and kill the spirit. A constitution is not a limb, but the brain. (We should notice that the metaphor is mobile: elsewhere Lincoln curiously called *slavery* the diseased limb that had to be cut off to save the Union's life, April 7, 1864, F, 83.) Yet I think that others in his place doubtless would have done as bad or worse by the Constitution and achieved who knows what, and others in high office since have mangled constitutional rights, often for no valid reason, but only for convenience and the purposes of discipline and mobilization.

I suppose that if slavery were not the cause of violent rebellion and of the attempt to defeat it, we might be less tolerant of Lincoln's thinking about the necessary suspension of major provisions of the Constitution. (Again, if slavery were not the issue in the *Dred Scott* decision, we could be made quite uncomfortable by Lincoln's general effort to shake the authority of Supreme Court decisions by setting down criteria for their "greater or less authority," [speech on the *Dred Scott* decision, June 26, 1857, LA, 1:393]. This passage on the political obstruction of judicial decisions is an apprenticeship in claiming extraordinary executive or political powers.) If the Constitution had been suspended for any reason in this period other than the defense of the golden principle of

equal liberty, our calculation of the necessary lesser evil would be close
to impossible to make, from the moral point of view. *Preserve the state,
whatever its organization,* is not a moral imperative; it is rather the su-
premely amoral political imperative. Yet Lincoln made the calculation
of necessity unhesitatingly. He was a man of state, and thought or acted
as if he thought that the preservation of the territorial integrity and au-
tonomous government of the Union as such was worth practically any
cost in life and wealth and in temporary abridgements of freedom. In
his First Inaugural Address he had said, "Perpetuity is implied, if not
expressed, in the fundamental law of all national governments. It is safe
to assert that no government proper, ever had a provision in its organic
law for its own termination" (March 4, 1861, LA, 2:217). Imagine, however, if secession took place, as some abolitionists desired, because a
group of Northern states wished to avoid continued complicity with
and support of slavery; Lincoln's argument for "exceptions of the Constitution" could have been used for military suppression of abolitionist
secession and, I suppose, with his endorsement.

In fact, Lincoln tried to avoid linking the preservation of the Union
and the abolition of slavery until the middle of 1862. The Union until
that time had been in Lincoln's mind an end in itself, apart from its nature, and when posited as an end in itself, even the higher purpose of
equality served by the Union appeared to recede. In his oath of office,
however, he swore to preserve the Constitution, not the Union as such.
Part of the explanation for his devotion to the Union as such is found in
the Conkling letter (see p. 87). The further part is found in his statism.
Henry Adams, who served as private secretary to his father, Charles
Francis Adams, the minister to England during the Civil War, reported
that British statesmen (Palmerston, Russell, and Gladstone), encouraged by Napoleon III, "had shown power, patience and steadiness of
purpose. They had persisted for two and a half years [1861 to mid-1863,
until Gettysburg and Vicksburg] in their plan for breaking up the

Union, and had yielded at last only in the jaws of war" because "they desired the severance [secession] as a diminution of a dangerous power" (Adams, 174, 115; see chapters 7–12 on the hostility of the English political elite to the North). An added reason for defending the Union was thus found in the hostility to it of European leaders of antiegalitarian regimes. Lincoln was fully aware of the great game of international rivalry.

In short, Lincoln as president felt two pressures that intensified the formality of his political realism: first, the will to preserve the political entity at its most powerful, no matter how temporarily resistant were some parts of it to accepting continued unification on the grounds they were only artificially and disadvantageously incorporated; and second, the will to preserve the political entity so that it could be a great power among the powers of the world, whether in the name of augmentation or active defense. Protect and strengthen the base so that it may sustain the country's power. But Lincoln never forgot for long his highest commitment, which was to human equality; thus formal realism, detached from a commitment to human equality, played, I think, only a minor part in his thinking as president.

Another part of the explanation of Lincoln's statism is perhaps found in an unexpected Hobbesian moment in his discussion of the military government in the loyalist slave state of Missouri in 1863 when proslavery Unionists and antislavery Unionists became embroiled in bitter controversy and had a little civil war of their own. Apart from opinions of right and wrong, order for Lincoln was the paramount consideration. He was worried that the intensity of the dispute was so great that it would become a war of all against all, not merely a civil war of sections or groups. "Thought is forced from old channels into confusion. Deception breeds and thrives. Confidence dies, and universal suspicion reigns. Each man feels an impulse to kill his neighbor, lest he be first killed by him. . . . Murders for old grudges, and murders for pelf, proceed under any cloak that will best cover for the occasion" (letter to Charles D. Drake and others, October 5, 1863, CW, 6:500; there is remarkable similarity to Thucydides's description of strife in Corcyra in 427 BC). But short of the realization of the worst possibility, the dispute had reached the stage where "one side ignored the necessity, and magnified the evils of the system; while the other ignored the evils, and magnified the necessity; and each bitterly assailed the motives of the other" (502). Military rule was needed to end the turmoil. Lincoln's point was that people should see the evils of the system and should also see the necessity for them.

In the Missouri case the evils of abridged rights were brought about by an unfortunately necessary military government. Lincoln, I believe, was teaching a general lesson and he meant it to apply to himself as chief magistrate and commander-in-chief. (See also the correspondence between Lincoln and Governor Thomas C. Fletcher on the later effort to end what Lincoln called the "mischievous distrust" in Missouri [308], where Lincoln revised his thinking and proposed an interesting Lockean piecemeal contractual solution to the problem and the governor asserted the need for a Hobbesian imposition of order, February 20 and 27, 1865, CW, 8:308, 319–320.)

Lincoln was clear-eyed about what he was doing. A succinct statement of his general view of military necessity in the loyalist states, even if it applied in this instance to conquered secessionist states, is found in a letter of 1864 to Major General Benjamin F. Butler on his duties as military governor of occupied Norfolk. Lincoln instructed Butler to make good the deficiencies of the civil government and override it where he had to. "But you should do so on your own avowed judgment of a military necessity, and not seem to admit that there is no such necessity, by taking a vote of the people on the question. Nothing justifies the suspending of the civil by the military authority, but military necessity, and of the existence of that necessity the military commander, and not a popular vote, is to decide" (August 9, 1864, LA, 2:617). Nothing could be plainer than that: in circumstances of necessity, consent has no place because refusal of consent would be self-destructive irrationality. Butler was supposed to act in Norfolk, but under Lincoln's authorization, as Lincoln was acting in the United States, but more sweepingly and with only congressional acquiescence or episodic but perhaps for Lincoln redundant authorization.

———

My main interest at this point is to return to the military necessity that required the emancipation of slaves by presidential action and hence unfroze the frozen Constitution of slavery. The connection between military necessity and emancipation was established over time. In the early stages of the war, there was the claimed necessity to abridge practically every personal right, except for the right to hold slaves as property, in order to make prosecution of the war successful and thus save the integrity of the Union. The right to hold slaves as property had to be respected as long as it was necessary to keep the loyalty of the Unionist slave states, but also to woo the South and entice it to end its rebellion. From the middle of 1862, however, the foolishness of continuing to honor the constitutional obligation to recognize the right to hold slaves by people who engaged in violence against the Constitution was manifest, and encouragement to general wartime emancipation began to emerge. The Union's repudiation of the right of secessionists to hold slaves was then confirmed in practice and buttressed by the idea of military necessity. Lincoln and other officials began to see that the blacks who had escaped and sought to fight in the Union army against their former masters might be useful, perhaps necessary, to the effort to defeat their former masters.

We could say that the emancipation of slaves signified that the slaveholders in secessionist states had *forfeited* their property in slaves; that is just as good as calling captured or runaway slaves "contraband," that is, prohibited or smuggled goods (useful to the enemy) that were seized when the opportunity arose. But surely the simple thought that even forfeited property was a notion that was just as philosophically inadequate as the notion of contraband to account for the status of runaway slaves; both legal ideas were contortions called forth in order to disguise the legal absurdity and moral atrocity of a constitutional entitlement to enslave human beings. Necessity clarified the situation and created an opportunity to force an immoral right to become void. A right that had never been in itself morally right lost the violent basis of its tyrannical existence. Counterviolent necessity created an opportunity to nullify the harmful practice of an "other-regarding" and immoral so-called right, which was never a right at all, but only a criminal practice—a criminal privilege, if you will—that prescription could never legitimate.

Lincoln went from calling the use of black troops, permitted by the Emancipation Proclamation that was issued on January 1, 1863, "very important, if not indispensable" (letter to Major General Nathaniel P. Banks, March 29, 1863, LA, 2:442) to saying the next year to Charles D. Robinson (a Wisconsin War Democrat) that if blacks were reenslaved after being promised their freedom, that policy would drive them back to the enemy who would use them to support rebellion, rather than being a Union force without which "neither the present, nor any coming administration, *can* save the Union"; "we can no longer maintain the contest" without them [gradually increased to 175,000 black men] (August 17, 1864, LA, 2:621). The subject of slaves turned into soldiers by a government that historically had kept them in the condition of slaves until it thought it could no longer do so was permeated by unsettled feelings among whites. There was some surprise that blacks fought so well, just as there was surprise that blacks rarely showed a spirit of revenge for having been enslaved; perhaps behind both was surprise at the infrequency of slave rebellion. It is noteworthy that at the time that Lincoln was drafting the Emancipation Proclamation in the middle of 1862, Lincoln had already defended, on grounds of military necessity, and in quite pugnacious language, the enlistment of runaway slaves in the army. Without the use of all possible means, prosecuting war would be like employing "elder-stalk squirts, charged with rose water" (letter to Cuthbert Bullitt, July 28, 1862, LA, 2:345–346).

On December 8, 1863, Lincoln told Congress in a passage to which I have already referred that "it had been hoped that rebellion could be suppressed without resorting to it [emancipation] as a military measure. It was all the while deemed possible that the necessity for it might come, and that if it should, the crisis of the conflict would then be presented. It came" (Annual Message to Congress, December 8, 1863, LA, 2:550). Otherwise, there was no "lawful power" held by the federal government that could have permitted emancipation: it was military necessity under the war powers of the president, or nothing. I would emphasize the clause "all the while deemed possible that the necessity for it might come" to show that Lincoln's calculation had been made at the start or very early in the war, and was perhaps foreshadowed by the House Divided speech in 1858. In a remarkably candid formulation Lincoln said that in regard to the policy of emancipation, "hope, and fear, and doubt contended in uncertain conflict" (550). We could add that, by 1863, there was enough (by no means preponderant) sentiment in the North, as Lincoln knew, for general emancipation as another purpose that made the war worth going on with. Lincoln left slavery untouched in the loyal slave states, though he did try to get them to agree to a compensated emancipation. Only Maryland complied, in 1864. He found it too hard to abridge the right of property—though it was defined to include property in human beings—until it was forced on him, but rather easier to abridge any other right.

If at the beginning of the war it was a military necessity not to emancipate, by the middle of the war it became a military necessity to proclaim emancipation. Lincoln was reported to have said that the Emancipation Proclamation "is my last card, and I will play it and may win the trick" (late 1862, F, 360). The "trick" (or move) had already been laid out in a message to Congress, March 6, 1862, before the draft of the proclamation was published in September. The strategy was to offer compensated (and gradual) emancipation to all states. His hope was that the loyalist slave states would accept the deal, and by doing so would let the secessionist states understand that they could not hope to secure the forces of four more slave states. "To deprive them of this hope, substantially ends the rebellion" (LA, 2:307). The "trick" did not work as planned. The real military value of the Emancipation Proclamation was that it officially encouraged the enlistment of blacks, especially fugitive slaves, into the Union army and thus added their number to the armed forces (LA, 2:425). In an interview with Alexander W. Randall and Joseph T. Mills for the *New York Tribune,* and as recorded in Mills's diary, Lincoln noted that the value of slave labor for the South's war effort was great and would be reduced by runaway slaves or by freed slaves in occupied territory. There was thus a double disadvantage to the South when the value of emancipated black manpower for the Union's war effort was combined with the loss of the South's black manpower subjected to slave labor. These effects made emancipation imperative for defeating secession, but the idea of necessity was extended to include in some statements the aim of the smallest possible cost in Northern white lives. The Union could not be restored without emancipation; without it, the war effort would "sacrifice all the white men of the north to do it" (August 19, 1864, CW, 7:507). Some abolitionists could speak of the readiness to sacrifice a whole (white) generation to the cause of Union and abolition, but Lincoln would not.

We must distinguish between using emancipated blacks as battlefield soldiers and using them as "servants, teamsters, and pioneers [construction engineers]" (Sherman, 724). Sherman is clear that "in our army we had no negro soldiers, and as a rule we preferred white soldiers" for the fighting. He quoted with approval the view of a member of a black delegation to the military that the enlistment of every black man "did not strengthen the army, but took away one white man from the ranks," while keeping the designated numbers steady. Sherman would not want to conscript blacks, yet he acknowledged that he called on [former] black slaves to help subdue General Hood's Confederate forces (726). And he also said that when he first saw a division of black soldiers a few days after Lee's surrender on April 9, 1865, he was much pleased (845). It need not be said that black soldiers served in segregated units whose officers were white. In sum, the military case for the necessity of emancipation was for some staunch antislavery Unionists in the armed services not quite as compelling as Lincoln said he thought it was.

The Union could not be preserved without the destruction of slavery; the Constitution had to be suspended both to preserve the Union and to destroy slavery. Lincoln seized the opportunity that necessity, or a situation more or less close to necessity (a sort of necessity), offered him. Necessity was not only an iron cage. Who can say how reluctant he was at the start of the process to exploit the opportunity of necessity? But is it not plausible to attribute to Lincoln, even at the start, the realization that victory would be victory only if slavery were destroyed on some terms or other? Short of that result, the status quo ante bellum would be restored with its furious political agitation over the containment or extension of slavery and the prospect of another attempted secession. That Lincoln really was indifferent to the fate of slavery, provided the Union could be restored without touching it, inspires disbelief. If the Union could be restored to what it was in 1860, then of course the horrors of slavery would still be intact, and the ferocities for and against slavery, despite exhaustion, would become even stronger, owing to the costs of war already paid. Even slight incidents would then be inflammatory. Hence there was a political necessity to emancipate that went beyond the aim of military victory.

On August 22, 1862, Lincoln famously answered Horace Greeley's indignant, at times searing, recent editorial in the *New York Herald*. Greeley wanted faster measures taken to emancipate the slaves; or at least he wanted the laws that Lincoln had already signed on freeing slaves to be enforced. Lincoln answered, "I would save the Union. I would save it the shortest way under the Constitution." He then asserted that what mattered was not that slaves be free; what mattered was the impact of his slavery policy on the effort to save the Union of states (that is, restore it as it was before any state had seceded). "If I could save the Union without freeing *any* slave I would do it" (letter to Horace Greeley, LA, 2:358). And he said the same principle held for freeing all slaves or only some. Reading this letter one feels that Lincoln was expressing reluctance to free *any* slaves by executive action anywhere in the Union. The words that stand out are the ones I have just quoted; it is the coldest clause in a cold letter. We know that as a general rule Lincoln would have preferred gradual emancipation on the grounds that the freed slaves, unemployed and homeless, could not handle freedom, or employment on market terms; and much of the white population would not know what to do when it found itself in the midst of millions of free blacks. At the least, a period of apprenticeship in freedom, even on plantations, with the right of unrestricted movement and other rights of former slaves not even sketched, would be desirable.

The important historical fact, however, was that the letter to Greeley has been regularly used by scholars not merely to emphasize Lincoln's supreme commitment to preserving the Union, but to show that he cared for nothing else. This is to carry scholarly skepticism too far. His behavior in office undercut what he told Greeley. Exactly one month before the letter, he produced for the cabinet a preliminary draft of the

Emancipation Proclamation, kept confidential until its release on September 22, after military successes had provided a more propitious atmosphere. I believe that Greeley, well informed though he was, did not know that this had happened, even though Allen Guelzo in his splendid book *Abraham Lincoln: Redeemer President* says that Greeley had sniffed out "the hint that Lincoln had composed an emancipation order" (340). In any case, how could Greeley have believed Lincoln's assertions in the letter to him when earlier in the year Lincoln had signed a bill abolishing slavery in the District of Columbia, approved a law that would abolish slavery in all territories, and approved the second Confiscation Act that authorized the seizure of the slaves of anyone found guilty by a court of supporting the rebellion? Yet there was merit in Greeley's editorial. One of Greeley's biggest complaints was that Lincoln had not pressed his generals to enforce the second Confiscation Act; just as bad was Lincoln's failure to criticize the refusal of some officers to accept runaway slaves into Union lines and thus take military advantage of their presence. (Greeley's editorial is readily available online in the Lincoln Papers at the Library of Congress.)

In emphasizing that Lincoln carried the day for emancipation solely on the explicit basis that military necessity was the supreme consideration that was incumbent on him in the line of "official duty," whatever his "personal wish" (letter to Horace Greeley, LA, 2:358), we are accepting his own emphasis. But I do not deny, despite what he found it convenient to say, that he would have thought the perpetuation of slavery after victory in a bloody war a stupendous catastrophe. In his last Annual Message to Congress, December 6, 1864, after his reelection, he said fiercely, "If the people should by whatever mode or means, make it an Executive duty to re-enslave such persons [those already emancipated], another, and not I, must be their instrument to perform it" (LA, 2:691).

In President Lincoln's mind at the start, military necessity was not a mere cover for promoting emancipation; it could be used and was used quite easily as a stated reason for retarding it. Yes, Greeley was morally right to condemn Lincoln for twice revoking emancipations decreed by his generals, early in the war, August 1861 (Frémont in Missouri) and April 1862 (Hunter in areas of three Southern states under his military control), giving as his reason that he lacked the constitutional power to authorize the liberation of slaves. He sent back to slavery people who had a respite of freedom. In the words of Edward Everett in his Gettysburg Address, bondage is "rendered ten-fold more bitter by the momentary enjoyment of freedom" (text as reprinted in Wills, 239–240). It was an almost inhuman calculation that Lincoln made, despite its putative constitutional correctness and its possible tactical advantage in keeping favor with the loyal border states. If, however, the transmission of Carl Schurz's recollection can be trusted, Lincoln had hoped to avoid the calculation: "I wanted him (Hunter) to do it, not say it" (already cited, F, 393). But until the time was ripe (at the end of 1862), when emancipation was said, it was then undone. Lincoln rationalized his earlier decision in the Frémont case in this way: "the powder in this bombshell will keep dry, and when the fuse is lit, I intend to have them touch it off themselves" (September 1861, F, 295). (His strategy of waiting had also been shown earlier in delaying violence so that a Southern state would fire the first shot in a war.) I suppose even this appalling decision of revocation, if carried through faithfully by the generals, was a necessary and lesser evil that could be and was vindicated only by ultimate success. (It was even worse when other generals sometimes refused to free slaves when they could have done so or, worst of all, enforced the fugitive slave law.) But perhaps if you take the perspective of a slave rather than that of a political leader, Lincoln's decision is impossible to vindicate at all. I suppose an observer must take both perspectives.

Not long before the war began, Lincoln wrote in the spirit of Emerson, "This is a world of compensations; and he who would *be* no slave, must consent to *have* no slave. Those who deny freedom to others, deserve it not for themselves; and under a just God, can not long retain it" (letter to Henry L. Pierce and others, April 6, 1859, LA, 2:19). Those who enslave should not be free; they deserve to be slaves. Lincoln enforced this historical compensation; that is, in order to free the slaves, he acted like a master or despot or tyrant and did so by suspending the rights of those Northerners who sympathized too publicly and vigorously with the armed defenders of the slavery cause, and far more importantly, by destroying through military despotic occupation the system of slavery in the South. He acted from military necessity, but that necessity was eventually turned into an opportunity to achieve more than the preservation of the Union. It was a necessity that was not only military but metaphysical. Lincoln made it happen that those who enslaved and those who befriended the system of enslavement should get a taste of what it meant to be enslaved; not of course in the full systematic way that they had enslaved others, but enough of political slavery carried to the point of actual despotism that the South could feel and the world could see. Lincoln emphatically denied the suggestion transmitted to him by Major General John A. McClernand that he had any "'purpose to enslave, or exterminate the whites of the South'" (January 8, 1863, LA, 2:428). Naturally, it was not his purpose to do so, but a taste of political slavery or actual despotism would have seemed fitting. It is worth noticing that Lincoln in this letter felt he had to deny that he wished to exterminate the whites of the South. In the last chapter we return to the idea of extermination.

Perhaps Lincoln hoped that the enslavers and their friends would learn a lesson: because they had enslaved or supported slavery they did not deserve freedom, and the proper response, when the right time came, was that their political and some other freedoms should be taken away for a while. But he probably had no such hope for the lesson to be learned. It was never learned. The slaveholders' mastery had to be taken away by a new master, who brought freedom to those who had been

denied freedom and in doing so, imposed temporary and limited un-
freedom as a necessity but also as tacit "compensation." Another word,
if not Emersonian, for enforced compensation is retaliation, but in this
case, painful as it was, it was much briefer and in most cases milder
than the original protracted wrong of the chattel slavery that millions
of blacks endured over more than two hundred years. It should be remarked that though slaveholders were regularly offered monetary
compensation for emancipation, and occasionally took it, the slaves
were never offered monetary reparations. As Emerson put it in his pref-
atory poem to his lecture of 1862 on the preliminary draft of the Emancipation Proclamation: "Pay ransom to the owner / And fill the bag to
the brim. / Who is the owner? The slave is owner / And ever was. Pay
him" (Emerson, 884).

The deaths of all those whites, in combat or from wounds or disease,
whether from the North or the South or both together, should not be
conceived as a substitute for reparations, any more than these deaths
should be conceived as justified capital punishment for the crime of
slavery. (I will come back to the theme of Lincoln's view of justified
punishment.) At the start of and throughout the Civil War, white deaths
and destruction of their property were caused not by the deliberate effort to end slavery but for the other causes we have discussed, including
most importantly the South's desire to perpetuate and spread slavery.
We cannot blame the incalculable evil of the war on abolitionism. The
South brought emancipation on itself by making a civil war to preserve
the Union possible. Not to say of course that in the North, everybody
saw emancipation as merely a by-product of the war.

On the subject of who deserves slavery, Lincoln in a speech to the
140th Indiana Regiment on March 17, 1865, said that those slaves who
agreed to fight for their masters deserved to be slaves, and that he would
"allow those colored persons to be slaves who want to be; and next to
them those white persons who argue in favor of making other people

slaves. I am in favor of giving an opportunity to such white men to try it on for themselves" (LA, 2:690). Perhaps he meant *forcing* such white men to try it on for themselves. Retaliation prescribes that those who enslave deserve slavery, but those who indicate, but perhaps not in so many words, that they want to be slaves are so far beneath mere contempt that they in a manner of speaking also deserve to be slaves. Lincoln could not resist philosophizing, even when half-joking. Moral chagrin lay behind the joking.

In his young-man's performance at the Young Men's Lyceum of Springfield, Illinois, Lincoln said, "Towering genius disdains a beaten path. . . . It thirsts and burns for distinction; and, if possible, it will have it, whether at the expense of emancipating slaves, or enslaving freemen" (January 27, 1838, LA, 1:34). (How peculiar to say that emancipating slaves would be just as transgressive as enslaving freemen or even be transgressive at all; in this context "disdains a beaten path" and "at the expense of" connote transgression.) There is no doubt that Lincoln burned for distinction. In 1866 his good friend Joshua F. Speed recalled that in early 1841, three years after the Lyceum Address, when Lincoln was deeply depressed because of personal troubles, he said (in Speed's words) that "he had done nothing to make any human being remember that he had lived—and that to connect his name with the events transpiring in his day & generation and so impress himself upon them as to link his name with something that would redound to the interest of his fellow man was what he desired to live for." Later skeptical about the Emancipation Proclamation, Speed went on to say that Lincoln rebutted Speed because he believed that in that document "my fondest hopes will be realized" (Wilson and Davis, 197). Here it seems that the beginning of abolition was more important to Lincoln's sense of his greatness than the preservation of the Union.

In the Lyceum Address, Lincoln uncannily warned against himself; he warned against titanic ambition and urged his audience to remain attentive to its depredations. We might say in accordance with Lincoln's prescience, but going further, that he emancipated slaves by enslaving freemen (if only in certain ways). It was morally necessary that this happen and, necessarily, there was no other way it could practically happen. Yet when on the eve of victory he gave his Second Inaugural Address, which was a summing up—but really a leap beyond any judicious summary—of the great situation of the period of Lincoln, the world outlook compressed in that speech was not simply vindictive or compensatory like the published letter to Pierce in 1859 on the theme that those who enslaved others deserved to be slaves.

7

Lincoln's World Outlook

IN THIS CONCLUDING CHAPTER, I take up Lincoln's world outlook in a little detail. We can call it metaphysical, theological, or quasi-theological. As with his political objectives and the strategies he employed to defend and advance them, so in regard to his world outlook: he is hard to pin down. He was as clear as can be, however, about his political religion. By urging it on his audience he told us what elicited from him his true piety and devotion. His political life bore witness to it. As the leader of the Union during an atrocious war, however, did he become religious in the ordinary sense? Did the scale of suffering, which stemmed from his political religion to the extent it was devoutly shared, at least to some degree, by others, especially in a patriotic variant, make him pious in the way many people were? Although he was not conventionally pious before the Civil War, did he when president seek relief from the consequences of his political religion in some standard religion? After all, especially during the war years, he mentioned God many times. But suppose you think that these utterances were only ritualized conformity, even if transiently heartfelt for the occasion. After all, most of these remarks could be interpreted as a way of saying

"I claim not to have controlled events, but confess plainly that events have controlled me" (letter to Albert G. Hodges, April 4, 1864, LA, 2:579). But any politician or man of state, whether he is honestly surprised or cynically self-justifying, could at any time say Lincoln's exact words and still not believe that some more-than-human force, possessed of a will if not a personality, was directing events.

It seems that according to Lincoln's outlook, God uses all of us in order to achieve his purposes, but some individuals have special importance. Lincoln, as president but perhaps before, thought that he in particular could be "an humble instrument in the hands of the Almighty, and of this, his almost chosen people," for preserving the promise of the American Revolution (Address to the New Jersey Senate, Trenton, New Jersey, February 21, 1861, LA, 2:209). At another point, close in time to the Trenton Address, Lincoln acknowledged that "he had sometime [sic] thought that perhaps he might be an instrument in God's hands of accomplishing a great work and he certainly was not unwilling to be" (as if his will, though ultimately powerless, was nevertheless independent of God's will and luckily coincident with it). But he warned those who pleaded for an untimely emancipation proclamation that "God's way of accomplishing the end which the memorialists [those who appealed to him for a proclamation] have in view may be different from theirs" (Remarks to a Delegation of Progressive Friends [from Massachusetts], June 21, 1862, CW, 5:279). The implication was that Lincoln's slower way was perhaps closer to God's. This, like the remark at Trenton, was an untypical utterance in which Lincoln singled himself out for a special divine role. It is also worthy of notice that soon afterward, Lincoln was no longer prepared to associate God's purpose unequivocally with the Union cause or the antislavery cause, or both together; what possibly existed was not merely a discrepancy between God's means and human means to the same end. There might be a discrepancy in ends, a discrepancy as important as any could be. This latter possibility appeared in Lincoln's Meditation on the Divine Will in regard to the issue of secession and the preservation of the Union.

There are six documents of particular relevance to thinking about Lincoln's metaphysical outlook. They are the Handbill Replying to Charges of Infidelity that he issued when he ran (it turned out successfully) for a seat in the House of Representatives from the Seventh Congressional District (1846); Meditation on the Divine Will (1862); letter to Albert G. Hodges (1864); letter to Eliza P. Gurney (1864); the Second Inaugural Address (1865); and the letter to Thurlow Weed after the address (1865). Obviously, Lincoln wrote no theological-political treatise. In Chapter 3, I have already said that Lincoln was never religiously orthodox; even though he sometimes dutifully attended church with his wife. It is clear to me that Lincoln never believed in God the creator as represented in Genesis or could possibly imagine that God could be the God of superabundant love (agape) as represented in the Sermon on the Mount and in epistles by Paul and John. The fact that as president he routinely invoked God as creator (of everything out of nothing) and God as the God of justice (defined only as retribution or retaliation) was not what it seemed.

But I would not deny the interest of an unsimple and perhaps strange remark Lincoln made to an acquaintance. He said that in view of the order and harmony of nature, "it would have been more miraculous to have come about by chance than to have been created and arranged by some great thinking power" (Herndon, chap. 14, 267). If the word *miraculous* was not pejorative for Lincoln, the systems of Epicurean or Enlightenment materialism (alluded to but not named) and Christianity were similar in at least implying the miraculous; but though the system of materialism was intellectually sounder than biblical Christianity, and eternal contingency sounder than divine purpose, Christianity had the advantage of being more useful and livable. It would be too difficult for people to live by the impious or even godless view that Herndon attributed to Lincoln: "Man is simply a simple tool, a mere cog in the wheel, a part, a small part, of this vast iron machine, that strikes and cuts, grinds and mashes, all things, including man, that resist it" (uncovered and quoted by Guelzo, 118). This sentiment took Lincoln closer to Melville than to any other major American contemporary. Or more moderately, Lincoln said to a not fully reliable source (Lucius E. Chittenden), "I know by my senses that the movements of the world are those of an infinitely powerful machine. . . . Such a machine requires an infinitely powerful maker and governor" (summer 1864, F, 106). He brought himself to say that "the system of Christianity was an ingenious one, at least, and perhaps was calculated to do good" (reported 1866, F, 278). But for himself he spurned the fantasy of an afterlife in heaven, and even found comfort in mortality and not because he preferred the thought of it to hellfire, in which he had no belief. He told Hannah Armstrong—for whose son he secured an acquittal on a charge of murder in 1858 (Herndon, 221–222)—and who worried that Lincoln would be killed as president-elect or president—that "if they kill me I shall never die an other [sic] death" (Wilson and Davis, 527). I doubt that not dying another death meant eternal life after death, but rather meant perhaps that with death, a person's apprehension of death would have ceased with one's consciousness. There was no Day of Judgment and its possibility of a second death.

Biblical religion, continued by Christianity, also appealed to Lincoln's imagination, as when he said that the sight of the heavens inspired the thought that "God had spoken those numberless worlds into existence" and that the human powers of discovering the immensity of the universe through the telescope meant that "beings endowed with such capabilities as man must be immortal" and made to "comprehend the glories and wonders of his [God's] creation" (late 1850s, F, 270). Whether a divine gift or a human achievement, language was the greatest miracle; it was, that is, the greatest cause of wonder though inexplicable in its origin. In general, when he was not being manipulative, Lincoln took scriptures more seriously than many religious people did because he did not read them literally, but only with frequent unpledged admiration.

More than a wondrous imagination was involved, however, when Lincoln specifically invoked providence, by which he meant some more-than-human directing force; but he did not worship it, any more than Machiavelli worshiped Fortuna. In Lincoln's case there may have been submission to the active directing force, but not worship, not reverence, and certainly not love. These feelings were lodged only in his political religion. In his extraordinarily brilliant address to the Washington Temperance Society of Springfield, Illinois (1842), he laid down a revealing but not-quite-forthcoming indication of his relation to the idea of divine providence; there is also slyness in it, especially at the end of the paragraph. He said that the "universal *sense* of mankind, on any subject, is an argument, or at least an *influence* not easily overcome. The success of the argument in favor of the existence of an over-ruling Providence, mainly depends upon that sense; and men ought not, in justice, to be denounced for yielding to it, in any case, or for giving it up slowly, *especially,* where they are backed by interest, fixed habits, or burning appetites" (February 22, 1842, LA, 1:85). This is indeed a backhanded endorsement. He placed himself above ordinary religious feeling while knowing that it was inevitable. He saw through it but worked with it, and sometimes with unexpected results.

For all his intricate accommodation to the prevailing religiousness, and for all his sympathy with aspects of it, Lincoln candidly said at last, "I have often wished that I was a more devout man than I am" (Remarks to Baltimore Presbyterian Synod, version 1, October 24, 1863, CW, 6:535). He explained more than once that if the only criterion for membership in a church were love of God and love of neighbor, he would join, but there was no such church (after 1862, F, 137, 374). I find no love of God in his writings but ample love of people, even though this love had to struggle hard with his always deep and eventually single-minded hatred of slavery—a system made and defended by people all of whom we were supposed to love as our neighbors, our equals, and our kindred.

Lincoln produced an idea of God that was complex enough—sometimes to the point of contradiction—to suit his conflicting responses to his presidential moral and political burdens. Aware of the metaphorical nature of his idea, he nevertheless could not do without it. If it was neither a faith nor a doctrine, it was a thought-experiment that functioned in his own eyes like a vindication he needed not only for himself but also for the whole country; but it also functioned as an indictment. His idea of God was politicized; his idea of politics was religious. In vindicating or indicting the country he rebuked and blamed God; he exonerated God; he morally corrected God; he resisted and co-operated with God; he used God—to the point of exploitation—to justify what he knew to be humanly unjustifiable; and he felt he was cruelly used by God almost beyond his endurance. Some of the time, God is God; sometimes he or it is providence; at no time was faith in the commonly worshiped God the center of Lincoln's religious piety. He did not wish to convert others to his idea; he did not want to be closely understood. I infer that he hoped that he would sound religiously familiar enough, even if a bit eccentric, to permit people to think that they did not disagree with him. If they did not disagree, it would have been for the same reason we now do not usually think he was saying anything terribly heterodox: they were either too shocked or too full of preconception to believe he could have meant what he was saying, just as we might now think he was saying something congenial or expect-able or in line with some inherited theology.

The problem of Lincoln's opacity is most acute when we study his religious or metaphysical views. When, however, he is elusive on a public political matter, there are other perspectives on it that we can use as a check or comparison for what he said or implied, whether Stephen Douglas or prominent abolitionists or yet others. But Lincoln's idea of God is his invention, despite its standard vocabulary, and despite its apparent reliance on common Protestantism. But it is not common Protestantism or even heterodox Protestantism, and must be seen, if we do see it, as his own, just as his political religion, supposedly all too familiar, contained the unusual, indeed original insistence that it was a political *religion,* moral at its core, untranscendental, and lacking mysticism or mystique; I touch on various facets of Lincoln's idea of God or providence in the following discussion.

———

In the Handbill (July 31, 1846), Lincoln told the voters that he had never denied "the truth of scriptures." The phrase avoided mention of what that truth was. Was the Bible truly revelation of God's word or did it give true accounts of distant ages or did it impart true moral teachings? Whatever Lincoln meant, his conduct throughout life showed that he took seriously the moral teachings of Jesus, especially the golden rule as a rule for private conduct, and as a rule to guide politics to whatever extent it could. But he did not indicate in the Handbill or anywhere else whether he believed any additional truth of the scriptures, Jewish or Christian. It is interesting that an acquaintance, John Hill, reported that Lincoln had written (c.1841) "a dissertation against the doctrine of the divinity of the scriptures" and then burnt it when he was reminded of the troubles and "ignominy" of skeptics like Voltaire, Thomas Paine, and Count de Volney (whose book *The Ruins* [1791], on empires and religions, was translated by Jefferson and Joel Barlow, [Wilson and Davis, 24, 61; see also the testimony of Abner Y. Ellis, 172, 179]). Lincoln later on challenged in a picky way Hill's truthfulness concerning his position on slavery through the years (CW, 4:104–108), but that fact does not necessarily impeach Hill's truthfulness concerning Lincoln's infidelity. But what was the meaning of writing "against the doctrine of the

divinity of the scriptures"? The most obvious meaning was to deny that
scripture is God's word and hence that scripture is fraudulent in its divine claims or the claims that believers made for it; it is all fiction of the
kind that is of service to sinister interests. Herndon emphasized the
doubts that religious people had about Lincoln's acceptance of the Bible
as God's revealed word (172). But if the divinity was truly what scriptures said or suggested, Lincoln's whole tendency was to think that
then it would not be worthy of worship but only of being endured with
resignation. Such meanings seem to be close to the surface of Lincoln's
other religious reflections, culminating in the most public Second Inaugural Address.

In any case, his Handbill did not deny the charge of infidelity by af-
firming his belief in the God of the scriptures or any god, but by repudi-
ating a metaphysical opinion he had held five years earlier and even
before then. That opinion concerned what he called in quotation marks
the "Doctrine of Necessity." He thus redefined the very meaning of infidelity as thinking that "the human mind is impelled to action, or held in
rest by some power, over which the mind itself has no control" (LA,
1:139). *Infidelity* was thus a belief in a power that was greater than the
human mind, and therefore not human and perhaps not benign. That
would take his infidelity close to orthodox faith in the course of denying his infidelity. But was infidelity, as perhaps Lincoln understood it,
actually faith in the God of the Jewish Scriptures, selectively understood? Was he slyly equating infidelity with acceptance of orthodox religion? If so, he would have had to plead guilty to infidelity, but his guilt
would have consisted not in denial of deity, but in refusing to worship
with his fellows what he could not bring himself to believe was worthy
of worship. The whole society rested on infidelity (a good Emersonian
thought). Lincoln was insinuating that his infidelity was to reject the
infidelity of society by refusing to worship its object of worship.

But if the reading that I just proposed is too much of a stretch, let
us look again at the definition of infidelity that Lincoln said he once

held and now repudiated. At first sight, it appears that when he was a younger man the ungovernable but not undetermined dream life of any person seemed to be his model of the mind awake. But Lincoln intended some other phenomenology than that of the dream in his remark about how the mind works or is worked. Thus, his proposed definition of infidelity was not the deliberate denial of theism, but rather an insistence on the impotence of mind; perhaps it was not an impotence caused by human passion or appetite, as was often thought. Lincoln replaced the charge against him by something like a denial of free will, which was and is, however, a rather common doctrine, both secular and religious, and one that is of course not foreign to Christianity. But if the power that controls the mind is inside us, is in fact passion and appetite, Lincoln surely sounded as if he had absorbed scientific materialist doctrines. Materialism had usually taught "infidelity" in the form of the denial of the creative freedom of the mind, and substituted for it the helplessness or unreality of the mind, and still does. We are helpless under the pressure of nature in us; our passions and appetites shape us and override our rational will. The body is our master. Nature, the nature in us, blindly rules us; but if we overcame delusion—how could we, if our mind is impotent—and looked hard, we could see that it does, even though we remained helpless despite our freedom from delusion. Lincoln eventually put forth God or providence as the master, but a purposive master, unlike nature. In his Handbill his redefined infidelity seemed to pertain to lack of belief in human beings, not in God. The charge against him therefore was not quite answered, or answered too ingeniously.

It is hard to imagine that anyone who was worried that Lincoln was an atheist unbeliever would be satisfied by the Handbill, despite its reference to "some power," which is not named or described and could be merely human as easily as it could be something more than human, depending on the inference one was prepared to make. But if it was true that Lincoln had abandoned his earlier form of infidelity, he nevertheless

adopted afterward an idea of providence—sometimes he called it
God—that put human beings under a domination that produced unin-
tended outcomes of their actions, or even more disturbingly moved
them to perform their actions in ignorance of the fact that they were
not the deepest cause of what appeared to be their own actions. Was
this idea of providential determination a further expression of his infidelity or a profession of his religious faith? Something like this idea, he
claimed rightly, is the "same opinion . . . held by several of the Christian
denominations" (LA, 1:139). Our actions are our own only passively;
we act, but suffer our actions more than we initiate them. Yes, with
these beliefs we are not utterly remote from Calvinist theologians and
preachers; but—except for the postulate of providential determination
of the whole course of history—we could also be in the company of the
gods in Homer and the Greek tragedians. Now and then Lincoln undeniably sounded similar to Greeks, Jews, or Christians. (For a resourceful study that assimilates Lincoln almost completely, and therefore too
much, to "Old School" Presbyterianism, see White, *Lincoln's Greatest
Speech,* especially chapter 6). Did he not, however, hold to a metaphysical outlook that was in some important respects distinctive? I think he
did, and will try to say why. A tentative conclusion is that there are sim-
ilarities between the infidelity he said he abandoned and the unconven-
tional fidelity he adopted whether sincerely or not, and which he later
expressed in troubled language in a recurrent effort to try to understand, and explain to others, the obscure meaning of great events and
the role of political actors, including himself, in them. We cannot say
with confidence, however, that we know for sure what his heterodoxy
was, what he really believed metaphysically, in the years of his life as
president. He was always a free spirit.

In Lincoln's mind, the idea of all-powerful providence had to compete with the idea of human free choice, which was all too often blame-
worthy. It is not clear which idea won in the struggle for Lincoln's ac-

ceptance. Perhaps neither one ever definitively did, which would be an anomalously inconclusive conclusion for a true believer in God's omnipotence. There is undated testimony from a longtime friend that Lincoln confessed that he found it "hard to reconcile that belief [predestination] with responsibility for one's acts" or "reconcile the prescience of Deity with the uncertainty of events" and that therefore "it was unprofitable to discuss the dogmas of predestination and free will" (F, 168). All these terms apply to the incompatibility between the force of providence and human responsibility for putatively free choices. He was double-minded; occasions dictated that one part or the other would represent him, and in a fairly extreme form; the two parts did not because they could not qualify each other. He himself was aware of double-mindedness, but illustrated it by the conflict in a person between a sense of wrong and a will to gain profit from the wrong of slavery. This conflict will "make a riddle of a man" (speech at Hartford, Connecticut, version 1, March 5, 1860, CW, 4:3). So Lincoln's mind becomes a riddle to us when the antagonistic ideas of personal responsibility and overmastering providence coexist independently, and neither one can defeat and thus banish the other. The riddle is solved when we simply say that both ideas have their profoundly important tactical uses. Lincoln's sincere espousal was not and is not the issue. But let us not be too quick. This almost reflexive capacity not merely to entertain antagonistic thoughts simultaneously, but to advocate them, showed itself in a personal, but in a more-than-personal symptomatic way, in letters proposing marriage to Mary S. Owens and giving reasons why she should not accept him. "My opinion is that you had better not do it"; she agreed with his conclusion, and did not marry him (May 7, 1837, LA, 1:19).

The riddle is solved if we affirm that *as a materialist*, Lincoln did not accept either the idea of providence or the idea of personal responsibility, but found both rhetorically expedient, together, or now this one, now that one, when speaking to people who did accept one or the other or both and who would have found it hard to accept an unadorned story of cause and effect with good luck and bad luck thrown in as contributory factors. That Lincoln recurrently felt an urgent rhetorical need to speak of both responsibility and providential determination is worth keeping present to mind, especially when we try to confront the difficulties of comprehending the Second Inaugural Address. But let us not be too eager to believe that we have solved the riddle just by insisting that Lincoln's sincere espousal of metaphysical ideas was and is an unimportant issue; or to say instead that his sincere metaphysics was only and always remained Enlightenment materialism, with no purpose in the world and where necessitous bodies constantly pushed against each other in inevitable conflict.

———

After the Handbill, the five other texts that I have mentioned contained explicit reference to providence or God as behind or otherwise implicated in the course that events took, while simultaneously indicating the effects of human choices as if these choices were free of superhuman influence. Lincoln never stopped blaming and praising political actors, as if they acted freely, but the divine enforcement of human impotence always lurked in the background when not in the central position. A purely secular mind could have recounted the story of the Civil War and the events that led up to it without invoking providence. Though greatly outnumbered in population, the South was more united and more driven in its secessionist purpose. But Lincoln felt impelled to insert providence. His political religion reached out to divine support but not in the form of ritualistic invocation of the Creator's endowment of all people with inalienable rights, but rather to God's omnipotence. Now, if there is a possibility that Lincoln was in fact purely secular and used metaphysical or religious language in the service of rhetorical persuasion, it is evident that such language also served such other purposes as making the historical period more dignified by investing it with divine significance or making its story more aesthetically fascinating. I think he would have appreciated Whitman's interpretation of his death.

It seems that for Lincoln a factual account of what happened, of cause and effect, of human intention and miscalculation, of the accidental and unforeseen, of earned practical success and deserved failure, was insufficient. The course of the war had also to be conceived as God might have conceived it, as a divine allegory in which human cause and effect were subsumed and transcended. Or Lincoln felt the need to have two parallel systems of interpretation of the same facts, one secular and one not, both necessary though each was offered as if it were sufficient. It seems impossible that Lincoln could have publicly presented a divinity uninterested in human affairs, if he were to present a divinity at all. But did Lincoln believe in providence? It is not possible to say for sure. But if we suspend that question and simply take what he said at face value, a complex and knotty metaphysical outlook emerges. One feature of it was meant to give a more-than-human cause for why things had not gone as they practically and morally should have.

Before coming to the central text, the Second Inaugural Address, some reference, in particular but not exclusively, to the Meditation on the Divine Will and the letters to Eliza P. Gurney, Hodges, and Weed is needed.

———

The great metaphysical problem that Lincoln set for himself was to infer God's purposes in the Civil War. Perhaps the largest immediate question was why it was taking so long for the North to win, given both the superior resources of the North and the rightness of its mission. You would expect the God of justice to favor the side of justice—equality and reciprocity—which was represented by the North, because it stood for the basic principle of equal human freedom, which supposedly had its foundation in God's endowment, and was waging a war that after the Emancipation Proclamation (but only then, and never without internal opposition) the North had come to see as aimed at defending that high principle and extending it to black people by ending their enslavement and thereby ending the North's immoral complicity. The first thing to notice is that Lincoln in his letter to the Quaker widow Eliza P. Gurney, September 4, 1864, said with bemusement, "The purposes of the Almighty are perfect, and must prevail, though we erring mortals may fail to accurately perceive them in advance. We hoped for a happy termination of this terrible war long before this; but God knows best, and has ruled otherwise" (LA, 2:627). Although God had ruled otherwise by prolonging the war, Lincoln claimed two years earlier in a cabinet meeting, held on September 22, 1862, to discuss a draft of the Emancipation Proclamation, and despite and because of Union battlefield failures, that "God had decided this question [of whether to declare emancipation] in favor of the slaves" (recorded by Gideon Welles, secretary of the navy, F, 474). This statement to the cabinet showed more spoken confidence that Lincoln understood God's purposes than almost any other statement he made before the Second Inaugural Address. Yet God seemed intent on exacting a great cost for a victory he willed.

Once again we can say that there was of course a purely secular way of telling the story of Southern tenacity and Northern frustration or ambivalence in the war up to September 1864, but Lincoln chose instead to involve the divinity in it. It is crucial that Lincoln's divinity might have other purposes than saving lives—at least Union lives—by a shorter war, even though the process of emancipation was well underway by the time of the letter to Mrs. Gurney. Did God want to inflict the greater punishment of a longer war on both sides? Lincoln in a slightly earlier letter to a newspaper editor in Kentucky said just that.

"Now, at the end of three years struggle the nation's condition is not what either party, or any man devised, or expected. God alone can claim it. Whither it is tending seems plain. If God now wills the removal of a great wrong, and wills also that we of the North as well as you of the South, shall pay fairly for our complicity in that wrong, impartial history will find therein new cause to attest and revere the justice and goodness of God" (letter to Albert G. Hodges, April 4, 1864, LA, 2:586). Of course, impartial history has not done any such thing.

Defeat for the South but joined to abundant suffering for the North as well added up to a story of God's retaliation on the whole United States for its practice and enjoyment of slavery. In fact in a public statement when the course of the war was not yet clearly in favor of the Union, Lincoln had said that a long war, "the awful calamity of civil war" that now "desolates the whole land," was perhaps meant by God to reform the whole people, whose "presumptuous sins" had been owing to the intoxication of unbroken national success (Proclamation Appointing a National Fast Day on March 30, 1863, CW, 6:156). (In the Peoria speech almost ten years before, Lincoln had warned "that feeling prosperity we forget right," LA, 1:337.) But the account of God as the rather undiscriminating force of comprehensive retaliatory punishment for great wrong was not the whole story of Lincoln's metaphysical outlook, though it would have been sufficient for the outlook of others.

We should notice that at one point in his presidency Lincoln seemed to hold human beings to a higher moral standard than God. God does not obey his own moral commandments, especially against killing, and what is more, teaches the wicked idea that retaliation is justice. Informed about the rebel massacre of black prisoners of war at Fort Pillow, Tennessee, Lincoln refused to order massive killings of Southern prisoners, certainly not as retaliation (as some wanted) and not even as a deterrent. In a message to Edwin Stanton, secretary of war, Lincoln said, "Blood can not restore blood, and government should not act for revenge" (May 17, 1864, CW, 7:345). The message, however, was not signed or delivered. But in a moment of moral truth, Lincoln denounced retaliation as morally unacceptable when done by human beings to each other. Frederick Douglass reported that in his meeting with Lincoln on August 10, 1863, when Douglass had complained about the Confederate murder and brutal treatment of black prisoners of war and asked that Lincoln retaliate by killing Confederate prisoners, Lincoln refused on the grounds that he could not kill innocent prisoners to avenge what the Confederates had done to their prisoners; but if the guilty were in his power, "the case would be different" (F, 145). Fehrenbacher tells us that Lincoln had already signed "a draconian order of retaliation" on July 30, 1863, but it was never put into practice (F, 145). The fact remains that Lincoln was inveterately made uneasy by the practice of punishment, whether or not it was justified on retaliatory grounds. He often overturned death sentences on Union deserters, and his leniency to defeated Southern soldiers after Appomattox went beyond generosity; there were good prudential reasons for it, but Lincoln's motivation was not merely prudential.

If the God of the Old Testament has other purposes than those of human beings, he must correspondingly have other moral standards in the light of which the practice of retaliation, an eye for an eye, which is the reproduction of immorality, figures centrally; or God may have higher, other than moral standards. When we therefore come to Lincoln's conceptualization of many deaths in war as punishment for the crime of slavery, with its numerous associated crimes, we should see that the punishment that Lincoln seemed to approve, though administered by God through human agency, he approved only as part of God's plan; human beings could not allowably intend the depth and scale of such suffering. Under God's plan, human actions, however intended, were compelled to serve God's purposes. For Lincoln, true morality did not regard retaliation as a moral deed, much less as morally required;

perhaps it was immoral, even when God did it or allowed human beings to do it for whatever purpose. Lincoln was a rationalist: immorality does not become morality when God does it. We could imagine that some shrewd cynic in power who was aware of the near impossibility of justifying massive slaughter could insincerely use the purposes of the deity as a convenient cover for as bloody an enterprise as the US Civil War. Another secret benefit would be to make vivid the appalling nature of the God that people claimed to love.

The unconventionality of Lincoln's metaphysical outlook, then, consisted in the willingness to believe that providential purpose and enlightened human judgment (including the best moral judgment) might not coincide. Slavery and war had driven Lincoln's mind into a metaphysical wilderness. Even apart from man, there is no innocence anywhere in the nature of things. (Lincoln once clubbed a sow, "the unnatural old brute," until it stopped eating its offspring, 1855, F, 496. Even nonhuman nature could be unnatural.) If the God of retaliatory punishment presided over Lincoln's reflections on the incalculable cost in death and suffering to whites for practicing or allowing and benefiting from slavery, another God was also present. That was the inscrutable God, the God whose designs were not understandable, and were certainly not in conformity with moral judgment, even when retribution is allowed to count as moral. Neither is this God Job's God, who we know had adopted a plan to test the sincerity of Job's virtue; but at least Job's God does not claim that he acted justly in tormenting a just man; God is beyond good and evil, and he not so much justified himself as spurned justification by pointing to the unmatchable aesthetic phenomena (whether beautiful or sublime) his power created in nature.

Nor is Lincoln's God Calvin's God who unaccountably spares some souls from eternal punishment even though all souls deserve it. A few get off, not for good reasons, not for any reasons, but because it pleases God, just like that. (Apparently, Lincoln did not believe in eternal punishment,

c. 1850s, F, 198. God's punishment in this life is a different matter. This is an odd combination in a Christian age, but perhaps not for some Jewish believers.) Protestant interpretation thus makes the Bible prepare the way for an unjust or capricious God. Yet in Calvin's Augustinian system, the primary sin is the primal sin of disobedience of a nonmoral command: disobedience of a scarcely comprehensible but easily obeyed taboo; the disobedience directly harms no one but God, who punishes everyone thereafter for the original disobedience of their progenitors, and punishes them by death, by mortality. If the original sin harmed all later human beings, that harm was owing to the same kind of divine arbitrariness as shown by the original prohibition. Harm to God—sin—is thus pronounced altogether worse than intentional harm done by human beings to human beings; the two kinds of wrongdoing do not always merge. Recall the murky doctrine of Christian atonement, in which only the bloody death of Jesus the son can appease the anger of God the Father. Divine anger comes not from all the killings human beings inflicted on other human beings; the crucifixion is not blood for blood. The anger does not come therefore from human disobedience of the moral law, but perhaps from violation of ritual procedures. God's anger is inscrutable, and yet perhaps it can be appeased, but only by the bloody death of the highest innocence. However, Lincoln's providence was apparently angered by humanity's profound commission of immorality, whereby some human beings made a system, indeed a way of life, that cruelly oppressed others; and yet providence or God governs events in a way that did not seem unambiguously to answer to moral expectations. I doubt that this view is Calvinist. Does Calvinism think that God is immoral? God forbid, as Paul said to speculative possibilities not remote from this one, and so would Calvinists, even if we think they should consider God immoral. Much is lost and only a little gained by seeing Lincoln's sensibility as essentially Calvinist, as some scholars do.

In a letter to a Republican politician, Thurlow Weed, not long after the Second Inaugural Address, Lincoln said, "Men are not flattered by being shown that there has been a difference of purpose between the Almighty and them.... To deny it ... is to deny that there is a God governing the world" (March 15, 1865, LA, 2:689). Didn't God—Lincoln's God—will the end of slavery? Were God's purposes different from moral purposes? Did he or it prolong the war not to intensify everybody's punishment but for some other inscrutable and more important aim, some undecipherable teleology?

———

When the war was not going well, in early September 1862, Lincoln wrote a short paragraph, Meditation on the Divine Will, which was found after Lincoln's death by John Hay, who thought that Lincoln did not want it seen by others. If Lincoln did not want it seen, he could have burnt it; but he let it survive, and so did John Hay. It is unorthodox, but not more so than the very public Second Inaugural Address. In some respects the Meditation is a preliminary statement of some ideas in that address. Roy Basler speculates that when Lincoln wrote the Meditation, he was depressed by the recent Union defeat at the second battle of Bull Run (CW, 5:404, n. 1). Yet there is some important continuity between the Meditation in depression and the Second Inaugural Address in hopefulness, delivered when total victory in the war was close to certain.

In the Meditation, written in early September 1862 and therefore after Lincoln's thoughts about an Emancipation Proclamation had begun taking form that summer, Lincoln acknowledged that both sides in the war claimed to act in accordance with God's will. Could both sides be right in such a claim? Lincoln's first inclination was not to say that both sides had to think that they were right; what else would they think? Rather, "Both *may* be, and one *must* be wrong. God can not be *for*, and *against* the same thing at the same time" (LA, 2:359). The meaning of the second sentence is that if one side is right, then the other must be wrong. But the immediately preceding sentence says both sides may be wrong. Lincoln was thus not consistent in holding that if the cause championed by one side is wrong, the opposing side must by definition be right; rather, both sides *may* be wrong. But if one side *must* be wrong, can the other and radically opposite side be wrong at all? Perhaps the other side is at best less wrong. Perhaps neither side is right; both sides, though radically opposite, are definitely wrong. There is a tangle here that I cannot straighten out. Let us persist.

The issue of the Meditation is the preservation or destruction of the Union. But by early September 1862 the issue had to be, what side did God want to prevail? The side that wished not only to preserve the Union but also to initiate emancipation or the side that wished to destroy the Union by secession in order to preserve slavery? One surprising but logical implication of the Meditation is that the North may be wrong and therefore that the South may be right. Actually, a good friend reported that Lincoln said in the summer or fall of 1861 that "suppose God is against us in our view on the subject of slavery in this country and our method of dealing with it" (F, 62). The next year, Lincoln had to hope but without total confidence that the cause of justice, which had become the cause of human freedom, "is the cause of God, and then we may be sure it must ultimately triumph" (November 1862, F, 302). But suppose that justice and freedom were not God's cause? Another surprise, perhaps the larger one, is that Lincoln went on to say in the Meditation, "In the present civil war it is quite possible that God's purpose is something different from the purpose of either party—and yet the human instrumentalities, working just as they do, are of the best adaptation to effect His purpose. I am almost ready to say this is probably true" (LA, 2:359). Are opposite sides, then, both acting in accordance with God's will? Can the South in its decision for secession for the purpose of defending slavery be an instrumentality of God equally with the North as an instrumentality for the purpose of saving the Union and perhaps ending slavery? Wouldn't that make God for and against the same thing at the same time? In a book of countless excellent formulations, John Burt says that in Lincoln's Meditation, "at each moment the divine will renews the killing power of the opponents against each other" (Burt, 674). Would that not make both sides right, neither of them wrong? Or can both sides be wrong, while still obeying God's will, without knowing it, or if suspecting it, without knowing why?

What divine pattern would be served unwittingly by two fierce enemies, one for a broken Union and bondage, the other for an integral Union and liberty, fighting each other for conclusive victory? Can only one side be morally wrong but still be necessary to the completion of God's pattern? Near the end of 1862, Lincoln is reported to have said to the pastor of the First Presbyterian Church in Washington, "I believe we are all agents and instruments of Divine providence. On both sides we are working out the will of God; yet how strange the spectacle!" (F, 436). Perhaps God knew, as Lincoln did, that only if the South seceded could the North find a way to abolish slavery. Then Lincoln had to step back from his metaphysical audacity while talking with a pastor and blame the South for its heretical Christianity.

It is useful to learn from Herndon that Lincoln, while still a practicing lawyer, said about Brutus and Caesar that "the former was forced by laws and conditions over which he had no control to kill the latter, and vice versa, that the latter was specially created to be disposed of by the former" (Herndon, 264). Lincoln offered no explanation or interpretation of the creator's purpose in giving life to Caesar and his assassin, not just to one of them but to both, if to one then necessarily to the other. If God intends to give life to both, no human being except an aesthete, a nihilist, or one made totally abject by piety could endorse God's double intention. No one could morally endorse it because no moral interpretation seems to fit the facts unambiguously, unless one wants to be earnest and say that a tyrant appropriately engenders his assassin.

But the murder of Caesar was not only the assassination of a tyrant by a republican; it was also the assassination of a populist by an unreconstructed aristocrat. Lincoln's choice of an illustration uncannily anticipates the contending interpretations of his own murder. Or is God an Olympian spectator that has no moral or teleological intention? Or is he more like a playwright that thrives on uncertainty? He or it just enjoys a good show, defined in every case by those events that can inspire human beings to write either scripture or literature, the ultimate tribute to God, whether addressed to him as spectator or supreme playwright. If I have departed from Lincoln in asking these questions, it would only be by a little.

In the Meditation, Lincoln then restated the point. "God wills this contest, and wills that it shall not end yet. By his mere quiet power, on the minds of the now contestants, He could have either *saved* or *destroyed* the Union without a human contest. Yet the contest began. And having begun, He could give the final victory to either side any day. Yet the contest proceeds" (early September 1862, LA, 2:359). We are left in the dark about what God's purposes could be and therefore how they could be served by the South's final victory. Lincoln appeared certain that God had purposes but claimed no knowledge of the nature of those purposes. Once providence was invested in the war, Southern victory would mean that the Union, beacon of freedom, would be destroyed and that slavery would be strengthened and perpetuated. Was providence, God, not on the side of morality, but immorality? No consideration of retaliatory punishment for slavery was present in the Meditation; the subject was deferred. But if God was not on the side of the North, then obviously those who enslaved could retain their power to enslave for a long time; this would be contrary to what Lincoln said in the letter to Pierce (1859) that I quoted. Lincoln's God becomes to our eyes an alien God. Was the less moral or more criminal South closer to being in the image of Lincoln's God than the North? If so, no wonder that Lincoln wanted the Meditation burned. Or is Lincoln's Meditation just incoherent?

———

The Second Inaugural Address was delivered on March 4, 1865; Lee surrendered on April 9; Lincoln was shot on April 14 and died the next day. This address is undeniably a majestic utterance. It concentrates more meaning than one would think seven hundred words on a political occasion could hold. It has great drive, but its course is not simple; it is almost wayward. In the core paragraph (the third of four), the course changes direction every sentence or two. The whole speech contains shifts and reversals. It puts into play ideas that do not go easily together, if they go at all. It condemns the South separately and the North separately, and both together; it praises the North, and it removes (not merely attenuates) the guilt of the South, not only that of the North. As far as I can make out, the exoneration of both sides, in regard to both slavery and atrocious war, is the metaphysical heart of the speech and takes the form of blaming providence or God for ordaining moral evil in the form of slavery and bringing about moral evil in the form of atrocious war to end slavery. But Lincoln did not abandon moral condemnation of human beings; he left it to others to reconcile blaming them and holding providence ultimately responsible for what they did. Thus, both sides were guilty, both sides were innocent; both sides were punished, guilty or innocent. Lincoln tried to explain, while not really explaining, the ways of God to men and thus justify, while not fully justifying, men to each other. Lincoln presumed to explain the ways of God because he did not think that God ever explained himself. Lincoln hated slavery and hated war, and attempted a perspective that was neither Northern nor Southern, but that of a god or ghost. The film *Lincoln* (2012), in an inspired displacement, showed him delivering the Second Inaugural Address in a scene that comes after Booth's attack on him is first announced and after his death is shown. In our minds he should be figured as speaking from the grave, an immaterial speaker whom we are able to look through, at last transparent. A ghost image of him, in premonition, flashes twice briefly to stand in for him as the living Lincoln builds up to the heart of his speech. He gave reason to hate God, the unforgiven father, or not to love him.

One thing that Lincoln did not do in the Second Inaugural Address was to give way to unqualified anger toward the South, an anger that he would have been entitled to feel on behalf of the North, and that many people of the North did feel, and not only Union soldiers, not to mention the slaves. That the South had enslaved millions of people was an atrocity just by itself; but then in order to strengthen their system they seceded and thus tried to destroy the Union by violence—they compounded the evil. But Lincoln resisted the most natural temptation. In his place, who would have resisted the temptation, no matter how many others in private life wished him to be conciliatory?

The most general point is that the entire subject of the speech was the institution of slavery; the instigation of the war was the national division over slavery and nothing else. Lincoln did not impute to providence any view of the Union other than that it was engaged in a war that was resulting in the end of slavery. In contrast the issue in the Meditation of 1862 was the role of God in saving or destroying the Union, though slavery was tacitly present. One side wanted to destroy the Union, the other side to save it. It was uncertain which side God favored. The word *slavery* did not appear in the Meditation and thus the reason one side wanted to destroy the Union was not given, nor was the reason the other side wanted to save it. The Second Inaugural Address specified slavery as "this interest" that was "somehow the cause of the war"; the interest created the determination to "strengthen, perpetuate, and extend" slavery, while "the government claimed no right to do more than to restrict the territorial enlargement of it" (LA, 2:686). If slavery was the reason the South went to war, the reason the North responded with war was left for listeners and readers to determine as long as they saw that without slavery there would have been no war. Lincoln did not simply say that secession, whatever its cause, had to lead to the North's attempt to undo secession.

"The prayers of both could not be answered; that of neither has been answered fully" (LA, 2:687). The prayers were to the same God of the same Bible read in the same translation. How were any prayers of the South answered: by many dead Yankees and a great expenditure of wealth? A little more than a month after the address, the North's prayers were answered fully, if all the North wanted was a victorious conclusion to the war, with the Union preserved. But the North of course did not want victory to be so costly to itself. So the North knew after a while its prayers could never be answered fully, even when it won. Lincoln did not want the victory to be so costly to the South, either. In an almost unprecedented political act he mourned his enemies, as if he were their mother. He would soon be president of the whole country not only in name, but for the first time in fact, if only for a few days.

Yet Lincoln's sobriety was not like that of General Grant right after he accepted Lee's surrender. The comparison is instructive. Grant went from being "quite jubilant" upon receiving Lee's capitulation to feeling "sad and depressed" at the fall of a valiant foe, who might even have been "inwardly glad that the end had finally come," yet who fought for a cause that was "one of the worst for which a people ever fought, and one for which there was the least excuse" (Grant, 735). Grant experienced powerful mixed feelings, but we could say that after a while he regretted nothing. I do not think that we should characterize Lincoln in the same way.

Lincoln condemned the South for being determined to destroy the Union because its interest was to "strengthen, perpetuate, and extend" slavery (LA, 2:686). He left no doubt about the South's responsibility, or at least the direct human responsibility, for starting the war, even though both sides shared responsibility for maintaining slavery. The condemnation continued when Lincoln said, "It may seem strange that any men should dare to ask a just God's assistance in wringing their bread from the sweat of other men's faces." Lincoln assumed that the South thought God was the God of justice as reciprocity and fairness; for himself, he surely did not definitively commit himself to that idea of God's nature, but contented himself with pointing out the inconsistency, bad faith, or hypocrisy of the South's avowal of faith in light of its system of slavery. As was the case throughout the speech, he left a good amount of work to the audience to do, if they wanted to understand him. Perhaps it is still not possible to do so. Then in the last fifteen lines of the core paragraph, the last paragraph before the famous ending about malice and charity, Lincoln compressed his metaphysical outlook. The idea of a strange God, not quite Greek and only eccentrically biblical if at all, was quickly introduced. No sooner introduced, it gave way to the principle of retaliatory justice.

Lincoln plucked from Matthew 18:7 words that are perhaps more Greek than Calvinist. Or are they Gnostic? It is striking in any case that they come not from the punitive Old Testament but from the gospels that sometimes preach the God of love. "Woe unto the world because of offences! For it must needs be that offences come; but woe to that man by whom the offence cometh!" The verses immediately before and after speak of offending "these little ones," and then how a person's hand, foot, or eye can as an instrument of desire lead that person to commit offenses; the person must sever any of them from the body rather being allowed to doom him. These surrounding verses, which he did not quote, have no relevance that I can see to what Lincoln was saying. They are opaque and un-Christian verses that resist the understanding, even when later translations say "stumbling" or "stumbling blocks" instead of "offences." The most straightforward meaning of

Matthew 18:7 is that God will punish some kinds of wrongdoing much more severely than other kinds, and inevitably; great severity is conveyed by the word *woe*. We should notice that if "offences" means stumbling blocks placed there by God or a person and hence causing another person to stumble, the offended person who stumbles also sins, perhaps through losing innocence, as Adam and Eve did because of the tempter. The offender, already a sinner, sins further and worse by causing others to sin. Did the already corrupted South (early 1862, F, 119) commit a further sin by beguiling the North into the terrible sin of enjoying the products of slave labor and otherwise facilitating and profiting from slavery?

Lincoln went on to say, "American Slavery was one of those offences which, in the providence of God, must needs come, but which having continued through His appointed time, He now wills to remove, and that He gives to both North and South, this terrible war, as woe due to those by whom the offence came" (LA, 2:687). I must say that the phrase "those offences which, in the providence of God, must needs come" means more than one thing. A pious reading holds that human beings will inevitably sin and will inevitably be punished for their sin. Their punishment is divine retaliatory justice, perhaps reserved for the afterlife when this life fails to administer justice understood as retaliation. But is this pious reading the only reading? The pious reading makes God's providence passive as history unfolds, but that is not how Lincoln claimed he understood providence. His stated view is of God's active governance, which means that providence does not merely allow things to happen; or that it brings nothing about; or that things happen solely because of human intention, and then providence sees that they are of some use, which is to us incompletely knowable. This divine passivity is not Lincoln's picture.

Lincoln said that certain offenses must necessarily come in the providence of God, that is, *by* the providence of God—what other meaning is there, if God's providence is active? And they continued "through his appointed time." Offenses continued because God willed them to continue; he could have ended them sooner rather than later. Or, more importantly, he could have prevented them altogether. Worst of all, God wills our offenses; he needs them or uses them; he plants them as he did a tree of forbidden fruit. God determines our will in the sense that he made us for sin; perhaps he makes us sin. We are—many of us or most of us are—the indispensable instrumentalities of necessary offenses. There are no fallen angels; only human beings are fallen. Without us, offenses could not happen, and without God's will, offenses would not have to happen. To offend is to play a role in God's scheme; this thought is foreshadowed in the Meditation on God's Will. The necessity to sin—so much in Lincoln's thought is about one kind of necessity or another—inheres in the nature of things, in the architecture of the world or in the play of transhuman forces and purposes, not in human nature, except derivatively, though indubitably.

When I speak of the removal or exoneration of Southern and Northern guilt, I have especially in mind this one sentence on providence in the Second Inaugural Address, a sentence that appears to me to transfer the ultimate responsibility for the crime of slavery to God, who nevertheless gave woe to those who practiced and supported slavery. This transfer was the basis of Lincoln wishing "charity for all" in the last paragraph of the address. Charity for all is hatred of God or his providence. The only hope for the future would be that human solidarity would prevail over attachment to incomprehensible providence and the accompanying theology of merciless retaliation and punishment. I imagine Lincoln saying to himself, "He that hath ears to hear, let him hear" (Matthew 11:15).

Then Lincoln returned to retaliatory punishment in the same core paragraph: "woe [is] due to those by whom the offence came." To be punished for offenses is to endure a necessary role in God's scheme. God causes what he then punishes. This sounds Greek, but also perhaps like St. Paul in Romans, chapter 7, when he introduces the idea that prohibition creates or at least solicits transgression. Yet Lincoln never abandoned awareness of the human vices that made it possible for the offenses to occur and that God took advantage of in order to further his scheme of first ordaining or permitting slavery and then after a long time ending it. God "gives to both North and South, this terrible war, as the woe due to those by whom the offence came" (Second Inaugural Address, LA, 2:687). The North deserved punishment almost as much as the South because the North gladly bought the goods that slave labor produced, and in other ways invested in slavery; perhaps the guilt of the North was equal to that of the South, not lesser. After all, Lincoln in his last campaign speech for the Illinois seat in the US Senate in 1858 had said that he did not express "harsh sentiments towards our Southern bretheren [sic]" because "the only difference between them and us is the difference of circumstances" (October 30, 1858, LA, 1:827). It was as if all whites wherever they lived and whenever they became aware that blacks existed in the world had no choice but to procure blacks and then enslave them and their progeny. The mere existence of blacks was felt as an affront to human dignity, as a horror. But, no, Southern whites had desire and then chose to act from their desire; they created the necessity they always loved. It was a necessity only because it was an ungovernable passion for excess. Most simply, circumstances determine the actions of necessitous bodies; greater strength and ruthlessness prevail. But how could necessitous bodies, how could brutes with impotent minds, be judged?

It is curious that Lincoln concentrated his most vivid hatred of slavery, when human not divine agency was its identified source, not first on the slaveholders and, second, on those who supported them, but on slave traders, especially foreign ones. In his Annual Message to Congress on December 6, 1864, he referred to slave traders as "enemies of the human race" and recommended that provision be made for "effectually preventing foreign slave traders from acquiring domicile and facilities for their criminal occupation in our country" (LA, 2:649). Earlier he had refused to rescind the execution order for an American slave trader in 1864, though Fehrenbacher says that Nathaniel Gordon of New England was the only one of seven slave traders arrested during the war who was executed; four were pardoned (F, n. 3, 515). In regard to Gordon, however, Lincoln had a counterimpulse: to the US district attorney in New York who urged Lincoln to reject pleas for clemency in Gordon's case, Lincoln said "that you do not know how hard it is to have a human being die when you know that a stroke of your pen may save him" (F, 409). But Lincoln overcame scruples, yet voiced them with unsparing accuracy. In an attribution of doubtful authenticity but fully consonant with his attitude, Lincoln said that a slave trader was "the perpetrator of almost the worst crime that the mind of man can conceive or the arm of man can execute" (F, 2). One wonders how it could be worse than hold-ing slaves, whose reproduction created millions of new slaves without the assistance of slave traders. This is too much like blaming the pro-curer and exonerating the customer, but even this analogy does not begin to reach to the evil of the quantities of slaveholders and slaves. There is a willful displacement of anger from a large category of associ-ated human beings to a much smaller aggregate, and that goes well with one principal tendency of exoneration in the Second Inaugural, the exoneration of the South.

Then Lincoln gave a new possible reason to explain why the war lasted so long: it did not last too long and perhaps should have lasted even longer. This thought is in his single greatest sentence, and it seemed to keep providence but made God entirely moral—but only if retaliation is part of morality. He said, "Yet if God wills that it [the war] continue, until all the wealth piled by the bond-man's two hundred and fifty years of unrequited toil shall be sunk, and until every drop of blood drawn with the lash, shall be paid by another drawn with the sword, as was said three thousand years ago, so still it must be said 'the judgments of the Lord, are true and righteous altogether'" (687). The sentence is shocking; we should not allow its magnificent rhetoric to do to us what we automatically expect ceremonial rhetoric to do: muffle the shock. By itself, it strengthens the judgment that the Second Inaugural Address was, is still, unlike any political statement ever made, and for a lasting moment it set Lincoln's mind apart from the whole country and all politics.

Let us notice that God's retribution would be inflicted not because the South tried to end the old Union but because it practiced slavery with the complicity of the North. If Lincoln's supreme purpose had been to preserve the Union at whatever cost and, if it came to that, without ending slavery, then God's purpose by imputation was not to preserve the Union but now to end slavery, and extorted its enormous cost in death and destruction as punishment for slavery; slavery is the offense, not disruption of the Union. The secular point would be that the only possible justification for the enormous cost was the successful effort to end slavery, a cost, however, that could not have been countenanced if known beforehand and that could have been paid, as it was, only if imposed incrementally and at least in part for some other purpose. In the sight of providence, as Lincoln presented it, the preservation of the Union was purely instrumental to ending slavery. By God's reckoning, the Union at last deserved to exist: but only to undo what it should never have done. Perhaps Lincoln came to believe secretly, as some people accused him of believing, that the abolition of slavery was the true war aim, and that the preservation of the Union mattered above all because it was necessary to that end. This was the reverse of everything he had ever said before. If to a secular mind only abolition could possibly have justified the actual cost, but not before the fact, to

Lincoln's mind only a religious idea, God's retribution, in which he did not believe, could possibly have justified the cost after the fact. The decision to be psychologically prepared to spend any number of white lives to end slavery before the war began was not and is not justifiable, but it is also true that slaves were justified in killing their masters and those who fought for their masters.

Although the sentence on the lash and the sword is only in the conditional mode, it should not pass through our minds as a gesture of reassurance, much less as a tidy way of interpreting the conclusion to the ordeal of a long war or as a preparation for the attempted emotional healing of the last magnanimous paragraph. It was not intended to provide catharsis because the whole situation of defending slavery and abolishing slavery was beyond tragedy. It hints at a great risk of total ruin that was barely and perhaps undeservedly escaped. The address was the opposite of a celebratory or consolatory statement, and if rightly understood, would have been enough to pull the trigger to kill Lincoln. It was his bitterest moment of truth, truth at its most disturbing and dangerous, even if barely present and easily overlooked. It conjured a hell of deserved suffering vastly worse than what actually came to pass, as if victory was coming too soon, even when Sherman's march was added to the account. Grant said confidently that Lincoln "thought blood enough had already been spilled to atone for our wickedness as a nation" (Grant, 761). But perhaps Lincoln was not sure. You cannot possibly sink all the wealth piled up by the slaves, or shed all the blood drawn by the slaveholders' lashes, short of destroying all the living white population in an apocalypse of extermination; but perhaps an apocalypse, and nothing less, is what whites really deserved for the evil accumulated from the beginning of the slave trade to the end of slavery. By embracing whites in the North and South, this reckoning obviously had nothing to do with military necessity, but only with their God's possible moral economy.

The terrible thing was that in regard to those who held slaves and the many others on both sides who approved of slavery and allowed it to go on, Lincoln was trying to convict them of the worst crimes by using against them their own religious devotion to the idea and practice of retribution or retaliation, call it what you will. He was applying their own scriptures and religion, not his own, to them, against them. He was turning their religious weapon on them. Their aggression or masochism was met with greater aggression. If he truly believed in the idea of retribution, he would have been as extreme, perhaps more extreme, than the most radical abolitionists had ever been. Lincoln seemed in the short term the avenger president, no matter how reluctant he might have been; and he was, if he ever was, if any person of politics could ever be, the redeemer president only in the very long run, surely not yet, probably never. (Guelzo's term is borrowed from Walt Whitman, who in 1856 expressed a hope for a president in the new election who would redeem the country one day by achieving every individual's freedom; Guelzo, 205.)

Lincoln's moral lesson was that the American people had to take seriously the principle of equality that they professed. If they had done so from the beginning, they would never have practiced or tolerated slavery. Then at the end of the war, if they took seriously the scriptural God they professed at his most vengeful, a murderous (we could say a genocidal) God, they must see that they deserved the worst possible retribution, even worse than what they endured. Under God's retaliatory punishment they had to kill (and wound and waste) each other, even though their original unforgivable sin had been not to kill (yet many died in the voyage to slavery) but to enslave and typically to exact cruel but not typically lethal punishments on the slaves, and to profit enormously from what they did. Traditional religion could be made to come to the aid of the political religion of human equality, but only in accordance with a savage but scarcely detectable irony. As an identifiable group, the great majority had always refused and will always refuse to be self-condemned. It is interesting, however, that George Fitzhugh, one of the most prominent apologists of slavery, could cheerfully call all those who lived off the unrequited labor of others "cannibals." He claimed that in every society a few lived off the many, and that it so happened that black slaves were the ones exploited in the South, while the allegedly free white laborers in the North were actually treated worse than the black slaves. His argument is clumsy and disingenuous, but at least he dared to use the word *cannibal* about Southern slaveholders, while knowing that the word, if used at all polemically, was used about the ancestors of the slaves.

In Joseph Conrad's *Heart of Darkness* (1899), Mr. Kurtz, the European agent for collecting ivory in the "Inner Station" (in Africa, though not named), scrawled in a postscript to his pamphlet for the International Society for the Suppression of Savage Customs, "Exterminate all the brutes!" These were his last written words. But Conrad left it an open question through the ambiguities of his narrator (who is not Marlow, the narrator's source, the good European and recurrent figure in Conrad's fiction) as to who the brutes were: the savages or the whites who brutalized them by horrible slave labor. The book's title has no definite or indefinite article, although Marlow early in his reported narrative does speak of how his vessel "penetrated deeper and deeper into the heart of darkness" (35). Suppose we add an article and think that the title would be more accurately *A Heart of Darkness* rather than *The Heart of Darkness*, and we ask whose heart is darkness, rather than assuming that the heart of darkness is inland Africa. The primary meaning of heart of darkness was not geographical or topographical but cultural. The reader makes the journey to a heart of darkness, to a person named Kurtz, who is the representative of a system and the wider European culture. He was the worst of the worst, deranged by the economic system, and after embracing its most extreme possibility of exploitation,

embraced the thought of the system's self-destruction through the destruction of the people whom the exploiters controlled. If the whites'
heart in Africa was darkness—I believe that Conrad thought that all
invaders, including the supposedly civilized Romans who invaded Britain, had hearts of darkness—did they deserve extermination whenever
they enslaved or otherwise degraded people? Was their civilization the
deeper barbarism, the true site that ought to have elicited Kurtz's cry,
"The horror, the horror" (75)? The cry should come out of astonish-
ment not at what the degraded people have done to me by enabling
their own degradation but at what we have done to them. Perhaps those
people who had a heart of darkness knew better or should have known
better than to do the evil they did, whereas the savages were innocent
in their ignorant adherence to their customs, no matter how dark their
customs were found to be. There is no doubt that Kurtz was dreaming
of exterminating the exploited laborers and the people who lived with
them as kin, not exterminating people like himself. Slavery was too
good for the savages and profits not as good as ridding the world of an
unclean mass whose touch contaminated those who came in contact
with them.

Perhaps only those people who desire or bring on the extermination
of multitudes deserve extermination. But human morality prohibits
that they should be subject to it at human hands, even in retaliation. To
exterminate those who carried out the original extermination in order
to make them atone for the original extermination is the worst possible
thought for human beings to act on. Only God can act this way, and
this way is not for anyone to adopt, even in imitation of God. But if it
must needs come, then say hypothetically as Lincoln did, God has
willed it and only human instruments could accomplish it and were
made by God to accomplish it. We must remember, however, that the
great offense of slavery was not murder but cruelty and degradation—
the lash; Southern fantasies of extermination came only after tens of

thousands of slaves had stood up to fight. Black manhood was an unendurable conception, worse even than full black humanity.

Conrad enters our picture because in the Civil War, when Southern soldiers killed black Union soldiers they had captured, they were saying or implying that if blacks escaped enslavement and then fought and thus forcibly resisted their re-enslavement, they deserved to be massacred. Blacks presumed to have virile equality. As descended from brutes and not capable of becoming much better than brutes, blacks had to meet one fate or the other, lifelong slavery or premature violent death. The true meaning of the monstrous arrogance that sustained slavery was revealed in the Southern determination to slaughter those blacks who dared to resist their enslavement with weapons and who were captured. Every black soldier carried a potential Southern sentence of death, in battle or surrender.

The will to exterminate designated groups, almost all of them nonwhite, at home or abroad, has frequently expressed itself in American life, but from the start it has usually had Native Americans as its real or imagined target. John Witt cites the words of Vattel (an influential Swiss theorist of natural and international law in the eighteenth century) that urged the slaughter of ferocious prisoners of war who were just like beasts. Jefferson then echoed and applied these words to Indians in a letter to George Rogers Clark in 1777: "the end proposed should be their [the Indians'] extermination" (Witt, 32). Because of white slaveholding, did Lincoln speculatively attribute the will to exterminate American whites to God—that is, not to the ideal observer of justice, but to the God of scripture? Of course I am not saying that Lincoln himself willed extermination of whites so that he could turn the will to exterminate inside out. I only mean that his outrage at the white race's prolonged and remorseless violation of human equality, which the white race defended tenaciously, was so great that he contemplated the possibility that God's mercy or grace alone could be an adequate basis for a pardon, which therefore could only be in intention and effect inscrutable and to us therefore apparently arbitrary. If Lincoln had a Calvinist residue or fell into a Calvinist pattern, this is where it showed itself, but Calvin would have been outraged by the thought that it was Lincoln's commitment to the secular Enlightenment aspiration to earthly human equality that had moved his mind in this direction.

Perhaps God's plan was to draw out not only the evil of war but also the evil of slavery in order to intensify the punishment for both. In such retaliation God would show malice toward all, the most extreme cruelty, as he did in the Old Testament, starting with the expulsion of Adam and Eve from the garden and thereby condemning them and all their descendants to mortality. And if God did now show malice toward all, one more time, by delaying victory indefinitely, it would apparently be with Lincoln's understanding but of course not by Lincoln's wish. Unlike God, Lincoln did not want the South or North to suffer more than victory for the North necessitated, and he certainly did not want a prolonged war: it would prolong all its horror along with the horror of black slavery. Slavery would keep on winning as long as the South did not lose.

The coming abolition of slavery, however, still would not settle the moral account just because all the blood drawn by the lash could never be paid for and all the consumed wealth that derived from exploitation and was therefore robbed from its rightful owners could never be paid back. The New Testament speaks of offenses that cannot be forgiven (Matthew 12:31); perhaps Lincoln thought to add chattel slavery to those offenses. Perhaps the original offense of entrenching slavery in the Union was so great that at last, but of course only when the Union was saved, could one feel that God's judgment was that it should never have existed on the terms by which it came to be; that the Union never deserved to exist; that its appropriate destruction would not of course have been successful secession but rather the common ruin; that the silver setting had poisoned the golden apples from the start. Lincoln would have stood repudiated by his own words, if his words had been quite understood, and repudiated in his own mind unless in a different mood he had looked away from them.

The greatest sentence in the Second Inaugural Address makes it hard not to think, though it is necessary not to think, that from 1854, not just from 1864, Lincoln had harbored the aim of working to end slavery, *no matter what it cost the country;* but obviously he hoped that the cost would not be equal to what was owed. It is needless to add: no matter what it cost him; but for sure we cannot say what he thought he owed. To understand Lincoln toward the end, we need the help not of Emerson and Whitman but of the apostate minds that created not only Satan but also Samson *agonistes;* not only Captain Ahab but also Ishmael; not only Billy Budd but also Captain Vere. From another angle and perhaps best of all would be the influence of Kierkegaard's re-creation of Abraham's mentality of sacrificial obedience in parts of *Fear and Trembling,* even though Kierkegaard himself felt he had to seek out analogies (and found unpersuasive ones) for Abraham's renunciation closer to home and in everyday life.

The North was punished by tremendous suffering on the battlefield, but was also the instrumentality by which victory over the crime of slavery was won, and it inflicted tremendous trauma, suffering, now conceptualized as punishment, on the South, in ferocious battle and devastation among civilians. The sword that compensated, though perhaps incompletely, for the lash of degradation and unrequited toil was in the hands of the North. The South, the wielder of the lash and of the sword to safeguard the lash, was the punished aggressor, as the North was the punished avenger. The North and the South were the punishers and the punished, but perhaps in their common human disaster, neither was punished enough for the incomparable moral disaster of slavery, for which both bore responsibility. They shared everything but what they could not possibly share, military victory, and with the North's victory, the preservation, not the destruction, of the Union, and with that victory, the end of a way of life devoted to slavery.

Looking back at the conclusion of this study, I find that I have been driven in different directions, all of them rather extreme: extreme praise of Lincoln but not before he became president; sharp criticism before and after he became president; great sympathy for him with a touch or more than a touch of unforgiving censure. I cannot offer a balanced judgment or a steady attitude or a portrait other than rough. He was always a good man and a great writer, but he became a great man only as president when among politicians he grasped better than any the fullness of the situation in its moral and practical complexity. His mind, despite his disclaimers, was adequate to such a situation; perhaps no other political mind was. I doubt that any historian or analyst could have told him, or could now as it were tell him, anything that he had not already thought. But we should remember that political greatness almost always comes with an exorbitant moral cost, even if that achievement, by some method of reasoning, exceeds in worth its cost.

On the eve of victory, Lincoln's highest qualities were consummated in the speech he gave; it was for the time and place he gave it. But it was somewhat mysterious, except for its final paragraph; it remains so. He painted as grim a picture of victory as one can imagine a victor painting. A month later he was murdered. He was, in Frederick Douglass's words, "the first martyr President of the United States" (Douglass, 2). But if a martyr, he was that uncanny thing, a martyr wading in blood. Did he think he deserved to die because of all the death his policies necessitated? He had a great enough soul for that, and he was unfriendly enough to himself for that, though he strove "to preserve one friend within me . . . to tell me that I have not been a tyrant" (September 30,

1863, F, n. 215, 529). I doubt that he could have completely reconciled himself to the victory of his political religion, which could have been perfected only by a long war and the breaking of the fundamental law, at such a cost in the number of dead, whatever the imputed will of providence. Among American presidents, only Lincoln suffered almost as much anguish from victory as he would have suffered from defeat.

ABBREVIATIONS

BIBLIOGRAPHY

INDEX

Abbreviations

A   Angle, Paul M. *Created Equal? The Complete Lincoln-Douglas Debates.*
Chicago: University of Chicago Press, 1958.

CW   Lincoln, Abraham. *The Collected Works of Abraham Lincoln,* ed. Roy
P. Basler. 8 vols. New Brunswick, N.J.: Rutgers University Press, 1953.
Index, Volume 9, 1955. Supplementary Volumes: 10 (1974) and 11
(1990).

F   Fehrenbacher, Don E., and Virginia Fehrenbacher, eds. *Recollected Words
of Abraham Lincoln.* Stanford, Calif.: Stanford University Press, 1996.

LA   Lincoln, Abraham. *Speeches and Writings,* ed. Don E. Fehrenbacher.
2 vols. New York: Library of America, 1989.

Bibliography

Adams, Henry. *The Education of Henry Adams* (1907, 1918). New York: Modern Library, 1931.

Angle, Paul M. *Created Equal? The Complete Lincoln-Douglas Debates.* Chicago: University of Chicago Press, 1958.

Briggs, John Channing. *Lincoln's Speeches Reconsidered.* Baltimore, Md.: Johns Hopkins University Press, 2005.

Bromwich, David. *Moral Imagination.* Princeton, N.J.: Princeton University Press, 2014.

Burt, John. *Lincoln's Tragic Pragmatism: Lincoln, Douglas, and Moral Conflict.* Cambridge, Mass.: Harvard University Press, 2013.

Carwardine, Richard. *Lincoln: A Life of Purpose and Power* (2003). New York: Vintage, 2006.

Conrad, Joseph. *Heart of Darkness* (1899, 1902). Edited by Robert Kimbrough, 2nd ed. A Norton Critical Edition. New York: Norton, 1971.

Donald, David Herbert. *Lincoln.* New York: Simon & Schuster, 1995.

Douglass, Frederick. "Oration in Memory of Abraham Lincoln: Delivered at the Unveiling of the Freedmen's Monument in Lincoln Park, Washington D.C." (April 14, 1876). Available at http:/teachingamericanhistory.org.

Emerson, Ralph Waldo. "The Emancipation Proclamation" (1862) and "Abraham Lincoln" (1865). In *Complete Essays and Other Writings,* ed. Brooks Atkinson. New York: Modern Library, 1950.

Faust, Drew Gilpin. *This Republic of Suffering: Death and the American Civil War.* New York: Vintage, 2008.

Fehrenbacher, Don E., and Virginia Fehrenbacher, eds. *Recollected Words of Abraham Lincoln.* Stanford, Calif.: Stanford University Press, 1996.

Foner, Eric. *The Fiery Trial: Abraham Lincoln and American Slavery.* New York: Norton, 2010.

Grant, Ulysses Simpson. *Personal Memoirs of U. S. Grant* (1885–1886). Edited by Mary Drake McFeely and William S. McFeely. New York: Library of America, 1990.

Guelzo, Allen C. *Abraham Lincoln: Redeemer President.* Grand Rapids, Mich.: William B. Eerdmans, 1999.

Guyatt, Nicholas. "A Topic Best Avoided." Review of Foner (op. cit.), *London Review of Books*, vol. 33, no. 23, December 1, 2011, pp. 27–31.

Herndon, William H., and Jesse Weik. *Herndon's Lincoln: The True Story of a Great Life* (1889). Edited by Douglas L. Wilson and Rodney O. Davis. Urbana: University of Illinois Press, 2006.

Hofstadter, Richard. "Abraham Lincoln and the Self-Made Myth." In *The American Political Tradition: And the Men Who Made It* (1948). New York: Vintage, 1973.

Homer. *The Odyssey.* Translated by Robert Fitzgerald. New York: Doubleday, 1961.

Jaffa, Harry. *Crisis of the House Divided: An Interpretation of the Issues in the Lincoln-Douglas Debates.* Chicago: University of Chicago Press, 1959.

James, Henry. *The American Scene* (1907). Edited by Leon Edel. Bloomington: Indiana University Press, 1968.

Jefferson, Thomas. *Writings.* Edited by Merrill D. Peterson. New York: Library of America, 1984.

Kaplan, Fred. *Lincoln: The Biography of a Writer.* New York: HarperCollins, 2008.

Lincoln, Abraham. *The Collected Works of Abraham Lincoln.* Edited by Roy P. Basler. 8 vols. New Brunswick, N.J.: Rutgers University Press, 1953. Index, Volume 9, 1955. Supplementary Volumes: 10 (1974) and 11 (1990).

———. *Speeches and Writings.* Edited by Don E. Fehrenbacher. 2 vols. New York: Library of America, 1989.

Madison, James. Federalist Paper no. 54 in Alexander Hamilton, James Madison and John Jay, *The Federalist Papers.* Edited by Garry Wills. New York: Bantam Books, 1982.

McPherson, James M. *For Cause and Comrades: Why Men Fought in the Civil War.* New York: Oxford University Press, 1997.

Neely, Mark E., Jr. *The Fate of Liberty: Abraham Lincoln and Civil Liberties.* New York: Oxford University Press, 1991.

Oakes, John. *Freedom National: The Destruction of Slavery in the United States, 1861–1865.* New York: Norton, 2013.

Randall, James D. *Constitutional Problems under Lincoln* (1951). Rev. ed. Urbana: University of Illinois Press, 1964.

Sherman, William Tecumseh. *Memoirs of General W. T. Sherman* (1875; 2nd ed., 1885). Edited by Charles Royster. New York: Library of America, 1990.

Smith, Steven B. "How to Read Lincoln's Second Inaugural Address." In *The Writings of Abraham Lincoln,* ed. Steven B. Smith. New Haven, Conn.: Yale University Press, 2012.

White, Ronald C., Jr. *Lincoln's Greatest Speech: The Second Inaugural.* New York: Simon & Schuster, 2002.

Whitman, Walt. "Death of Abraham Lincoln" (1879). In *Collect* published with *Specimen Days* (1882). In *Complete Poetry and Collected Prose,* ed. Justin Kaplan. New York: Library of America, 1982.

Wills, Garry. *Lincoln at Gettysburg: The Words That Remade America.* New York: Simon & Schuster, 1992.

Wilson, Douglas L., and Rodney O. Davis. *Herndon's Informants: Letters, Interviews, and Statements about Abraham Lincoln.* Urbana: University of Illinois Press, 1998.

Wilson, Edmund. "Abraham Lincoln." In *Patriotic Gore: Studies in the Literature of the American Civil War.* New York: Oxford University Press, 1962.

Witt, John Fabian. *Lincoln's Code: The Laws of War in American History.* New York: Free Press, 2012.

Index

Caste, rejection of, 96
Christianity: and denial of human
 equality, 77–78, 85; Lincoln's views
 on, 181–184. *See also* Calvinism
Citizenship, of blacks, 72
Civil religion of Rousseau, 51–52
Civil War: providential and tragic
 determinism in, 5; suffering in, 7;
 death toll and division in, 14–15;
 patriotism in, 17; Northern
 reluctance to fight in, 19–20, 21–22;
 South's anger as cause of, 31–32;
 Union sacrifices in, 32; ferocities in,
 53; preservation of Union and
 Union's aim in, 56; suspension of
 Constitution during, 63, 138–145;
 and amendment of Constitution,
 64–65; likelihood of abolition
 without, 65–66; conditions in South
 following, 92; cost of, 118–120, 203,
 209–210; pursued for moral reasons,
 121–122; suspension of habeas
 corpus during, 145–150; justification
 for suspension of Constitution
 during, 152–157, 159–161; providence and human choices in,
 190–193; as God's retaliation for
 slavery, 193–195; God's will
 concerning, 197–200; blame for,
 201–204; slavery as cause of,
 202–203; duration of, 208–209
Colonization of blacks: Lincoln's
 defense of, 61; Lincoln endorses,
 90–91; as necessity, 136. *See also*
 Segregation
Compromise: Lincoln on, 20, 29–30,
 31; and Northern reluctance to fight,

21–22; regarding slavery, 61,
 120–121; Lincoln's willingness for,
 125
Confederate Constitution, 61–62,
 66–67
Confiscation Act, second, 173
Conkling, James C., 90, 135–136
Conrad, Joseph, *Heart of Darkness,*
 212–213
Conscription, 142, 150. *See also* Black
 recruitment
Consent: Lincoln's idea of, 76, 99; and
 military necessity, 166–167
Constitution: and legality of slavery,
 34; state slavery laws and, 55–56;
 commitment to preservation of,
 56–57; as tenet of Lincoln's political
 religion, 59, 60; human equality and,
 60–61; suspension of, 63, 111,
 138–145, 151–152; as worthy of
 obedience and reverence, 63–65,
 110; slavery established by, 66–67,
 124, 135–136; Lincoln's reverence
 for, 67–68; Douglas's views on, 103;
 as constitution of slavery and
 freedom, 105–108; entrenchment of
 slavery in, 110–118; three-fifths
 clause in, 116–117; preservation of,
 127; justification for suspension of,
 152–157; purpose of suspension of
 rights, 159–161; slavery as reason for
 suspension of, 163–164; preservation of Union and suspension of,
 164–165. *See also* Confederate
 Constitution
Constitutionalism, 162–163
Conway, Moncure D., 113

Second Inaugural Address, 197,
201–210, 216
Segregation: as proof of racism, 28;
Lincoln endorses, 89. *See also*
Colonization of blacks
Self-determination, national, 81
Self-evident truths, 68–69
Self-sacrifice, 83–84, 90
Sherman, William Tecumseh, 134–135,
170–171
Slavery: and group ferocity of whites,
12–14; abolitionists' horror to
conscience caused by, 15–17;
sympathy toward victims of, 17, 59;
conceptual gap regarding, 18–20, 22;
morality of, 22–27, 83; racism as
foundation of, 25–28, 71–73, 75,
85–86; compromise regarding,
29–30, 61; responsibility for
continuation of, 31; moral disapproval of, 32–33, 70–71; as violation
of Constitution, 34; ending, as
Lincoln's sole aim, 42, 47–49; and
House Divided speech, 43–46,
125–127; war abolishing, 45–46;
containment of, 54, 64, 87–88, 122,
123, 124; Constitution versus state
laws regarding, 55–56; under golden
principle, 59; defenders of, 59–60; in
Confederate Constitution, 61–62;
and preservation of Union, 62,
120–121, 137–138; and due process
clause, 66; established by Constitution, 66–67, 105–108; constitutionality of, under *Dred Scott* decision, 72;
as tyranny, 73–75, 104; ancient, 75;
effects of, 76; as exploitation, 76–77,

100, 212–213; Christianity and,
77–78, 85; whites as victims of, 79;
political religion and, 79–80; human
equality and condemnation of,
80–82; grounds for resistance to,
81–82; Jefferson's thought-
experiment regarding, 82–85;
Lincoln's hatred of, 97–104; as
oppression, 100–101; and Constitution's worthiness of obedience and
reverence, 110; entrenchment of, in
Constitution as political necessity,
110–118; as lesser evil, 114–115, 120,
135–136; Framers' expectation of
extinction of, 115–118; and cost of
Civil War, 118–120; peaceful
extinction of, 127, 128; as reminis-
cent of damnation, 127; true motive
for keeping, 130–131; military
necessity and dismantling of, 133; as
reason for suspension of Constitutional rights, 163–164; as right,
167–168; Lincoln on deserving,
176–177; retaliation for, 193–195,
209, 215; God's will for, 198; as
subject of Second Inaugural Speech,
202–203; as cause of Civil War,
203–204; as offense, 205; responsibility for, transferred to God,
206–207; as unforgivable, 215. *See
also* Abolition; Abolitionism;
Emancipation; Political slavery;
Slaves
Slaves: humanity of, 6, 108, 124;
traumas of, 10–11, 12; treatment of,
100; insurrection of, 130–131. *See
also* Slavery